Settlin'

SETTLIN'

*Stories of Madison's Early
African American Families*

MURIEL SIMMS

WISCONSIN HISTORICAL SOCIETY PRESS

Published by the Wisconsin Historical Society Press
Publishers since 1855

The Wisconsin Historical Society helps people connect to the past by collecting, preserving, and sharing stories. Founded in 1846, the Society is one of the nation's finest historical institutions.
Join the Wisconsin Historical Society: wisconsinhistory.org/membership

Publication of this book was made possible thanks to the generous support of the Wisconsin Historical Society Readers Circle. For more information and to join, visit support.wisconsinhistory.org/readerscircle.

The cover illustration was inspired by a sketch by Billy McDonald of buildings from Madison's first Black neighborhood, in the 600 block of East Dayton Street.

Printed in the United States of America

Cover designed by Andrew Brozyna
Typesetting by S4Carlisle Publishing Services

22 21 20 19 18   1 2 3 4 5

Library of Congress Cataloging-in-Publication Data

Names: Simms, Muriel, 1944– author.
Title: Settlin': Stories of Madison's Early African American Families / Muriel Simms.
Description: Madison : Wisconsin Historical Society Press, 2018. | Includes bibliographical references and index. |
Identifiers: LCCN 2018017487 (print) | LCCN 2018018445 (ebook) | ISBN 9780870208867 | ISBN 9780870208850 (pbk. : alk. paper)
Subjects: LCSH: African American families—Wisconsin—Madison—Biography. | African Americans—Wisconsin—Madison—Biography. | African Americans—Wisconsin—Madison—History—20th century. | Oral history—Wisconsin—Madison.
Classification: LCC F589.M19 (ebook) | LCC F589.M19 N47 2018 (print) | DDC 306.85/08996073077583—dc23
LC record available at https://lccn.loc.gov/2018017487

To the African American families who settled in Madison in the 1800s and early 1900s. They showed strength, courage, and pride as they made a better life for themselves and for others in the community.

And especially to my mother, Mary Esther Simms, who came here in 1935 and helped to make the city a more welcoming place for everyone.

CONTENTS

A group photo taken outside St. Paul's A.M.E. Church on East Dayton Street in 1944 includes members of many of Madison's early African American families. Back row: Doris Barlow, Colleen Johnson, Dorothy Newville, Billy McDonald, Paul Washington. Third row: Mr. Glover, Mrs. Glover, Laura Hoover, Paul Henderson, Sam Dixon, David Simms, Mr. Russell, Mamie Owens, Mamie Anderson, Effie Dunn, Mrs. Russell, Joe Washington, Blydena Newville Lucas, Mrs. Arthur Mosley, Myrtle Daniels, Emily Miller, Effie Stamps, Mrs. Givens, an unidentified woman, "Deep Stuff" Johnson, Mrs. Earl Muldrew, three unidentified people, Ellen Waldon with baby, an unidentified man, Mrs. Virgil Woods, two unidentified UW students. Second row: Sadie Bostick, two unidentified women, Mrs. Newville, Mr. Charles Daniels, Reverend Fulton, Mrs. Fulton, an unnamed presiding elder, Freddie Mae Hill (John Hill's daughter), Mary B. Hawkins, Ida Henderson, Myra Allison, Fannie Weaver. Front row: Charlene Hill, Roland Anderson, Freddie Mae Hill, Beverly Hill, Bobby Newville, Colenthia Hill, Dickie Miller, Jack Mitchell, Emma Jean Anderson, Carl Satterfield. ST. PAUL'S AFRICAN METHODIST EPISCOPAL CHURCH

INTRODUCTION

As Alex Haley wrote in his book *Roots*, "When a griot dies, it is as if a library has burned to the ground."[1] He was referring to the value of information carried by West African storytellers and oral historians, but looking around the African American community in my Midwestern hometown, I realized the relevance and urgency contained in those words. Only a fraction of what is known about Madison's earliest African American settlers and the vibrant and cohesive communities they formed is preserved in archives and libraries. The rest is contained in the hearts and minds of successive generations. As the carriers of these families' stories age and pass on, something of great value was at risk of being lost. I saw a pressing need to gather their stories into a volume, one that would give substance to the lives of the pioneer families who settled in Madison.

While some researchers, scholars, and freelance writers have published works on Wisconsin's earliest African American settlers, they offer only a partial picture. Journalists of European descent wrote many of the accounts, often singling out Blacks who they deemed to be influential or to have accomplished something significant. While these stories are important to the historical record and give a sense of African Americans' lives in Madison, they fail to represent the breadth of forces that shaped their experiences. In the words of Linda Shopes, an editor of oral histories, such articles only rarely discuss "the unequal and conflicting relations among people . . . or . . . explore the way the internal experience of the community is shaped by the economic and social forces external to it, the way the actions of banks, employers, landlords, schools, planners, and developers have structured the dynamics of the place."[2] This book is intended to help fill the gap by capturing the internal experience of a people who came to Madison to improve their lives and the lives of other Black people and who did so in spite of many challenges. As Shopes wrote, oral history projects with their accompanying artifacts and written accounts demonstrate the

> sturdiness of ordinary people, their ability to cope in difficult circumstances, their capacity to create lives of meaning. . . . They are generally

1

organized around broad social categories like work and leisure, family, church and community, to suggest that people's individual experience really isn't individual at all, but social. . . . These projects enlarge people's sense of identity, and encourage people to see themselves as living . . . lives embedded in a broader social and historical context.[3]

Oral histories have long been used effectively by scholars to record the histories of early African Americans, especially those of former slaves. In 1929, John B. Cade enlisted his students at Southern University in Baton Rouge to record the stories of ex-slaves and their masters in Louisiana. Other scholars engaged in similar efforts to collect interviews of former slaves in Tennessee, Kentucky, and Indiana. In 1937, George P. Rawick compiled a nineteen-volume set of slave accounts from seventeen states. These early scholars took the lead to document the African American experience, knowing that oral stories were the only way these individuals had to fill in the "gaps and disprove many of the distortions of written history."[4] Their narratives, supported by records and corroborating evidence, cannot be viewed as simply reminiscing or nostalgia, but instead should be regarded as important historical evidence, as well as our best insight into the hearts and minds of those who have experiences to share with the interviewer and with the wider community.

Knowing more about the past lives of African Americans in Madison can be instructive to Madison's wider community, especially the children. Teaching and valuing the stories of Madison's Black ancestral families, as well as those of other ethnic groups, is an approach that teachers can use to construct a bridge from home to school—showing how stories originate from someplace, from someone's parents and grandparents—and yet assist children with learning to read and understand social studies concepts.[5] Oral history is a teaching tool that broadens student knowledge about others and debunks negative perceptions they might have about people who do not share the same background and experiences.[6] These narratives disrupt the dominant culture's reality and force it to incorporate the reality of others, to develop a more inclusive cultural consciousness. Dr. LaVada Taylor Brandon, associate professor of education at Purdue University, wrote about the benefits of this type of learning:

When urban African American students use oral history to document the tales of their cultural community, through voices of other urban

African Americans, in my view, oral history empowers them to
w/right historical narratives of their greatness.[7]

Valuing oral traditions gives children an important resource beyond tra-
ditional instructional practices. From listening to family stories related to
their past, African American children learn about surviving and persever-
ing through times of struggle and about appreciating signs of progress.
The oral history genre is a modality in which people become informed,
linked to the past, grounded in the present, and led down a pathway to
intelligent thinking and action for the future.

In their interviews with me, the descendants of these pioneer families
emphasized that their ancestors came to Madison to find work or attend
school. Most arrived with some formal education and even various academic degrees but were relegated to the domestic, janitorial, maintenance,
and other menial work that was available to African Americans at that
time. Some Black pioneers of Madison were able to open barbershops,
restaurants, or other small businesses. No matter what field of endeavor,
no matter how humbling or humiliating, three aspects of their lives became clear in their stories. The first African American families of Madison
worked hard, with quality in mind and dignity at heart, no matter what
jobs they had or positions they held. They did not let their anger at White
neighbors or at institutional racism deter their dreams or corrupt their
children. And they passed down the values of education, family, and community as well as a love of recreation and play to their descendants. Sometimes conflicts with Whites occurred in the workplace or in school, which
meant that they had to act to protect themselves and their children from
mistreatment or find ways to fight for their individual rights. Regardless
of the social and economic conditions of the time, the stories, told in their
own words, reveal that the families survived, thrived, and even had fun.

It is important for newcomers in the African American community
and in the wider Madison community to recognize that the city's African
American history began as early as 1847. The lives of these pioneers were
not easy, as they tried to further their education, find employment, and
raise families in the midst of a wider community that did not always want
them to be successful in these areas. The stories told by the descendants
of these earliest settlers, supported by newspaper clippings and other records, show a diverse but unified Black community that has supported its

members through these trials. These ancestors and elders—regardless of individual economic, educational, or professional status—consulted with each other about issues, worked with one another to overcome adversities, and often acted as one when confronting the wider community. In the words of Cornell West, "The genius of our black foremothers and forefathers was to create powerful buffers to . . . equip black folks with cultural armor . . . of meaning and feeling that created and sustained communities . . . ways of life and struggle that embodied values of service and sacrifice, love and care, discipline and excellence."[8]

Most of the oral histories that begin on page 31 are from my interviews with the descendants of Madison's African American pioneer families. I conducted most of the interviews between 2003 and 2013, and their words are presented with only minor edits for clarity. Adding to my own work I have included three oral histories that were collected by the Wisconsin Historical Society for the Coming to Madison project in 1989. Additionally, to supplement the stories of Madison's early Black families, I have also included the oral histories of two people whose accounts help to shed light on aspects of the local African American experience: a White realtor who helped Black families find housing in Madison, and an Italian American who recalls the multicultural Greenbush neighborhood that was lost to urban renewal.

A Brief History of African
American Settlement in Madison

Before its statehood, very few African Americans lived in Wisconsin. Some of these had been brought to the area as slaves by the English fur traders of the 1700s or by the White settlers who streamed into the state to mine lead in the 1820s and 1830s, later to be freed or sent back to slave states. As of 1840, Wisconsin had fewer than two hundred Black residents.[1] Black settlement in Wisconsin increased dramatically with the passage of the Fugitive Slave Act of 1850, which allowed slave catchers to capture escaped slaves and return them to their masters, as well as detain free Blacks and force them back into slavery.[2] To avoid this fate, many Blacks fled to free states such as Wisconsin, where local officials resisted enforcing the federal law. In the years before the Civil War, a growing number of abolitionists in the state helped slaves escape through the Underground Railroad. By 1860, the number of Blacks in Wisconsin had grown to about twelve hundred.[3]

Some Blacks first settled in other Wisconsin communities, such as in and around Milwaukee, Baraboo, Lancaster, and La Crosse, while others came directly to Madison. Both groups were drawn to the state capital, also the state's first university town, hoping to find work and educational opportunities. A few came to Madison to visit and decided to stay because they liked the geographic location, surrounded by four beautiful lakes and in close proximity to bigger cities, such as Milwaukee and Chicago.

Because of the methods used to track populations before the 1900s, it is difficult to ascertain the identities or be precise about the numbers of Madison's first Black residents. The US Census began recording race in 1847, but the surveyors had the responsibility of recording someone's race and often mistook an olive-skinned person for Black or mixed race, or a light-skinned Black or mixed-race person for White. Racial mixing sometimes allowed offspring to pass as White or to live in Native American societies out of the reach of census takers.[4] In other words, racial classifications and therefore the numbers of Blacks reported may not be accurate. Another complicating factor in determining the first Black residents of

Madison was slave owning. Many Blacks came to Madison because their owners brought them. For example, in 1827, slave owner James Morrison and his family brought their slaves to Iowa County, where he took a position as a probate clerk. Approximately ten years later, Morrison saw an opportunity to advance his position. He moved from Iowa County to Madison, bringing his family but only one female Black servant. One census reports that other Blacks came to Madison between 1836 and 1847, but they could not be identified by name. One lived in the home of a man by the name of Abrum Yokey, three lived in the Madison Hotel, and two lived in the home of J. Burk.[5] Although unidentified African Americans may have lived in Madison as early as 1836, Darkey Butch was the first African American resident listed in the Village of Madison records in 1847.[6]

According to the 1850 federal census, twenty-five African Americans had settled in Dane County communities including Madison, Oregon, Montrose, and Rutland. These Black settlers listed their birthplaces as Virginia, Ohio, Michigan, Louisiana, North Carolina, and Wisconsin. The records show that only six of the twenty-five people settled in Madison, three with the last name of Anderson, two with the last name of Mitchel, and one named A. Jackson. Outside of Madison, eight African Americans with the last names of Marshall, Volintine, and West lived in Rutland, the nine-member Valentine family lived in Oregon, and the two-member Freeman family lived in Montrose. Strikingly, the number of Black people who lived in these small communities at the time totaled more than three times the number of Black people living in Madison.[7]

The 1850 US census did not record vital information such as age or occupation about Blacks living in Madison, but the limited information available on some of these residents shows that at least several of them were astute businessmen. No information was found on A. Jackson, but reports show that William and Catherine Mitchel moved from Louisiana and settled in Madison about this time. They worked at the American House Hotel as cooks. With their earnings, they purchased a lot on the corner of Lake Street and University Avenue and other lots near the intersection of Hamilton and West Wilson Streets. These properties were valued at one thousand dollars, a considerable sum for that time. Forty-seven-year-old J. Anderson and his son or brother, Alexander, were barbers. The Andersons came to Madison before 1850 and immediately made plans to own a barbershop, which they did in 1850. The Andersons earned enough to purchase several pieces of land, valued at four hundred dollars. They bought one lot on the corner of Gilman and Henry Streets and the other lot on the corner of Hamilton and Dayton Streets. Eventually, both the Mitchel and Anderson families moved to Janesville, where they acquired more property. Both used their respective properties to establish their barber and restaurant businesses, which collectively were valued at two hundred and fifty thousand dollars.[8]

One of the most prominent Black families discussed in Madison history is the Noland family. William H. and Anna M. Noland migrated from New York to Kentucky and then to Madison with three of their children. Their two youngest children, Charles and Frank, were born in Madison's Fourth Ward in 1848 and 1850, respectively. The Nolands were considered the first permanent Black family of Madison, and Charles and Frank were considered the first native-born Black residents. William Noland not only was a skilled laborer and businessman, like other Blacks who came to Madison, but also applied his skills and knowledge in the areas of barbering, food production, manufacturing, animal husbandry, and the fine arts as a musician and bandmaster. He became a law clerk for Madison attorney William B. Jarvis, who nominated Noland for the post of notary public and put up the cash bond required. Governor Coles Bashford accepted the nomination and made the appointment, but Secretary of State David W. Jones refused to accept the bond. His notation on the records reads: "This man is a n——, and the secretary refuses to file his bond."[9] Although Jones's refusal was denounced throughout the state, Noland was not appointed to the position. This incident may have motivated Noland to become an early civil rights activist. As a citizen, he denounced the Democrats for putting his name on the ballot to be mayor of Madison in 1866 without his permission. Noland refused to accept this nomination because the Democrats of this time period had showed hostility toward the idea that Blacks should have equal rights. Even though he did not campaign, Noland garnered 306 votes. Noland died in 1880.

Noland had an acquaintance, Jonathan J. Myers, who came from Milwaukee to Madison in 1857. Myers owned and operated an ice cream parlor as well as a fruit, poultry, and game store at the corner of Main and Webster Streets. Myers's wealth captured the interest of the African Colonization Society, which promoted the idea of returning Blacks to Africa and raising money for their passage. Due to a civil war in Nigeria and little momentum for the movement in the United States, Myers moved back to Milwaukee in 1860.[10]

William H. Noland, pictured in costume for a parade. The Noland family were among the first permanent African American residents of Madison. WHI IMAGE ID 5082

In 1852, Eston Hemings Jefferson, widely believed to be the son of Thomas Jefferson and Sally Hemings, moved to Madison with his wife, Julia, and three children, John Wayles, Anna, and Beverly. Eston, a skilled woodworker who had been free since 1827, died shortly after arriving in Wisconsin. The rest of the family passed as White until the 1905 census showed that they had identified themselves as being of Black ancestry. The two brothers, John and Beverly, used the inheritance from their father to buy the American Hotel in Madison. During the Civil War, both brothers enlisted in the Union Army. After the war, John moved to Memphis, Tennessee, and Beverly returned to Madison to live with his mother. In 1868, they opened the Rasdall House on King Street between Webster and Butler.[11]

1860S

During the 1860s, William Anderson, Notley Henderson, and Benjamin Butts came to Madison. William Anderson, raised on a plantation in St. Louis, Missouri, had been sold, along with his brother, Stephen, to a

---

RESIDENTS OF THE 1860S

A few other African American men resided in Madison during the 1860s, but only sparse information can be found about these four men:

- John Smiley came from Pennsylvania, where he served as cook and hostler, and settled in Madison in 1860. He worked for Madison mayor Andrew Proudfit. The March 20, 1895, edition of the *Wisconsin State Journal* reported that John Smiley was the oldest Black resident in Madison, having lived in the city since 1860.

- Elijah (or Elisha) Williams, a Georgian slave, came to Madison sometime after the Civil War. He served in the Twelfth Wisconsin Regiment of the Union Army.

- Dennis Hughes was from Tuscaloosa, Alabama. After running away from a master in Mississippi, he later signed on as a hostler with a northern army unit, after which he joined the US Colored Infantry. In Madison, he found work as a janitor and doing odd jobs.

- John H. Boggs, who came to Madison in 1867, operated the Williams Barber Shop on Pinckney Street. He was found dead in a water-filled boat on Lake Monona. Authorities described the event as mysterious.

Forest Hill Cemetery Committee, *The Biographical Guide to Forest Hill Cemetery, Volume II* (Madison, WI: Historic Madison, Inc., 2002), 197–199.

planter in Humboldt, Tennessee. When the Thirteenth Wisconsin Regiment of the Union Army came through the Humboldt area, Anderson joined as a cook. After the war, this regiment brought Anderson to Madison, where he married Phoebe Van Valkenburg, a European immigrant. They apparently had four children, three boys and one girl. Even though some discrepancies exist about the number of children they had, the records show that the oldest son, William I., was born in Madison in 1868. He attended and graduated in 1885 from Madison High School, later known as Madison Central High School. William entered the University of Wisconsin in Madison in 1886 but one year later abandoned his studies due to an illness he contracted while on a hayride with classmates. Another son, Charles, died of tuberculosis. The third son, George, born in Madison in 1878, also attended Madison High School and played football and baseball, for which he achieved some fame. He died of tuberculosis. A girl, Grace, apparently died young as well. The family lived at 315 North Henry Street.[12]

Another prominent man who settled in Madison was Notley Henderson. He moved from Kentucky to the town of Madison in the late 1860s. He worked as a farmhand for Seth Bartlett and soon earned enough money to marry Martha in the 1880s and buy a tract of land that was on the south side of the UW Arboretum. The Hendersons had one son, Allen, who eventually ran the farm along with his two sons, Paul and Walter. The family often took in newcomers; reportedly, William and Anna Mae Miller honeymooned on their farm.

Due to a bizarre double murder, the Hendersons lost their farm. On March 5, 1927, Charles Nelson reportedly shot Walter Henderson, and the body was found in the woods near Nakoma Road. He then allegedly went to the farm and killed Allen Henderson. Nelson, a former mental patient and son of a real estate developer, had been known to be upset about what he believed were slanderous words he heard one of the Hendersons say about White people. After officials approached Nelson about the crimes, he committed suicide. Soon after the murders, Mrs. Allen Henderson sold the farm and moved in with their only living son, Paul. Both lived on 641 East Dayton Street.[13]

Another prominent man in the Madison community, Benjamin Butts, was born in 1851 in Petersburg, Virginia. As a runaway slave, Benjamin became attached to the Fifth Wisconsin Battery, which occupied Petersburg

A detail of an 1890 land tract map shows the location of the Henderson farm.
WHI IMAGE ID 137508

An 1885 portrait shows Martha and Notley Henderson with their three children.
WHI IMAGE ID 4175

during the Civil War. He tended the soldiers' horses. After the war, Colonel Butts brought Benjamin back to Richland Center, Wisconsin—an offer Butts accepted without saying good-bye to his family—and gave Benjamin his last name. In 1865, Benjamin Butts moved to Madison, where he was able to find work as a clerk in an auction store. He took a room with Virginia Wonzer and her sons and daughters. The sons were barbers, an occupation that Butts learned and used to support his family later in life. He returned to Richland Center, where he worked as a waiter

Benjamin Butts.
WHI IMAGE ID 45156

and valet. He married Amy Rogers, the daughter of a Black family that originally came from Vernon County in Wisconsin, and the couple had eight children, several of whom died in infancy. Returning to Madison, the family rented a house at 633 East Johnson Street and later, in 1907, bought a home at 639 East Dayton Street. Benjamin opened a barbershop in the basement of a bank. Robert M. La Follette Sr., a young university student who later became a congressman, a US Senator, and governor of Wisconsin, was one of his customers. La Follette could not pay him at that time but said that when he earned some money, he would return. La Follette kept his promise by offering Butts a lifetime messenger job at the State Historical Society. Butts earned a salary of twenty-five dollars a month.[14]

Butts was known as affable, courteous, and energetic. Lucile Miller, who knew the family through the church Amy Butts attended, said:

> Mrs. Butts joined St. Paul's African Methodist Church; Mr. Butts belonged to the First Methodist Church. You know what he would do? In those days they had stoves in the church. He would clean our church, make the fire on Sunday morning, then go home and change his clothes and wash up. He did that all his life. He never did join. Mrs. Butts did, but he never did. But he always did that for the church. You never had to worry; Mr. Butts was always there.[15]

From all accounts, Benjamin Butts was a well-respected man. Amy, who preceded him in death, was a resident of Madison for forty years and a charter member of the Order of the Eastern Star, an auxiliary church women's group at St. Paul African Methodist Episcopal Church.

Leo Vinton Butts, the Buttses' second-youngest son, had an outstanding football career at the University of Wisconsin. Born in 1898, Leo attended Madison High School. In 1918, he enrolled in the University of Wisconsin's pharmacy school. As a Badger, Leo Butts demonstrated his athleticism by participating in football, track, and basketball and became the first African American to play on the varsity football team. The *Daily Cardinal*, the university's newspaper, reported in 1918, "He has shown lots of pop and action and promises to put up a good game."[16] He also was one of four substitute linemen to make the traveling squad for the team. Because football was taking time away from his studies, he gave up the sport to concentrate on his courses and became the first African American to graduate from the School of Pharmacy in 1920.

Although the reported Black population in Madison increased from thirty-two to sixty people from 1860 to 1865 due to the number of Black Union soldiers at Camp Randall who decided to stay in Madison following the war, the number fell to forty-three by 1870.

Leo Butts was the first African American to play varsity football at the University of Wisconsin–Madison, where he graduated from the School of Pharmacy. KREMERS REFERENCE FILES, AMERICAN INSTITUTE OF THE HISTORY OF PHARMACY, UNIVERSITY OF WISCONSIN SCHOOL OF PHARMACY

1870S–1880S

During the 1870s, one hundred fifty African Americans settled in Dane County. Of the eighty-eight who settled in Madison, seventeen were born in Wisconsin, and the rest came from a variety of southern, northeastern, mid-Atlantic, and Midwestern states. The 1870 federal census began listing

Black people by race and gender. While most of the eighty-eight residents living in Madison were identified as Black, twelve were listed as "mulatto." The number of Black men was fifty-two and the number of Black women was thirty-six.

One Black man who reportedly settled in Madison after the Civil War made a name for himself in the later part of the century. William T. Green, who is not noted on any of the Madison census reports, led a crusade for the passage of the Wisconsin Civil Rights Act of 1895. When he arrived in Madison, he was hired to do janitorial work at the State Historical Society. Later, he entered the University of Wisconsin Law School in Madison, graduating in 1892. He moved to Milwaukee, becoming the city's first Black lawyer, and engaged more actively in the civil rights movement there. His civil rights activity led him to be elected to the Wisconsin State Republican Conference representing Milwaukee's mostly Black Fourth Ward. He introduced a bill in 1894 granting Blacks their civil rights in Wisconsin in the areas of public transportation, restaurants, and recreation. The bill passed, with fines up to one hundred dollars and possible imprisonment for violating its stipulations. However, the new law did not stop many Whites from practicing prejudice against Blacks in Madison.[17]

As the number of African Americans settling in Madison increased, so did discrimination. Thus, Blacks decided to form their own organizations for unity and support. Two organizations that formed before the 1900s were the Douglass Literary Society and the Good Templar Lodge. The former, named after abolitionist Frederick Douglass, provided social activities and education to Black people.[18] The Good Templar Lodge was organized nationally as an all-White temperance organization whose primary objective was to speak against drinking alcohol. However, in Madison, the lodge, exclusively composed of Black citizens, was not reported to have had temperance as an objective. In fact, an 1870 advertisement said that the "colored lodge" held a festival and social activity in Madison's City Hall.[19]

1890 TO 1910

Because a fire destroyed most of the 1890s census data stored in a US Census Bureau building in Washington, DC, not much information about Madison's early Black settlers is available for this period. Between 1880 and 1900, the population of African Americans in Madison fell to 79, then rose again to 89 by 1905. By 1910, that number surged to 143. In the early 1900s, several Blacks who may have been members of the Douglass Literary Society organized St. Paul African Methodist Episcopal Church, the first Black church in Madison. One founder, John Turner, and his wife, Martha, visited Madison on their way to Minneapolis and decided to stay. They lived at 118 North Blount Street, which became the meeting place for the founders of St. Paul African Methodist Episcopal Church when it was formally established in 1902.[20] Other founders of the church were Richard M. Miller, Albert Roberts, William Martin Miller, Moses Jefferson, William Hughes, and Henry Jameson. Reverend Sam Miller and J. S. Wood were the first ministers. The small congregation also met at 649 East Dayton Street,

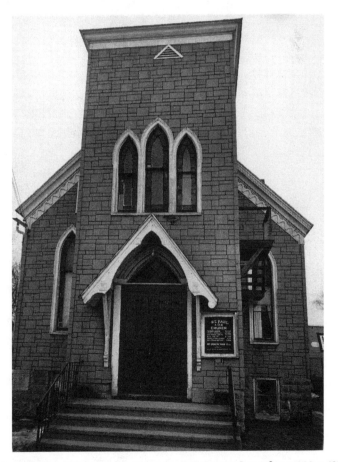

This St. Paul A.M.E. building was located at 625 East Dayton Street from 1902 to 1928, then moved to 631 East Dayton Street in 1928. It was torn down in 1964. WHI IMAGE ID 37662

the site of John Hill's grocery store, now a historic landmark. In 1902, they bought the First Norwegian Lutheran Church located on the corners of Hamilton, Butler, and Johnson Streets and moved it from there to 631 East Dayton Street, where the congregation met for sixty-three years.[21]

One of the founders was also a community activist. William Miller was a law graduate of Berea College in Kentucky. He met his wife, Anna Mae Stewart, a graduate of Knoxville College in Knoxville, Tennessee, while she was teaching at the Kentucky State Reformatory. Because Blacks could not obtain a license to practice law in Kentucky, Miller moved to Chicago, where he thought he could get licensure. Having no success in Chicago, he moved to Milwaukee. While working at the Plankinton House in Milwaukee, Miller met Governor Robert M. La Follette, who asked Miller to work for him as an executive assistant and expert on the needs of Black communities. After coming to Madison in 1902 to work for the governor, Miller and his wife bought two homes, at 645 and 647 East Dayton Street, and a home on land that is now Truax Field. They rented the home at 645 East Dayton Street to Black students and other Black families who came to Madison. The Miller home at 647 East Dayton Street is now a historic landmark, recognized as the oldest known Black-owned building remaining in Madison.

The Millers were considered social and educational leaders in Madison during the early 1900s. William Miller belonged to the Niagara Movement, an organization founded in 1905 by W.E.B. Du Bois and William Monroe Trotter, who was the first Black graduate of Harvard University. The National Association for the Advancement of Colored People (NAACP) contacted Miller in 1913, asking him to advise the organization on ways to defeat a bill proposed in Wisconsin that would have prohibited interracial marriages. Miller, along with V. C. Turner, Leo Butts, W. C. Johnson, A. Brown, and H. H. Starks, played a part in protesting the showing of the film *Birth of a Nation*.[22]

In 1909, a few Black men and women gathered at the Miller home to organize a club designed to improve African American intellectual development by reading articles and poems by prominent Black people and discussing the issues of the day. This club became known as the Book Lovers Club. The officers were listed as Anna Mae Miller, Asa Washington, O. P. Mack, W. W. Johnson, and M. A. Richardson. The club stayed active for four years (see appendix A). Besides the Book Lovers Club, other organizations

William and Anna Mae Miller and three of their children, Geraldine, Bill, and Lucile, in 1907.
COURTESY OF BETTY BANKS

emerged, such as the Madison chapter of the NAACP and Friendship
Chapter No. 2 of the Order of the Eastern Star, which was formed in 1910.
The Eastern Star women's group associated with St. Paul A.M.E. Church
raised money for the church, presided over funerals and weddings, and
assisted the pastor with various church activities. It disbanded in 1933
but reemerged in 1946, keeping its status as Friendship Chapter No. 2.[23]
On September 24, 1912, Wisconsin governor Francis E. McGovern

John Hill, owner of Hill's Grocery at 649 East Dayton Street. He and his wife owned the grocery store from 1915 until his death in the 1980s. WHI IMAGE ID 37661

appointed Anna Mae Miller to be a delegate to the National Congress of Colored Educators, held in Washington, DC.

John W. Hill and his wife, Amanda Carmichael Hill, came to Madison from Alabama in 1905. He worked in a restaurant, was a train porter, and operated a shoeshine shop in the Tenney Building. In 1915, he paid forty-five dollars for the building at 649 East Dayton Street to establish a grocery store, which Amanda ran while he operated the shoeshine parlor. This store became the longest-running family-owned grocery in Madison.[24]

Another early Black settler was Sam Pierce, who was born in 1870 in Virginia. As an adult, Pierce moved to Chicago, where he became a porter on the Chicago–Minneapolis railroad route. When working this route affected his health, he received a transfer and became a porter on the Madison–Milwaukee route for fourteen years.[25] In 1908, he brought his mother, Hettie; wife, Mollie; and nephew Ted to Madison. His mother had been born a slave in North Carolina in 1829. For thirty-six years, she lived in Madison with her son Sam at 1438 Williamson Street. Hettie outlived all eleven of her children, dying in 1944 at an estimated age of 115.[26]

Sam Pierce works in the executive offices of the governor in 1930. WHI IMAGE ID 37461

After working for the railroad, Sam Pierce obtained a position as a messenger working for governors John Blaine, Fred Zimmerman, Walter Kohler, Philip La Follette, and Albert Schmedeman. Pierce was more than six feet four inches tall and carried himself in a dignified manner. His main duty was to deliver important state documents and executive messages between the offices in the Capitol. In addition to this duty, he kept the reception areas for visitors spotless and well arranged. Highly regarded in the community, Pierce was described in a tribute to him that ran in the *Capital Times* as "actively identified with Negro advancement work here and he had business interests in Madison."[27] At one time Sam owned a shoeshine parlor and a tailor shop in the Loraine Hotel, as well as a car wash. Sam used his money and influence to help other Black families who moved into Dane County. He lobbied against housing discrimination in Madison and tried to drum up support for a community center for Black youths.[28]

Sam abandoned the idea. Sam Pierce died in 1936, but to honor him, his portrait was hung in the State Historical Society building during National Negro History Week, February 9–16, 1968. Sam was the first African American from Wisconsin to be honored in this manner.[29]

Sam Pierce with his mother, Hettie Starks Pierce, in 1929. WHI IMAGE ID 37458

Another Black man who came to Madison in the first decade of the twentieth century was Louis W. Anderson. He arrived in 1906, opening a shoeshine stand on South Pinckney Street and living at 141 South Franklin Street. He also was a news carrier for the *Capital Times* and originated an honor system of selling papers by placing stands around the city with coin boxes. The customer dropped the money in the box and took a paper instead of waiting for a newsboy.[30]

1910 TO 1920

Blacks who came to Madison in this decade were not only early settlers, but early community activists as well. They established another church and created organizations, such as the Utopia Club, founded in 1918 to promote interracial understanding and perform charitable, educational, and civic work.[31] African Americans in Madison also opened businesses during this time, including the *Wisconsin Weekly Blade*, the state's first Black publication. This decade signaled a time when African Americans began developing community and entrepreneurship.

From 1910 to 1920, the Black community grew from 143 to 259 people. Some of the families who arrived in Madison during this period were the Bosticks, Charlie and Myrtle Daniels, the Frazer family, Joe Gentry, John Mosley, the Shephard family, Frank Hoover, Albert and Fannie Weaver, Oliver Davis, Oscar Shivers, Zachary Trotter, William Hopkins, and Carrie Williams. This growth led to the creation of Mt. Zion Baptist Church in 1911. Its first location was on West Johnson Street. The men who helped found this church were J. N. Wilson, T. E. Hines, A. J. Jones, and J. Anthony Josey, who served as the chairman of its board of trustees.

Born and raised in Augusta, Georgia, Josey started the first Black newspaper in Wisconsin. After high school, Josey attended Atlanta University, a historically Black college and university, and while there began his journalistic experience at the *Atlanta Independent*. After graduating, he married Chestena M. Carmichael, and in 1905 the couple moved to Madison, where he entered law school at the University of Wisconsin in 1910. Josey worked as a janitor and waited tables.

During this time, Josey recognized that the Black community did not have a newspaper, and that existing publications in the city failed to cover issues and happenings in the Black community. To fill this gap, Josey debuted the *Wisconsin Weekly Blade* on June 8, 1916.[32] The paper operated out of Josey's home on Henry Street. L. J. Quisely and Z. P. Smith, pastor of Mt. Zion Baptist Church, were Josey's coeditors, and George DeReef, a Black lawyer, was a contributing editor. The paper sold at a subscription rate of $1.50 per year. The opening lines of the newspaper stated,

> We are about to speak and we wish your attention. In the first place we have started a newspaper and have named it "The WISCONSIN WEEKLY BLADE." We have done this because we feel and believe that there is a demand for this kind of paper we propose to run. We have studied the matter carefully and we believe we are going to succeed.[33]

The front page of the inaugural issue of the *Wisconsin Weekly Blade*, June 8, 1916.

Josey wrote that the paper's intent was to lift up and not pull down, and to produce a good paper. He further described its aim:

> The mission of a newspaper in these times was two-fold: to publish news from the north, south, east, and west, as the letters of the word news imply and also to help create a healthy sentiment. . . . We have no grudges to settle and shall avoid all internal church and society differences. . . . We believe the Negro has in his own hand his destiny.[34]

J. Anthony Josey.

The articles in the *Wisconsin Weekly Blade* often focused on issues of social justice for Blacks. For example, Josey opposed the war policies of President Woodrow Wilson, who had retreated on his promise of providing equal justice for people of color.

Josey's editorials alleged that President Wilson was institutionalizing racial segregation in the federal bureaucracy and destroying all that had been done for civil rights. He and other Black editors led an antienlistment campaign, discouraging Blacks from joining the armed forces. After federal government agencies began investigating the *Chicago Defender* and other Black newspapers in an apparent effort to suppress their voices, Josey changed his tone about enlistment but still continued to speak out against Wilson. He reminded his readers that Blacks were loyal to the war effort regardless of the ways that Whites treated them, and that Black soldiers demonstrated bravery against the Germans in France. On March 31, 1917, as Americans became increasingly aware of the war and loyal to the effort to defeat the Germans, Madison officials held a parade in which Blacks "turned out in full force." However, when Josey announced that he had arranged for Black soldiers of the 365th Regiment, Ninety-Second Division to be welcomed home with another parade, the festivities were mysteriously cancelled.[35]

Josey also wrote articles on behalf of Black women's rights. At a national convention, the General Federation of Women's Clubs refused to admit women of color from Wisconsin and from across the country. This incident created great indignation among the club members of color, who did not make efforts to join the national organization but instead "redoubled efforts for their own organizations."[36]

Beyond being an advocate for change, the *Wisconsin Weekly Blade* also covered the social activities of clubs, churches, and organizations and noted personal news, such as the arrival and departure of visiting friends and family. In addition to fostering a sense of community and giving recognition to the daily events in the lives of Madison's Black citizens, these reports provide valuable historic evidence of the scope and activities of their growing community.

The *Blade* worked with a variety of businesses that were not afraid to advertise in a newspaper that was owned and operated by Black people. Some of the *Wisconsin Weekly Blade*'s advertisers were John Hill Groceries, a Black-owned grocery, as well as White-owned businesses, such as Harvard Shoes on Washington Avenue and Pinckney Street, Lewis' Drug Store on State and Gilman Streets, Kennedy Dairy Company at 618 University Avenue, Capital City Cigar Company at 108 South Pinckney Street, and Madison Gas & Electric Company.

A SAMPLING OF COMMUNITY NEWS
IN THE *WEEKLY BLADE*

- Mayor George Sayle today named fourteen colored citizens of Madison as delegates to the first annual convention of the Co-operative Development and Progressive association at Oshkosh June 22. The delegates are the Rev. Z. P. Smith, T. E. Hines, V. C. Turner, S. S. Steele, Asa E. Washington, Harry Allison, Joseph Gentry, A. L. Weaver, J. S. Mosley, Allen Henderson, Z. A. Trotter, W. R. Harris, John W. Hill, and J. Anthony Josey. (June 8, 1916, p. 1)

- The Dane County Colored Club, of which Messrs. Allen Henderson, T. E. Hines, Geo. E. Buckner and Asa E. Washington are the advisory board, are planning for its members and followers at 222 E. Main St., June 23rd. The occasion will be a full dress affair. (June 15, 1916, p. 3)

- Mrs. Daisy Gentry leaves today for two months stay visiting her parents in Gourdin, Ark. She will stop in Chicago, being entertained by her many friends. Before returning she will visit Louisville, Ky., Memphis, Tenn., and Oklahoma. (June 15, 1916, p. 3)

- The Blade is operating an employment agency; all kinds of work furnished. (June 15, 1916, p. 3)

- The Blade is planning on issuing a special edition of Madison children. Let us have the photo of your boy or girl. (June 15, 1916, p. 3)

- The Blade is on sale at the following places: Mosley & Smith, 202 E Washington Ave., Trotter & Hopkins, 222 E. Main St., Hill's Grocery Store, 649 E. Dayton St., Weaver's Grocery Store, 522 E. Mifflin St., and all Local News Stands. (June 18, 1916, p. 3)

- Mr. and Mrs. William Hopkins [are] now housekeeping at 643 E. Dayton Street (July 20, 1916, p. 3)

- Mrs. Ida Carmichael is confined to her home for an indefinite period [recovering] from a very painful scalding of her foot. Her condition is serious. (July 31, 1919, p. 5)

- Mr. Harry Allison and daughter, Miss Marguerite, returned to the city after a month's visit in St. Louis, Kansas City, Mo. and Independence, Mo. While away both father and daughter were the recipients of many social functions. (July 31, 1919, p. 5)

- Hill's Grocery carries a full line of groceries. Phone 7975 (September 14, 1916, p. 3)

- Mr. and Mrs. J. Scott Mosley, 821 Milton St. At Dinner in honor of the Misses Myrtle D. Smith and Robertha Echols of Chicago, At the palatial home of Mrs. and Mrs. J. Scott Mosley on last Sunday afternoon an eight course dinner was served. . . . The guests consisted of Mr. and Mrs. J. Anthony Josey, Miss Pauline Battice, Messrs. H. De Voe Canney and W. Randall Carmichael. (September 14, 1916, Page 3)

- Andrew Mehlas, restaurant proprietor at 207 State Street, was brought into court to answer the charge of refusing to serve W. R. Harris. It was brought out that the Greek's refusal to serve was solely on account of color. He pleaded guilty and was fined $15 and costs with a thirty-day jail sentence as alternative. (March 1, 1917, Page 1)

Even though the local newspaper publishers of the *Wisconsin State Journal* and the *Capital Times* did not report many news items about the Black community, they did respect Anthony Josey as journalist and citizen. When a World War I veteran fatally shot a Racine Baptist minister and wounded Josey in Josey's home over a dispute about religious differences, the *Capital Times* and the *Wisconsin State Journal* reported on Josey's condition almost daily. A month later both papers announced his release from the hospital. Media coverage of the incident "indicated their esteem for their brother of the press."[37] In 1925, Josey moved to Milwaukee, where he continued to publish the *Wisconsin Weekly Blade*.

1920S ONWARD

The Black population in Madison continued its upward climb from 1920 to 1930, with the 1930 federal census showing 367 Blacks in Madison.[38] Despite the growth of the Black community in Madison, other than what was reported in the *Wisconsin Weekly Blade*, little other information exists to indicate what opportunities or obstacles they faced during this time. Scattered reports hint at a tension between African Americans and other Madison residents who were less than welcoming toward the newcomers. In 1925, the NAACP recorded that "a journeying Black was arrested on the grounds of the murder of a White couple. As the Blacks believed that he was innocent, they formed a committee to free him. They were successful in that attempt."[39]

The Ku Klux Klan also was active during this time, using Prohibition-fueled violence to sow fear and support for their organization. A *Wisconsin*

Members of the Ku Klux Klan march through the Greenbush neighborhood on South Park Street in 1924. WHI IMAGE ID 1902

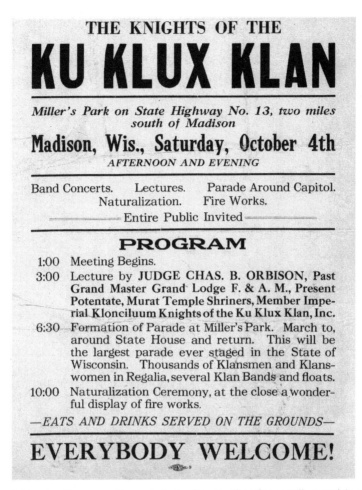

A broadside advertises a meeting and picnic of the Ku Klux Klan at Miller's Park in 1924.
WHI IMAGE ID 51778

State Journal photo taken on December 4, 1924, shows two hundred Klan members marching down King Street to attend the funeral of a police officer who was allegedly slain by Italian immigrants in the Greenbush neighborhood.[40]

During the 1930s and 1940s, the Black population almost doubled. The local newspapers covered some events and activities in which Blacks participated, or printed the death notices of prominent Blacks of the time. The *Weekly Blade* had been the main outlet for recognition, promotion of their events, and social sustenance and satisfaction, but coverage became sparse after it began publishing in Milwaukee. Blacks had to get news related to their interests from national newspapers such as the *Philadelphia Inquirer*, although a gap remained in community coverage. In the 1940s, a group of young African American women began publishing the *Alpharetta News*, Madison's first Black youth newspaper. It published local community news, including wedding announcements, funeral information, recipes, and school and church events.

In 2004, Jonathan Gramling, publisher and editor of the *Capital City Hues*, wrote a four-part series based on interviews with James Braxton, a Black southerner who came to Madison in 1937. Like the other stories detailed in this book's oral histories, this personal account fills in details of life for Blacks living in Madison during this period. Braxton was born in 1918 in Ruleville, a small town in northwestern Mississippi, where cotton was king. Sharecroppers such as Braxton often owed more to landowners for seed and tools than their crops were worth. Black sharecroppers did not have the same ability to borrow funds from banks that White farmers did and struggled to provide basic necessities for their families during hard years. "When you're sharecropping, they own you," Braxton told Gramling.[41] Growing up in this system, Braxton was often unable to go to school because he lacked proper clothing and had to work on his family's land. He recalled White children riding by in buses, throwing stuff and yelling racial slurs. Braxton said, "I don't care if you had one individual or five kids, you worked for ten cents an hour."[42]

The poor treatment and pay that Braxton experienced in the South motivated him to leave home and move north during the Great Migration, when millions of African Americans were doing the same. In 1937, Braxton bought a train ticket to Madison, where his Uncle Jake lived on the corner

James Braxton. JONATHAN D. GRAMLING

of Baird and Center Streets, an area of town that was mostly cornfields at the time. Later, he moved from his uncle's to Dane Street, and then to live upstairs in the building that used to be Mr. P's tavern at 1616 Beld Street. Braxton received an education in Madison through a federal program funded by Franklin Roosevelt's administration. The program gave him twenty-five dollars a month to go to Madison Adult Vocational School, where he studied arc and acetylene welding. One man put obstacles in Braxton's way: "The man, Mr. Straeman, didn't like me and didn't want me to graduate. But I did. I had to take [those] classes twice to graduate and he finally let me graduate."[43]

During World War II, jobs opened up at Oscar Mayer, where only three African Americans had worked prior to the war. At first the company told Braxton that they needed welders and many other types of workers, but he was later told that there were no such openings, even as the company continued to hire for jobs he had been told did not exist. After much persistence, he finally was hired, but not for the job he had trained for. "They put me down in inedible," he said. "We had to cut them up, cook 'em, and grind them up into a powder. We'd put it in a machine and put some bags under that. We'd sew up the bag. That was my job. We'd have to do that for 16 hours per day."[44] He later quit because he did not get the welding job he had originally wanted. Braxton then worked for 3F Laundry, located in the 700 block of East Dayton Street, for forty cents an hour. He then returned to Oscar Mayer for seventy cents an hour, after they again dangled the promise of a welding job. After working for another year and a half in the inedible section, the company still did not give him the job for which he had trained.[45]

Like many African American families who migrated to Madison at that time, Braxton held two or three jobs at a time. While working at Oscar Mayer, he also cleaned up at the Badger Candy Kitchen on the Capitol Square. After 1950, Braxton worked at the Veteran's Administration Hospital, where he became a union activist, serving as president of the American Federation of Government Employees until 1980, after which he bought Lee's Cleansers at 1216 Williamson Street. During his life in Madison, he owned a pool hall attached to a restaurant owned by Zach Trotter on Washington Avenue, a cleaning business, and two homes.

Braxton lived in Greenbush, which he described as a beautiful and friendly neighborhood. "Everyone got along. Jews, Italians. They'd make that wine and moonshine. You name it," Braxton recalled. "We had something of everything going on there. People looked out for one another. No, you don't hurt your neighbor; I don't care what they do. I loved it down there. . . . I stayed in the Bush until they tore it all down and ran us out of

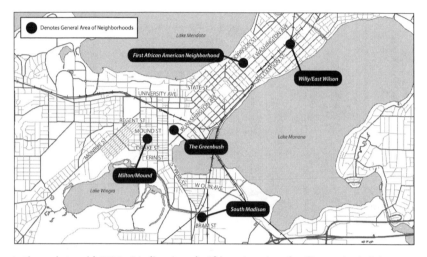

In the early to mid-1900s, Madison's early African American families made their homes in five main neighborhoods, as shown on this map. CITY OF MADISON, PLANNING DIVISION

there."[46] He noted the political and social scene of Madison at the time, commenting that only three or four families were involved in the NAACP early on, and the organization took off only after a group of southern segregationists came to Madison to make Blacks feel unwanted. He remembered conflicts in the United Service Organization at Truax when Whites mistreated Blacks and did not want to mix with them, just as they had been used to doing in the South. "We said, 'Oh, no, this ain't Mississippi. This is Wisconsin!' This is when the NAACP started up again." Later in life, Braxton became an active participant in the civil rights movement, joining the Madison Equal Opportunities Commission in 1963, and then serving as its housing committee chair for eleven years. He praised civil rights activists of the time, such as James Wright, Odell and Dimetra Taliaferro Shivers, Hilton Hanna, Anna Mae Mitchell, Mary Louise Symon, and Helen Vukelich.

Braxton came to Madison in 1937 as a bitter man because of the life he led in Mississippi, but here he met people who shared a common purpose. The White and Black residents who worked together to fight segregation and discrimination caused him to lose his bitterness and contribute to that purpose. His story is one of the many that has survived to show the vibrancy and resiliency of Madison's African American community.

ORAL HISTORIES

MADISON'S EARLY BLACK FAMILIES
SHARE THEIR STORIES

"My mission in life is not merely to survive, but to thrive; and to do so with some passion, some compassion, some humor, and some style."

—MAYA ANGELOU

BILLY McDONALD

Billy McDonald, son of James and Anna Mae Miller McDonald, retired in 1990 from the University of Wisconsin–Madison after working there for thirty years as a campus mail handler. He volunteered for the Wisconsin Historical Society for two years. Since retirement, he has spent more time with his buddies, a few of whom are also Madison Central High School graduates.

Billy McDonald.
MURIEL SIMMS

My grandparents, William and Anna Mae Miller, came to Madison in 1901. They lived in Milwaukee before that for at least two or three years. William was a lawyer but couldn't find a law job. He worked for the Plankinton Hotel in Milwaukee as a waiter. One of his favorite customers was Bob La Follette, or "Fighting Bob," as he was sometimes called. Bob asked my grandfather, "Bill, I know you have a better education than you're showing here as a waiter. I don't doubt anybody for what they do with their education, but what did you do?" And my grandfather said, "I am a college graduate of Berea College in Berea, Kentucky." My grandmother, Anna Mae, graduated from Knoxville College in Knoxville, Tennessee, with a teaching degree. This was obviously before the turn of the twentieth century, when it was kind of rare for Blacks to finish college. By the way, my aunt Ernestine Mitchell was the first Black teacher to be hired by the Madison School District. She was hired as a substitute and taught well into the sixties. Her husband, Eddie Mitchell, was an accountant and a graduate of UW–Madison. Anyway, my grandfather told La Follette that he [had] finished in law but couldn't find a job. La Follette said, "How would you like to come to Madison and work for me as a legal consultant?" My grandfather said, "Of course." He came to Madison and started to work for him right away. He was here a couple of months, and then my grandmother moved to Madison and settled. At one time, we had accumulated five homes. The homes were rented one at a time: two of them on Dayton Street and three on Olin Avenue by where the old bridge used to be. Two are still up. One was torn down. To be more accurate, when my grandparents moved to Madison, they bought a house on Johnson Street and had it moved to Dayton Street, to the 600 block. They also moved the second house next door to the first one. The addresses were 643 and 647 East Dayton Street.

There was a fire at the Capitol. My grandmother told us that my grandfather ran up there in his nightshirt to get the papers and books out of Senator La Follette's office, and it just so happened that the fire didn't reach that wing, but he was removing things so that the fire wouldn't get them. My grandfather later died of pneumonia in 1922.

My grandparents had six children: Geraldine, Lucile, Anna Mae, Caroline, William, and Dubois. Geraldine died young, in her early twenties. When my grandfather died, my grandmother had to go to work for [the] first time, and the only job she could do was domestic work. Back then, the neighborhood on Dayton Street was half Black and half White. The neighbors always said, "Well, it's going to be funny not to see Mrs. Miller sitting [on] the porch all day and her husband working and now she was going to have to go to work." We were fortunate to have the antiques, the old furniture. We were able to keep it all during the Depression because we were fortunate. My grandfather and grandmother never kept any money in the bank, so when the banks folded, nothing was lost. At one time we had a country home on the [future] property of Truax Field. My grandmother held onto everything throughout the Depression and the mid-thirties. My grandmother sold the property out there so we could keep our homes together and sold the other three homes except the two that were on Dayton Street. She said if we had the foresight and had looked a couple years ahead, we could have been millionaires, because the government paid top money for Truax Field. I'm not sure who they sold it to, but the government turned right around to build the airfield there, the army and air force. She said we would have been sittin' pretty the rest of our lives. It was like in Truax Field proper, not on the other side or way out; it was there. It was a morning trip back in the days when they had a Maxwell or a LaFayette. They used to ride on Dayton Street and East Washington

Avenue. Everybody on the east side knew the Millers. My grandmother was the matriarch of the family for quite a few years.

They were fortunate. I think it had a lot to do with my grandfather working for Senator La Follette. The kids went to Lincoln grade school, which was on Gorham Street. They went to Central High School with all the money people at that time, like the doctors in Madison. They all lived up around Sherman Avenue and Maple Bluff. My family knew everyone along there, and the people who were of any importance in Madison who had money. They had no problems. My neighborhood was fine. Now, my mother had problems when they wanted to move from the Bush to different homes. They had problems getting places to live. However, when you said you were a Miller, you had no problems in Madison because everybody said, "Oh, you're William and Anna Mae's grandsons, or Mae's kids." It was nice to be known and that the Miller family had a name, and it was nice to have a good name. My grandmother said that other Blacks had problems with jobs, with living, but our family didn't have any problems with living because we owned property and homes, which made it much easier than renting. My mother used to do a lot of babysitting and my grandmother used to do a lot of work around the house, but in the later years, I'd say she worked in different families' homes.

My mother said that my grandmother and my aunt Lucile would say what they pleased. Lucile used to correspond with every senator, state or national, that was from Madison. She knew them all. She would handwrite them daily and tell them what she thought they should be doing. My grandfather was very political. He was one of the original Niagara Eleven, the beginning of the NAACP. My grandfather couldn't go [to] the meeting in Niagara Falls because he was sick. He knew W.E.B. Dubois. Of course, working for La Follette, we were progressives, and in fact, Bob La Follette and my grandfather were part of the reason William Evjue started the *Capital Times*. Evjue's ideas were different from those of the *Wisconsin State Journal*, so La Follette and my grandfather talked Evjue into starting his own newspaper. They were all good friends. My grandmother used to brag about this. She would say, "Your grandfather was in the middle of this, and that [is] why to this day, I still read the *Capital Times*." I wish I would have known more about my grandfather than I did because at the time there were tidbits that [my] grandmother would tell us about our grandfather.

There were no conflicts between our family and other families. But there were some Black people who thought that my grandmother was too high and mighty for the rest of the Black people in town because she had so many White friends and because of her education, intelligence, and knowledge. My grandmother didn't look down on people but felt she was walking a different step from everybody because of her upbringing and the way she taught. She said, "I want to teach you and you to know that you are going to be able to sit down and talk to anyone, whether he is a street sweeper, a ditch digger, a janitor, or the governor or the president. You will be able to sit face-to-face and talk to him as well as you can talk to anyone. You will never feel that you are beneath them. You are on their level or above their level." I've always followed that theory. They always said that we thought we were different. I would say back, "No, you thought we were different. We didn't." My grandmother always said that what you know about yourself is good enough. What they don't know about you is their problem. We were brought up to believe that there was no such thing as separate but equal. We are put here all together and treated all together. My grandmother told one youngster one time, "God never made one color of flower. Go look at flowers. How many colors are there? You can't count them. That's the way people are." My mother said that they misunderstood Grandmother because she was a fighter for all rights, and without all rights you wouldn't have any rights for anyone. My grandmother fought for Black voting rights and for women's voting rights. If there had been conflicts, Grandmother and Lucile would have been in the middle of everything, wondering why the Whites are treating the Blacks that way.

My dad, Ernie, told us, "I don't want to ever hear you come home and say, 'They did it' or 'I did it because they did it.' You guys better be the leaders. If you're in trouble, it better be because you're in trouble, not because he's in trouble and you're with him. You better be the one. You better be the leader. You are not a follower." I can remember an incident. My youngest brother, Ralph, was coming home from school with a bunch of guys from Lapham School. They took a shortcut through the marketplace. There was an abandoned building. Some of the kids threw rocks through the windows of this building. Ralph knew better. He walked away. The police came. Everybody ran. Ralph didn't run. The police said, "We got you." Ralph said, "For what?" The police said, "For breaking windows." Ralph said he didn't do it, but the police insisted, saying, "You didn't run like the rest of them. I'm going to take you to your parents." Obviously, the police didn't know our parents. My mother asked what happened. Ralph told the story about kids breaking windows and said that the police think he did it. My mother asked Ralph whether or not he did it and why he didn't run. Ralph said he didn't do it and didn't run because he didn't do anything wrong. My mother said, "That is good enough for me and it better be good enough for you." The cop said, "Yes, ma'am" and turned around and walked away.

There was an incident at Central High School. The only thing that people knew was that there were Black boys involved. My brother Ralph was the youngest one in the group and happened to be in this particular age group, and who had never been picked up by the police. The other kids worried about that. They wondered why, but yet they knew better than to believe that he squealed. There were a few other boys that weren't in on it, but the reason Ralph was not called by the police was because his last name was Mitchell and his mother's name was Miller. Having the right name and [being] the right type of person helped. Some kids' families didn't have a name that the police knew. So the police took those they didn't know to the station.

We didn't have problems with other ethnic groups either, because a lot of them had the same problems we had. When we lived in the Bush, we were like all family. In my mother's era, they may have had a few problems with other ethnic groups, but the problems were gone just like that; they didn't linger. We practically lived at each others' houses, whether White or Black. It didn't make any difference. We were always grouped together. We were taught that if any parent said it's time to go home, we never argued; we never talked back. We went home. If invited to stay for dinner, we stayed and ate. Sometimes my mother would get mad at us, saying that just because they invite you doesn't mean you have to stay and eat. Then you come home and you eat again. You don't need that. You leave by five. I seldom heard the N-word. I heard a guy say the N-word once when my brother Scrammy and I were walking to school. Scrammy punched him and that was it. We were good friends after that. The guy knew better than to punch Scrammy back. It never happened again. We were always told by Ernie, "Don't you ever say the N-word in this house or ever let me hear or have me find out you have said it, because if you don't like them to say it, then you shouldn't say it." We couldn't call anybody names. We couldn't call Polish, Italians, or Jewish people names. The neighborhoods we lived in were very good that way.

Just to show you how the Bush neighborhood was: During the war, my mother worked at a small box factory on Regent Street. It was in the ten or twelve hundred block of Mills Street. We lived on Murray. It was a night job, and my mother would get off at midnight. Ernie would walk from our house to meet her to walk her home. An Italian man saw him and said, "Hey, Ernie, what are you and your wife doing out here so late?" Ernie told him that Mae just got off from work and that he was walking her home. The Italian guy said, "You don't have to worry about her in this neighborhood. We know who she is. Nobody will bother her. If anybody bothers her, all she has to do is walk into any one of these businesses, the Italian Workman's Club, Josie's, any place along the way. She will be well protected." And that was the last time Ernie walked to meet my mom unless he wanted to.

We had no problem that I know of getting the Hilltop restaurant in 1952. The bad thing was we had a neighborhood where people did not go out to eat much because it wasn't a very rich neighborhood. We had bus drivers at the end of the bus route, we had police; we had people come in after the bars closed. Ernie barbecued chicken and ribs in their fireplace in the back and my mother made pies. The Uptown restaurant on State Street closed, and it would have been perfect for us to open a restaurant there because Madison could have used a good barbeque and chicken place at the time. Austin McClinton opened up a little restaurant there, but it did not survive either. We ended up losing money in the Hilltop and had to close.

I'm positive that our family was on the network for student housing because we had students at my grandmother's house on Dayton Street for many years. We rented the house next door to families. I think there was a silent list that Black families had that listed which Black families would rent to Black students or others who came to town. Newspapers didn't advertise because, even though Madison liked to look liberal, it wasn't. It wasn't an open thing that you would put in the paper. To my knowledge, there was never anything in the paper that said renting to Negro or White only. Look around now, Blacks are everywhere, but back then there were a number of places in Madison where Blacks lived that people didn't even know about because it wasn't advertised. The church played a role in helping with renting, too. That was another word of mouth. St. Paul had rotating ministers, which was too bad because they didn't live in Madison long enough to help people. The Baptist church had Reverend Joe Washington. He did a lot. He helped a lot of people get established in housing and jobs. I should mention Reverend Peroni, too. He was of the Italian Methodist. Italians, Whites, Blacks, Catholics were members of his church. He was another one who helped people living in the Bush, because his church was in the Bush on Lake and Milton Streets. He did help a lot of Black people who needed housing. People did not know he did a lot for Madison. In fact, a lot of Catholic Italians used to go to him without the Catholic Church knowing about it. He got a lot of stuff done. He and one of his sons went back to Italy because they had a big vineyard. Peroni's wine and beer are still produced there. Louis Arms and his half-sister Nedra Arms belonged to his church. I went to a family reunion in Hillsboro several years ago with Louis and Nedra. You saw Indians, Blacks and Whites. That was one of the best reunions I've ever seen in my whole life.

Blacks who moved to the south side said that Blacks on the east side didn't know what it was to be Black. They had no idea. They just didn't want to do anything with us. We would go to the Loft. They never did, so they thought we were above everybody else. We didn't go to their parties because they were drinking parties. We got along with them, but we just didn't socialize. It was the established versus the newcomers. Like when the soldiers from Truax Field came to town. They wanted to bring their life in our town. It didn't mix. Like any army place, it didn't mix with the town. I'm not saying anybody was at fault. But somewhere along the way, we didn't get together. It may have been because so many of the soldiers, Black and White, came from the south, so there was no mixing there. Established people got along well and all knew each other through the churches and organizations like the NAACP. Voting was open for everybody, but many people had nothing to do with voting. My grandmother, mother, and aunt worked at the polling booth; they knew what was going on in politics. There were a few established people, people who were conscious of the community, not just themselves, and knew what was going on, like Dimetra Shivers.

When I was a kid, I used to think the Simmses lived in a castle. They lived and worked in the fraternity house on Langdon. But I used to think it was a castle because of the pillars. Lucile used to go there to visit, to see what was going on [laughing]. Grandmother used to work at one of the fraternities, too, cooking. In fact, Bud Foster, who was a big cheese in basketball as the coach, would not recruit any Blacks to play basketball, but he would help my grandmother clean the kitchen. She couldn't believe how he was there compared to how he was about basketball. She said he used to clean up, take things off the tables; he was such a good help around, but he wouldn't recruit Blacks. Anyway, some people were down on the Simmses because they lived in a neighborhood that had only four or five Blacks living there. They couldn't understand this. The Simmses didn't have to find somebody to get where they lived; they got where they lived because they got it. My grandmother told us when we were younger, "Don't you ever let me hear of you using a group of people to help you find a job. You better be able to sit down and interview for a job and get that job better than the next man, or I better know why you didn't get it. And if there is a reason why you don't get it, then we should look into it." I'll always remember Grandmother Miller saying, "You are as good as or better than anyone—Black, White, or any color. You were brought up that way; you are going to be that way and you better think that way." I'll remember that until the day I die.

We had a lot of discussions at our house, arguments and family discussions of current events. One guy at the university told me that I was spoiled because I don't have to worry about segregation. I told him that we weren't born or raised in a vacuum. We knew and discussed everything in our home. If something came up in the paper that we didn't understand, it was discussed in our home. Why do you think we formed an NAACP? We didn't want segregation to happen here. Why did we have an Urban League? Same thing. Why do you think we fought for voting rights? Same thing. We worked to prevent the problem. These discussions were family traditions. Sewing, knitting, crocheting, and playing sports, such as baseball, softball, touch football, track, were our family traditions, too.

My real dad died young; I didn't get to know him, but my mother said he worked himself to death. He died at twenty-eight. Our grandfather McDonald, who was half White, died in Madison. It bothers the daylights out of me that I never knew his age or never had a picture of him to show people. My grandmother McDonald said he was typical Irish, red ruddy face, short-cropped hair. My grandmother was African. The McDonalds were house servants and not considered slaves. They lived in the big house; my grandfather's father owned some slaves, but not very many because he wasn't that rich. My grandmother went to grade school and high school with my grandfather. They had the same upbringing; they played with each other when they were children. My grandfather thought he was going to defy his father by marrying her, an African. They all felt like it was going to happen anyway, so they never thought about it one way or the other. So that's the McDonald side.

There were many times when my dad, James McDonald, worked two full-time jobs. But he played all sports. He played basketball and baseball. I remember one time he had this job. I don't remember if it was ditch digging or what, but it was a street job. The foreman told him to do something and my dad looked down at his shoes and said, "I can't [do] the work in these shoes. These are one hundred dollar shoes." My dad wore size nineteen and twenty shoes. The man said, "You're fired. Anybody who can buy a one hundred dollar pair of shoes doesn't need this job." The guy fired him on the spot. My dad always said that you can't live without a firm foundation. My grandmother McDonald said that when my dad and his brothers sat in the living room anywhere, their feet would cover the whole room. She said they sure had a firm foundation.

My uncles, Dubois ["Duke"] and Bill Miller, left high school early. Duke said he could build a car and work on an engine as well as anyone, but that wasn't his vocation. The only time Duke could get mechanics is through vocational school. The vocational teacher told my grandmother that Duke learned everything there was to learn about mechanics. He knew everything about a car. He went into the army and learned about diesel engines. The army was segregated. He worked in construction on two airstrips: Wake Island and Midway Island. When Duke came back from the military, he and Leo Wiley had a car wash place together called Car Brite Auto Laundry. They washed and polished cars by hand. He also had a filling station in the Bush on Milton and Park Streets, at the bottom of the hill. A developer was going to tear it down to build something. After that, Uncle Bill opened his own garage on Butler Street, one block from Doty and Main Streets. What kept him going was that he used to repair the trucks for Ed Phillips and Sons, the liquor place. They were right across the street from the garage. That really helped him; he had steady work. Duke didn't have any problems because he was [a] good mechanic.

My uncles were so different. You could go to Duke and say, "Duke, my car is falling apart." He'd say, "Okay, I'll be right there." Well, a week later you call him again, "Oh, yeah, I'm coming." My grandmother would say, "I'm fixing lunch today. Come and get some food." He'd come over and forget about the job, but she got him there anyway.

Uncle Bill was a carpenter, electrician, and plumber. Uncle Bill worked in the Solomon Islands as the head of all the electricians because he knew everything. Sometimes he would get busted for things like when his commanding officer ordered him to make the men dig trenches and holes for fifteen minutes and then rest for five. My uncle noticed that these guys would come up wringing wet and breathing bad. He made them dig for five minutes and rest for fifteen. Sometimes he wouldn't come to chow; he would catch and cook his own food in the jungle and eat by himself. Like when the colonel came up to Bill and said, "Bill, will you take a crew and go over to such and such. It's electrical work." Uncle Bill said, "I can't do it. I was busted the other day down to corporal." The colonel said, "I just put you up to sergeant. Go take this crew." That's the way it was for him. But the officers depended on him because he knew everything about electrical work.

Uncle Bill had the first noncommercial radio in Madison. He built it himself in his backyard. He probably was a teenager then. It had a nice, high antenna. He attached a wire to that and ran it all the way down to the church. He climbed to the top of the church's steeple to get the ground for it. My grandmother said people used to come off of the streets to come listen to the radio. He could get WHA because that was the first station. Mrs. Bostick said to my grandmother, "Bill is up there and he is going to kill himself and my grandmother would say, "Oh, he knows what he's doin'; he's putting an antennae up for his radio." He also built a radio in a fountain pen.

DOLORES SIMMS GREENE

Dolores graduated from UW–Madison with a BS degree in secondary edu-cation, with a double major in English and speech and a minor in French. She did her master's work at UW–Madison, UW–Milwaukee, and Marquette University. Her predoctorate work was in Equal Employment Opportunity and Title VII law. Her first job was teaching English and citizenship to immigrants. Because the Madison public school system would not accept any qualified Black teachers at that time, Dolores's husband and sons moved to Milwaukee. The Milwaukee public school system hired her to teach reading to the college bound, and to serve as a reading consultant, a position in which she demonstrated how to create successful inner-city-school reading centers. Later, Dolores and family returned to Madison, where she filled administrative positions with the state Department of Labor and Department of Health and Social Services. There she supervised the initiation of affirmative action plans and programs. Before retirement, Dolores spent eight years as the chancellor's assistant at UW–Extension in Madison, where she steered the adoption and implemen-tation of policies prohibiting sexual harassment as well as led the Extension's services in civil rights compliance and affirmative action activities. Dolores had creative energy as well, becoming a novelist, poet, and oil painter.

My father, David Simms, taught students reading, writing, and math in grades one to eight in a one-room schoolhouse in Blackwater, Missouri, about one hundred miles from Kansas City, Missouri. He was often paid in farm food products to supplement his government salary. He was determined to seek a higher education, which he was convinced was the only way to rise above the standard of the poor farming communities in which he was raised. In the 1920s, Missouri had in place the policy of refusing to allow Black students into its public universities. Instead, the state would send qualified Black students to schools in other states that were racially integrated. Missouri picked up the cost. My father applied to the pharmacy school at UW–Madison in 1927, was accepted, and moved to Madison while my mother and me stayed in Missouri.

In 1934, my father received word from UW–Madison officials that he could not continue his education without more income from Missouri, and besides Missouri had a limit that it would spend for these out-of-state stipends. He took maintenance and janitorial positions to fund his education and at the same time took correspondence courses in engineering at UW–Extension. Someone he met in Madison told him that if he took janitorial work, and if he had a wife who could cook, then he and family could have free housing at fraternity houses. Dad took this chance for employment and sent for my mother and me, age five, to come to Madison. Mom could not cook well but had to learn quickly to prepare meals three times a day for twenty-five boys at this fraternity. We lived at Delta Chi fraternity for four years and then Phi Gamma Delta fraternity for three years. By doing the janitorial and cooking duties at the fraternity houses, they could have a free basement two-rooms-and-bath apartment. When the fraternity houses closed for the summer, my parents were allowed to stay in the apartment but had to seek other work for wages, which usually meant cooking and cleaning at the frats or sororities that didn't close for the summer. They found that menial jobs were easy to get. Dad found out that his two years of college education could get him nothing higher than custodial work. He also applied for other jobs, like a lithographer position at a printing plant. As soon as the interview was over and he was about to close the door behind him, he turned to see the employer crumple the application and throw it the wastepaper basket.

This fraternity housing arrangement allowed my parents to save money to purchase the house they wanted, a small three-bedroom house on the corner of Lake and Dayton Streets. However, they encountered difficulty. The realtors tried to limit their choices to the Bush, the south side, and the near east side, the three areas where most Blacks lived. My parents settled on a house they could afford at 201 North Lake Street.

The house was ideal, with enough space to rent to Black female UW students who were refused private housing on or near the campus due to racism and discrimination. Since the neighbors gave them problems trying to buy the house by circulating a petition, Mom and Dad filed a lawsuit under the city's fair housing laws, which were just developing in Madison. They won the case and bought the house, which they kept until 1955. While living on Langdon or on Lake Street, I don't recall being called a n——, but I was called "chocolate drop," "pickaninny," and "brownie." At age twelve, all that changed, and I became an aggressive and mouthy activist, challenging every name-calling and put-down toward me and my Black friends, who I had many more of now that I had moved from Langdon Street and fraternity row and could get about town on my own. After the housing incident, my folks got along well with everybody, both Black and White. Our family got to be known as a "don't mess with me" family and became well respected everywhere.

When my parents enrolled me in the old Washington Elementary School in 1935 (then located between West Johnson and West Dayton Streets at North Broom Street), they had little difficulty except to insist that I should go into first grade instead of kindergarten, where the authorities wanted to place me, even though I was six. My father had been a one-room schoolteacher of grades kindergarten to eighth, and I had attended kindergarten there. Not a genius, I still was a quick learner and proved to be as developed as the White students in the first grade. Also, I lived among adults in the fraternity house on Langdon Street and picked up adult ways from university students. However, my social life was limited to three or four White girls from well-educated families that I played with in the neighborhood. I only socialized with Black kids on Sundays and some Saturdays when I was involved in the activities of St. Paul A.M.E. Church. My best of all friend was Doris Barlow, close as sisters up through our retirement years in the 1990s.

I had been chosen as Central High School's track queen in 1947 because I had excelled in all subjects, had a pleasant personality, and had been a community activist. The annual track meet and parade were planned to celebrate this event. The queen and her court were to ride in an open convertible around the square, down East Washington Avenue to Breese Stevens Field. The court was made up [of] girls from West, East, and Wisconsin High Schools. I felt that these girls were all snooty anyway, but they made it a point to ignore me as queen. Most of these girls were upset, too, because they did not get any public recognition for their own activities. When city officials learned that I had been picked as track queen, they canceled the parade, the dinner, the photo shoots, and name recognition—all of those aspects that historically had been associated with the event. All I could do was hand out the awards and trophies to the winners as they came

Dolores Simms (right) with Doris Barlow. COURTESY OF DOLORES SIMMS GREENE

to the podium. The women's track coach was livid about the cancellations and the city's obvious attempt to obliterate any Black presence at the event. The coach tried to appeal to school and city officials but was unsuccessful. This coach was embarrassed, sad, and angry. Many of Central's students expressed outrage, too. However, my family and the students felt helpless to do anything about it. Even Black organizations, including the NAACP, did not act to protest this discrimination. The irony is that Central High School took all the track awards in the city meet that year. The Black athletes, such as Ed and Bill "Babe" Withers, Al Dockery, Jim Weaver, and Charlie Hopkins, ran track that year and took first place. People did treat us badly and kicked at us, but they couldn't keep us down.

A film company came from New York to Madison in the summer of 1947 to make a movie called *Make Way for Youth*. The film was about a group of teens trying to work toward social justice. The group created social activities that tried to reduce the disparities between Blacks and Whites in Madison. Many students, including me, auditioned, but I was cast in the major role. Adrenna Matthews was in the film, too. The filming was successful, with no one behaving in discriminatory ways. The premiere opened at the Wisconsin Union Theater with a capacity audience. After the showing of the film, state legislators authorized the funds for a teen center in Madison, which was named the Loft. Many teens from various ethnic groups came to the Loft to socialize. In effect, the film helped the city to break the barriers between Blacks and Whites at that time. Subsequently, the film was used as a training tool throughout the country. Oddly, the White girls cast in the film began acting in a civil manner by the time the filming was over. That was one experience of which I was particularly proud, even though we received no individual compensation and fanfare. My mom and dad attended and were thrilled.

I also performed in a high school play for which I did not audition. One of the leading characters was James McDonald, but we called him Scrammy. I don't know how he got that nickname. He was a popular guy among his peers. Tall, lean, medium-brown skinned, and personable. He was a willing participant in the annual school musical because he was bright and could sing. The drama was *Pirates of Penzance*, or some such frolicking light classic. The problem was it called for the chorus to split up into dancing couples two or three times during the play. At the risk of offending some White families, the musical director was reluctant to pair a White girl with Scrammy. Even though this was a junior class project, there was no Black girl in that class who could or would sing in the chorus. So an embarrassed White music teacher asked me to learn the lines, rehearse the choreography, and get into costume to be Scrammy's partner. After an in-depth discussion with his mother and aunt, who were royally upset at the audacity of this decision, it was agreed that I should accept the role so the show could go on without a big racist incident being exposed to the general public.

I had two other experiences that occurred in high school that centered on race. These incidents involved the principal and teachers who were in conflict over me. I was unaware of what went on until a member of the secretarial staff took me aside and told me what she witnessed. One incident was between the choir director, the band director, and the school counselor over selecting the soloists to perform in the spring concert. When the first draft of the program was circulated among the staff, the counselor noted that in spite of racial minorities composing nearly 10 percent of all participants, none had been chosen to play a significant role in this musical event. She felt this should not be, as at least six Blacks and one [Asian] had proved earlier to be excellent in their chosen area as vocalists and/or instrumentalists. Furthermore, three of the students played in the band and in the orchestra and sang in the choir. Surely, the counselor argued, there could be at least one soloist in each group for one selection out of the twenty to be presented. It turned out, after much bickering in-house and unknown by the general student body, the [Asian] was picked from the orchestra to do a solo cello part. The band director decided to duck the issue and revised his program to include no solo parts. The choir director chose me, an alto, to sing the whole song "Beautiful Savior" with the chorus humming backup. In spite of objections like "excessive," "overkill," "too liberal," and other conciliatory suggestions, such as, "Have each one do a verse," "Choose the Italian soprano instead," "Do a triple trio selection and include Dolores in that; it won't be so obvious," the choir director, bless her heart, stuck to her guns and the program went forth. After the spring concert, people commented that the "Beautiful Savior" rendition was the best in the show.

The second incident had to do with selecting those to receive monetary scholarships to attend higher education. No matter what the criteria

IIRROR   Page 3

Delores Simms to Reign as Queen at City Track Meet on Tuesday, May 13

Delores Simms will reign as queen of the city track meet on May 13 since she was chosen earlier in the year as Central's D. A. R. good citizen, and Central is in charge of the meet this year. The meet will be held in the evening at Breese-Stevens Field with Madison Central, Madison West, Madison East, and Wisconsin High participating.

Bad Fortune Dogs

Central's Faithful

May 24, 1946   T H

Dockery Ties High Hurdles Record At Kenosha; Central Comes in Sixth

Central's track squad finished sixth in the Big Eight track meet held at Kenosha two weeks ago. Many records were broken, and Central's Al Dockery tied the previous record in the high hurdles when he ran the event in :14.8 in the first heat.

Besides winning the highs in this excellent time he also won the low hurdles in the fast time of :23.5. Both of these marks are the fastest in the state in the respective events. Other Central trackmen to score points were Don Grubb, who finished fourth in the high hurdles and fifth in the low hurdles. A surprise was Charles Hopkins, little sophomore who finished fourth in the toughest competition of the day.

Dean Corrado, Janesville distance man, broke an old record set by Jimmy Dunn of Central in 1928, when he ran the half-mile in 2:03.4. The record had previously been 2:04. Bob Mansfield broke the record in the 440, when he circled the oval in :50.4. He cut almost two full seconds off the previous record set by Ken Hendrickson of Kenosha in 1941.

Henry Weinberger of Kenosha broke the broad jump record set by Wayne Williams of Madison West in 1938. West's relay team ran the 880 yard relay in the good time of 1:33.3. Central had been beaten by West earlier in the season in a dual meet and would surely have placed in this event if Jay Morey, Central's sprint star, had not been sick and unable to compete.

Beloit Captures Links Crown; Badger Prep Match Is Rained Out

Central took last place at the Big Eight golf meet at Beloit last Saturday. There were only seven schools represented with Kenosha absent as the hosts copped the Big Eight title.

Central was beaten decisively, finishing 44 strokes behind the sixth place golfers from East. Beloit defeated us by 99 strokes.

Vincent Stankewitz of Beloit was low man while Douglas Nordby of West was next. Stankewitz had a 76. Nordby was only one stroke behind him.

Bill Dillman was low man for Central. He tied for seventh place on the basis of individual scores. His total for 18 holes was 83. The other Central golfers, Paul Cleary, Larry Day, and Eugene Day had scores of 103, 110, and 120, respectively.

A golf match between Wisconsin High and Central scheduled for last week was not played because of the weather.

In a previous meeting, Central was very badly defeated with only Paul Cleary scoring.

The match, originally slated to be played on Wednesday, May 15, will be played next week if possible.

Headlines from the *Madison Mirror* (left and above) highlight the accomplishments of Madison Central High School track stars Dolores Simms and Al Dockery. DANE COUNTY HISTORICAL SOCIETY

Dolores Simms, seated right, is pictured with members of Alpha Phi Eta: in the back row, left to right, Rose Lee Matthews, Doris Barlow, Gwen Shellie, and Mary Alice Elvord, and Anna Banks seated in front. Not shown are Loretta Wallace and Addrena Matthews.
WHI IMAGE ID 80543

were for selecting a scholarship winner—whether by need, on grade point average during ten to twelve grade years, overall conduct, attendance—no matter how they did it, my name kept coming up in the top three for every type of scholarship administration had at its disposal. There seemed to be no way to exclude me from receiving at least one of the cherished honors. Since I was the only Black from that class to register such high achievement in academic performance, the faculty had to deal with it. So it came down to letting the chips fall as they may or skew the results so that Dolores gets only one, and if so, which one. I was later told that faculty hashed over that decision for the full last semester. Finally, the principal took the matter into his own hands, disgusted with the couple of bigots that kept botching the faculty vote. He proclaimed that the scholarship committee must evaluate according to established guidelines and let the chips fall where they may. Consequently, I received enough honorary money to fund my first three semesters at UW–Madison. The largest scholarship was one donated by the Daughters of the American Revolution. Imagine their surprise when they discovered who got it. I went on to the UW campus with glee. Doctors Frederick Haberman and H. W. Weaver, faculty in the speech department, were not going to intimidate me. I hit the ground running, as they say.

I also participated in an effort to form a city youth council, composed of representatives from each of the four high schools chosen by their respective student bodies. The council chose its own officers, of which I was secretary. The officers met once a month in the chambers of the Madison City Commission. We forged recommendations and debated any issue having an impact on youth in any section of the city. We were also able to persuade the *Wisconsin State Journal* to publish on Sundays a column written by a member of the youth council. Columnists rotated from school to school each week. I took my turn writing for Central High. In the meantime, I worked part-time jobs, one of which was at the Madison Public Library, where I was the first Black page. I also was able to stay on the high honor roll and be a member of the National Honor Society from 1942 to 1947. I also taught Sunday school, directed the St. Paul choir, and babysat during this time.

Speech education became a base for me, as the value of knowing how to communicate effectively rose more and more as an asset toward "making it" at that time. I had read literature about the abolitionists as they spoke and wrote about conditions for people and women in the 1800s. Frederick Douglass, Phyllis Wheatley, Laurence Dunbar, and Walter White influenced me in my thoughts and opinions about slavery and freedom fights, although I had not yet formulated my own course of action. But I was convinced that how one used words was important. I had experienced the example of what I could do when I delivered the senior farewell address on Central High School class night as part of the yearly graduation exercises. I was told I looked stunning in a long white satin gown in solo on stage, which I appreciated. But what thrilled me most were the comments that referred to my speech. A long-term faculty member said, "You had everyone in tears. It was the best oratory ever given on class night since I've been at the school." And one of my peers said, "I was so touched, you expressed just how we all felt."

I went on to graduate from the UW–Madison with a degree in speech. During this time, though, a group of us Black young women formed a monthly newspaper called the *Alpharetta News*, which stood for *first little one*. Our organization was called Alpha Phi Eta. Other women who belonged to this group were Doris Barlow (secretary), Mary Alice Elvord, Anna Banks, Loretta Wallace, Gwen Shellie, Rose Lee Matthews, and Addrena Matthews. I was the president and doubled as the editor. We collected local Black news and shared in dispersing the mimeographed paper throughout the Black community. Somehow, Doris found an old mimeograph machine for us to use. The paper covered church events, births, deaths, health hints, recipes from our mothers, new persons in town, and any Black person's accomplishments not covered in the *Wisconsin State Journal* and the *Capital Times*. Otherwise, no Black national or state news got to us other than that covered in a newspaper called the *Philadelphia Courier*, peddled by Mr. Stewart, an elderly Black man who had the paper shipped in.

My parents belonged to the NAACP, St. Paul A.M.E. Church, my dad with the Masonic Lodge, my mother with the Eastern Star, Urban League, often in leadership positions. We were in the forefront of racial integration efforts and tried to counsel and to advise new Blacks in town, who usually were from Chicago, on how to be assertive and look out for their civil rights. My parents were part of a core of older Black families that worked together to foster the attitude that Blacks, albeit only about .02 percent of the Madison population, need not take a backseat to anybody. At the same time, they encouraged stepping out and availing themselves of educational, political, and cultural opportunities in the White community. Consequently, it was easy for me to become the first in many avenues of leadership during my teen and young adult life. I was the first Black to be an officer (secretary) in the Dane County Junior Red Cross at age twelve, to be a high honor roll student, to be elected secretary of the City Youth Council, to write the column in the *Wisconsin State Journal's* Youth Section, to be a high school class officer, to receive a scholarship from the Madison Chapter of the Daughters of the American Revolution, to hold a rank in the city Girl Scouts, to be the track queen, and to be a part of the group to put out Madison's first Black youth newspaper. I also was the first local Black inducted into the national speech sorority, Zeta Phi Eta.

Our elders worked together to dispel unfair housing practices, to stop police from picking up every Black man when only one was a suspect, and to thwart job discrimination. Because at that time in Madison, no governmental agencies existed, no laws existed to regulate or enforce indecent bigoted behavior. People of good will had to step up and out and work together, both Black and White, to bring about conditions and attention to basic life needs for all. In Madison, these actions led into the activism of the 1960s. Blacks were supportive of one another in every way. There was little or no conflict among Blacks regarding obtaining work, housing, or educational opportunities. I remember when the emphasis in the Black community was on honesty, integrity, being self-sustaining, and not bringing shame or disdain on the rest. My own parents insisted on hard work, completing tasks, having a serious demeanor, and getting the highest quality possible results.

In fact, my family helped (as they had been helped) new Blacks in town to find places to live, shared knowledge of job openings, cautioned about social behavior, told of places to avoid because of bigotry—like which stores won't serve you or where you couldn't try on clothes, such as Yost's, Barons, and Manchester's. Instead of making a lot of noise, my mother quietly had a meeting with Mr. John Yost, owner of Yost's Clothing Store, to tell him of the discrimination he was doing by not allowing Black women to try on clothing. After her conversation with him, he no longer held to that practice. The churches played a big role in holding the Black community together and often worked together for community causes as well as cooperated with White churches and organizations for the good of all.

After I had graduated from the UW and had married Jim Greene, we made reservations at the Cuba Club on Madison's west side to have dinner to celebrate our one-year wedding anniversary. This was November 1951. After trying not to honor the reservations we made, they finally seated us at our insistence, but they ended up winning because they salted our food. We couldn't eat anything. The whole evening was ruined, with no recourse we could take. Also, during this time, I, along with other recent graduates, interviewed with school superintendent Philip Falk for a teaching position. But he never hired any Black applicants, claiming we were not qualified enough. However, when I applied, I was recommended by the University of Wisconsin placement office, the principal of my old high school, and other dignitaries from Madison, and I had nearly perfect grades and honors. At my interview, Falk told me he would hire no Negroes as long as he was superintendent.

Those of us who grew up together knew and talked with Oliver and Mamie Davis, Arthur Mosley, Curt Lucas, Albert Weaver, Frank Hoover, Zach Trotter, all who owned restaurants where we or our ancestors frequented. In talking with each other we brought up names, such as Gertrude Harris, Willie Lou Harris, Mamie Anderson, Charles and Myrtle Daniels, Edgar Caire, Joseph Gentry, Roy Rogers, the Russells, the Bankses, Baylus and Mamie Owens, Chef Carson Gulley, the Bosticks, Hopkinses, Riches, Newvilles, Mitchells, Elvords, Givenses, Mrs. Skenedore, Ted Pierce, the Shepards. I knew them all. Hannah Hopkins and I were inducted into the Milwaukee chapter of Delta Sigma Theta and later, along with Vel Phillips, received permission from University of Wisconsin president [Edwin] Fred to start the undergraduate chapter on the Madison campus.

LOIS WALDON MCKNIGHT

Lois Waldon McKnight, whose family hailed from Iowa, was born in Madison in 1935. She attended West High School and Madison Central University High School, and later Madison Area Technical College and the University of Wisconsin–Stout. She worked at General Motors in Janesville and then for the state of Wisconsin as a community specialist. Lois began playing the piano at an early age under the direction of her mother, a concert pianist, and played piano for churches and other civic organizations for sixty years. She and her husband, Bobby McKnight, had seven children. She received a Mother Full of Grace Award from Friendship Chapter No. 2, Order of the Eastern Star, and a certificate of commendation from the state of Wisconsin.

My father, Lawrence Waldon, migrated from La Crosse to Madison about 1930. The Waldons originally came from Iowa. My [great-] grandmother, Mattie Stein, was disowned and told by her father to change her name to Mattie Stone because he did not want anyone to trace her back to the family. Certainly, she told her children her plight, and as they got older and grown, they tried to find out about Grandpa and Grandma Stein. Uncle Charlie related a story about going back to Iowa inquiring, but he was met with relatives at gunpoint. He was told to leave and never come back there again. Mattie met Grandpa Wicks in Iowa. After Mattie Stone and Austin Wicks married, they left Iowa and went to La Crosse, Wisconsin, in Vernon County near Hillsboro in the 1870s, where they settled and had five children (Austin II, Grace, Gertrude, Charlie, and Nellie). There was also a cousin named Edna who was one of Grandma Wicks's sister's daughters. Nellie married Norman Waldon in Chicago and moved to La Crosse, where they lived on the 600 block of Main Street. Together they had seven children (Norman, Gertrude, Robert, James, Shirley, Gladys, and Lawrence). Most of them moved to places like Chicago and Milwaukee. Lawrence, or Leroy as he was called, moved to Madison. There were stories that made you know Dad's family was so dysfunctional that it should have been a crime, but they were a fun-loving family, and there were even ministers (mostly Methodist) in the family. I heard about Sherman Waldon and his escapades and knew that he was what we Black folks called "a mess." I thought it was my dad's dad, Sheldon, who was the mess. It's been about two years now, but I met a cousin named Anthony Stilter, and he's a direct descendant of the Waldons. He brought me a picture of Great-Grandpa Waldon. The catch was Sherman and Sheldon were twins, and Sherman never married.

Now, most of the Wickses passed as White. The Waldons were light-skinned enough to pass and did. It made them able to take care of themselves and eventually their families. In the 1940s, my uncle Charles got a job driving a bus for the city of Madison, and all of us were told to remember not to call him Uncle Charlie when we got on the bus. Uncle Charlie played with us, bought us toys, and gave us money and candy. He was good to us. Needless to say, we'd get on the bus and forget because we were glad to see him, and say, "Hi, Uncle Charlie." He'd smile, but looked away from us. It got the better of him, and he quit and found a job where we didn't see him as much. He had the most beautiful black hair and was fairly good looking, too. My daddy, Lawrence Leroy, called "Roy" for short, never passed. He didn't pass as far as getting a job as a redcap at the Greyhound bus station. When the passengers would get off the Greyhound bus, they thought that Dad was White, and he never said, "No, I'm not." He worked there for twenty-seven years, and then got a job as a security guard with the state of Wisconsin. One of the men in charge was showing my father around the building, going from floor to floor. And the second night he was there, he said, "God, Waldon, I'm sure glad they didn't hire none of them n——s. Daddy said he stopped and said, "Oh." He said he never said anything else. He wanted to see what else he would say. All week this guy talked about the n——s getting jobs with the state and taking White people's places. At the end of this training with this man, Daddy said, "You know them n——s you been talking about? Well, I'm one of them."

Let me go back and get my mom's family in here. Myra Denning was born in Lake Mills, Wisconsin, and stayed there with her parents until she grew up. She then moved to Chicago and worked as a maid and cook. She came to Madison around 1914. My grandfather, Harry Allison, was born in Stanton, West Virginia, and my great-grandmother Mattie Allison moved with Harry and Belle, his sister, to Kansas City, Kansas. Harry

Harry and Myra Allison, grandparents of Lois McKnight, in 1908. COURTESY OF
RALPH LEE III

grew up there. He moved to Chicago and worked as a maître d'. He came to
Madison in 1910. My grandmother Myra was an avid ice skater and went to
the park to skate near where she worked, and that's where she and Harry
met. They married and bought the house on 628 South Park Street behind
Schwartz Drug Store until they found the house on Dane Street, which
was built by a Black man named Clayton. They raised Harry Jr., Margaret,
Ellen, William, and Constance and a grandson, Ralph Lee, in that house.
Much happened in that house for us to learn how families should be to one
another. Harry worked as an ice cream maker at the Mansfield ice cream
shop located where the old Madison post office was on Monona Avenue
and which is now the Madison Municipal Building.

They raised some foster kids, too: Doris Barlow Kinney, Ila Mae Hines.
Doris grew up and married one of the Kinney boys from Beloit, Wisconsin.

Illa was killed in a tragic car accident when she was eighteen years old. I believe I was three when my sisters and brothers, Ellen, Phyllis, Carol, Larry, and two foster brothers, Lee Dufek and Dennis, moved into that house where we all grew up. Phyllis was killed in a car accident at sixteen. There were other foster children that came and went. The grandson, Ralph Lee (Aunt Margaret's only child), grew up and made a career in law enforcement in Milwaukee. Harry Jr. married Marie and had Roxanne and Billy. Margaret married Hosea Doxey, and they raised two foster daughters. Billy never married. He played drums. Duke Ellington wanted to take him on tour. My grandmother was adamant and said, "No." Constance had one child, Charles "Chuck" Matthews, who made his career as the city's affirmative action officer. Constance married Clarence Boles after he and his son, Clarence Jr., age five, came to Madison. Constance and Clarence raised Chuck and Clarence and fought in the courts for Christie and Connie, two foster children. They won, and also raised the two girls.

My dad married my mom, Ellen Allison Waldon. Now, my ma, Ellen, took piano lessons and became an accomplished musician. She could have got jobs with bands and stuff, but she did not want that kind of life with drinking and stuff. She taught piano in the park. Dolores Simms took lessons from her in Brittingham Park. She was really something. She had her own radio show when she was a teenager with WHA. Mom played the piano and dad sang for people like the Quislings of the Quisling Clinics here in Madison.

When Uncle Harry Allison got out of the service, Dad told him to come to the bus station and put in an application. He was hired, and they worked together for years. In terms of color, the Waldons were light enough to pass for White and a lot of them did just that. On the other hand, the Allisons were brown-skinned. There were slaves on my mother's side and on my father's side. My grandmother and her parents came to Lake Mills as slaves, and were freed there probably around 1851. I suspect that Grandpa Waldon and the Wicks were in La Crosse in 1872 and then came to Madison about 1890. As Blacks moved into Madison both sides of my family were instrumental in their being able to settle here. We lived on Dane Street in south Madison, so we went to West High School. Most of the Blacks lived [on] the other side of Park Street and on West Washington, so they went to Central High School. There were seven Black girls and one Black boy, Joe Brown, at West. The prejudice at West was blatant, and it not only hurt, it stung! It ran the gamut. Kids calling you "niggy bawl" and "blackie" from the stairwells. In physical education class, the White girls played with my rolled-up gym socks, throwing them to each other so I couldn't catch them. When I asked one of the girls to get the socks, the girl said that her mother told her "n——s were supposed to work for her." I remember during debate in a social studies class, a girl named Lucia stood up and said that she did not understand why Blacks went to school. They couldn't learn and even if they could, they would not be able to use it in life. This girl Lucia got Cs and Ds, and I got Bs and Cs. What was that?

My mom was scared to death for us girls. She did not want anything to happen to us and tried to get all of us to comply, to do whatever we had to do to get an education. Ma said to me, "You go there and show those White people what you can do." I told Ma that I didn't care about White people and did not want to show them anything! I know I made choices that made it hard for me to get through school, but I hung in there, and got what I needed. I'm okay. I like me and know that's what counts.

I looked out for my brothers and sisters. I really didn't like the way my sister Ellen was treated in school. Ellen tended to be the quiet one in the family and the one White kids seemed to pick on. I would beat up kids that would not leave my brothers and sisters alone. I fought a boy who called me a n——. When his sister tried to protect him, I beat her, too. I slapped a math teacher who kicked me out [of] his classroom, after he blurted out during a discussion "the n——s in Africa." I took issue with that! When I left the room, I slammed the door and he came after me. I stood on the stairs and slapped him when [he] got up close enough to reach. Protecting myself and my brothers and sisters spilled over to protecting my own kids. I lashed out at a teacher who grabbed my son.

I could play the piano. I could sing, but not in a play where the boy had to kiss the girl. The music teacher wanted me to sing the songs using Standard English, but in the southern Negro dialect. It was okay for me to sing the song like *Ole' Arks a Moverin'* in the music program. I practiced that song good, too. On the day of the program, I sang beautifully *The Old Ark Is Moving*, using no dialect. The teacher, Marion Huxtable, was livid. I was pleased as punch.

I had other encounters with White teachers, principals, and students. When I hear people talk about the North, I get irked—to think we had it

Velma Hamilton. WHI IMAGE ID 72167

better. I remember the principal at West High School calling my parents for a meeting to tell them Ellen was a slow learner and it would be better to put her in a trade school and that she should transfer from West to Central High School, where the White boys might take an interest in her. After I transferred to Central, I had encounters with Principal Vida Smith, who I called "Vicious Vida." It was unreal. I couldn't stand her and she couldn't stand me. She was the epitome of prejudice. I dropped out of Central, and went to Madison Area Technical College, where I met Velma Hamilton, the only Black teacher I knew in Madison. She taught English. She took me under her wing. Even though I left school in eleventh grade, I went back and took my GED exams and passed. I did it in one day. Thank you, Velma Hamilton.

I met Bobby McKnight when I turned sixteen and married him when I was seventeen. We had five kids, Walter, Carol, Robert, Patricia, and

Timothy. Carol was killed by a truck in the alleyway coming from school when she was eight years old. It took me years to accept that. When my own children started school, Patti, the oldest, was a handful. A Black teacher called her a bitch, so I went to school. I asked what happened and he said, "Well, she just made me so mad." I let him know that if he had called her n——, I wouldn't have answered, but instead, I would have called in my mom and her mom and everybody else in my family. I told him that I didn't want to run into him again, but he didn't listen. The next year, I had another run-in with him over Tim, my second child. This same Black teacher grabbed Tim by his arm, leaving nail and finger prints. Needless to say, I was furious. He said, "We didn't want him to call you."

I attribute my grandmother Myra Allison and grandfather Harry Allison for my faith and belief that God was in my life and that I just needed to stop and listen. He would take care of me and mine. Church became a real place of refuge for me, and looking back, I can't remember when I was a youngster not knowing about God and Jesus Christ coming to the Earth to die for my sins. Now, I [didn't] always remember that he loved me or that he saw what I was doing or not. Some of the knowledge and acceptance of that knowledge came in little spurts, but today I know that he kept me in his arms and at times long for periods of time. He never put me down to walk on my own. If he had, I wouldn't be here today. It was Jesus who made me let go of a girl who had picked a fight with me. I was getting ready to twirl her by her legs into a brick wall. My grandmother Allison was his instrument for my learning about him and his mercy and grace.

The Women's Federated Clubs of America and the Utopia Club kept me busy singing for their events, especially me and a man named Calvin Harris. My mom played for us. I remember the Loft on Doty Street. I sang "This Is My Country," and Barbara McNair sang the song "Because." I won, but I told my mom I didn't want to sing anymore and conceded the award to Barbara. Imagine my surprise when I saw her on TV years later.

My family did nothing in terms of business, except sell chickens. My Grandma Allison would bring three hundred to four hundred to our house and put them in the sheds in the backyard. It was the kids' job to feed and water them. Many a day I hid in the apple orchard across the street from our house so I wouldn't have to feed them and clean the chicken coops. Yuck!

I think the one thing that sticks out in my mind is Gram taking time to help people. She didn't care who they were or what they did. If they were sick, she was there. If they were hungry, she would make sure that they ate. She even gave out money, and most of the time she knew it wouldn't come back to her. Gram and Aunt Margaret went in together on a business venture and bought a sorority house, and called it the Allison House. The girls, most of whom were Black, stayed there while going to school at the University of Wisconsin.

First Margaret lived in the downstairs apartment and had the role of housemother. Then she decided to move to California and Gram took over. It was a fun time for us kids. Gram made a living out of that endeavor even though my grandfather never stopped working at cleaning windows for Parker's Jewelry and the Candy Kitchen. He took care of buildings at the end of Mound Street, stoking fires in the winter and the synagogue, too. He worked up into his nineties and passed away at ninety-seven years old. What a loss for me. The man told stories of his youth that would have you laughing and then crying. He could tap-dance, pour long and short drinks, and cook coon and curried chicken along with the best of 'em. He was my mentor and a dear friend, and he understood me. There has been no one since his passing that I can say that about. It hurts my heart sometimes that he is gone. But God knows best and I am on my way—glad to see him. I'll be thankful to God because I know he'll keep it straight and we'll know each other and speak of all the things I've told you about in these pages.

There are some other things I remember:

- Choir rehearsal at the Simms house. Dolores Simms, Jim Greene, George Greene, Rose Newville, Ed Hill, Ellen Waldon, Billy McDonald, Scrammy McDonald, Paul Washington, and me. We were St. Paul's A.M.E. Youth Choir.

- Duke Ellington coming to town. We could go and hear him for free, and then go backstage. He would hug my Grandma Allison and kiss us kids on the cheek. He sent us demos of his records. Margaret ended up with them. I bet nobody knows where they are.

- Gram Allison standing down by the bakery. If we were late getting home from youth group or swimming, she would be waiting for us to come down the street, sometimes with a switch that she never used, but it kept us on track nonetheless.

- When Ila Mae, Gram's foster daughter, was killed on her way to Milwaukee in a car with Hugh Stamps, Sam Dixon, and some White girls. They all died except one White girl, and I have no idea what happened to her.

- Ralph Lee as a teen when he got his first car, a red Oldsmobile, and singing "The Lady in Red."

- When there was a clothing store on the corner of Mifflin and State Streets. The museum is there now. We went there to buy a pea green suit for me and a blue one for Ellen to have our pictures taken. We were eleven and twelve.

- Miss Berhends, our piano teacher, hired us to clean her studio apartment. She was a buxom woman and kept coming into the room where we were cleaning her windows, asking Ellen and I how she looked. I almost fell from the second-story window laughing. Ellen vowed she'd tell when we got home. The chili she made for our lunch: one pound hamburger, one can kidney beans, one can tomatoes, chili pepper, salt, and pepper. It was plain, but we were hungry!

- When my sister Phyllis got killed in a car accident on the way to Beloit with Gordon Johnson, Joe Barlow, and her best friend, Wanda Moncrief, who also died in that accident.

GEORGIA HARRIS HENDERSON

Georgia, a lifelong resident of south Madison, has volunteered at the South Madison Neighborhood Center, at a middle school reading to struggling students, and at her church. She raised eight children and three stepchildren and became well-known for her bountiful vegetable and flower gardens.

My father, George William Harris, was born in Danville, Kentucky. His family moved to Cincinnati when they were small. He had two brothers, Richard and Henry. Now, my father rode a mule-driven moving van from Cincinnati, Ohio, to Wisconsin several times a year, mostly to northern Wisconsin around the Green Bay area. Madison was always the stopping point. It's where he planned to spend the night and then go wherever he had to go. He'd come back and spend the night here in Madison. At that time, [he knew] like fifteen or sixteen Blacks in Madison, but he liked it. He liked Madison. He finally moved to Madison in 1916. Uncle Zachary on my mother's side was in Madison already. Uncle Zachary had his tavern downstairs but rented out rooms on the second floor and that's where my father would stay. My father got a job at Madison Kipp Corporation. My mother, Willie Lou Mann, was born in Americus, Georgia. Because of all the racism, her father sent her to Madison to attend the University of Wisconsin. So my father, George, and my mother, Willie Lou, met and married in Madison. They had five children, Calvin, Donald, Charles, Richard, and me.

My dad worked as a janitor most of his life but performed that job with pride. They both basically came for a better life. My mother came to go to school and get a better life, and my father to get a job and a better life. There was so much racism in the South in those days and you could only go so far. My father worked at Commercial State Bank and worked there fifty-four years. My mother did domestic work and went

Georgia's mother, Willie Lou Mann Harris.

George Harris (left) with the mule-driven cart he brought to Madison. COURTESY OF
GEORGIA HARRIS HENDERSON

back to vocational school, is what they called it in those days, and became the first licensed Black practical nurse in the city of Madison, and
worked at Madison General Hospital. She was so proud. Now, with the
job at the Commercial State Bank, daddy was a janitor. It was a job that
he was so proud of. You would have thought that Daddy was president
of the United States. He kept that bank just so. Daddy was eighty-one when
he died. He had retired about six months before that, but they were calling
him every day saying to him, "George, this doesn't work or that doesn't
work." And Daddy would go back to work. He was more than just a janitor.
He could do everything. They were always nice to us. Our dentist was in the
Commercial State Bank and our lawyer, Mr. Wagner. They were pretty decent to Daddy. I think Commercial did not hand out too many mortgages,
but they did mortgage our house. I do remember Mama saying there was
a struggle, and I do remember it was just a struggle back then with all the
banks. My mother had the land from the post office down here on Wingra
Drive up to the Madison Newspapers office. That land was for sale. My
mother tried to buy that land. The bank wouldn't finance that. That's just
too much land, they said. They wouldn't sell it. She tried and tried to get
that land. They did purchase the seven lots on Bram Street. They did let

my family have that. So on the one hand they were decent, but on the other hand, they were not going to let them get ahead.

They believed in work and that if you wanted something, you must work for it. Nobody gave you anything, especially if you were Black. Our family saved money and divided it in certain ways. I can remember Daddy and Mama pulling out these envelopes that they kept in a box. Each envelope was marked for a certain bill. First of all, the church, the tithe to the church, and then Madison Gas, and the telephone and whatever bills they had. She would put the rest of the money away, as I believe most of the Blacks did because they took pride; they had to pay for everything as they got it. They brought those principles with them. They didn't owe anybody. You didn't ask for a handout. My dad said so many times that he was so proud of the fact that they never asked for welfare. You don't ask anybody for anything. If you want it, you get out and work, no matter what it takes to get it. Nobody owes you anything because you're Black. But we would lay-away what we wanted. You laid it away, and you paid so much. They would set up a payment plan. A car and a house were probably the only two things you made some kinds of arrangements to pay. You can say it's yours, but it's not yours until you have a receipt that says "paid in full." If you didn't have the money to lay it away or pay cash for it, you didn't need it. That's what Daddy said.

Finding housing was awful. The only places they would sell to Blacks were near West Washington Avenue, south Madison, or the east side, or you had to rent. Daddy bought the house on Bram Street when he married my mother. My mother lived with Uncle Bud and Dad was there, too, until he got the house. But it was hard. It was after that that my mother tried to purchase the land. She went to every bank in the city trying to get a loan. Both of my parents were working, too. They would say, "You don't need that." They were famous for those words, "You do not need that." Even in Calvin's day when Cal was in the building business. He would try to get financing. They said, "Oh, you can't handle that, or it's too much." That hurt. My house was the first house that my brothers built, and he had like two thousand dollars cash. That was enough to build the basement and put up the first floor. My mother went to Commercial first to borrow some money, but Home Savings and Loan was the only lending institution in Madison that would loan my mother the money. Later on, First

Federal loaned Calvin some money. Cal and Charles were the first Black apprentice, certified carpenters in Madison. They had a terrible time just getting a job before they even decided to open their business. White carpenters didn't want to work with them. When I was a kid, the Italians had all of the city of Madison jobs. And the Italians that lived in the Bush with Blacks and Jews bought homes in south Madison around Magnolia Lane. Cal built Maggie and John Davis's house on Magnolia Lane. A few Italians had fits. In fact, they'd go at night and do something to wreck whatever was up so Cal had to start over. These few Italians did not want John and Maggie Davis there. This little Italian lady and her husband would pull their lawn chairs right to the edge of the property and say, "Don't want you n——s here."

Let me tell you what made her change her mind about us. The old man died, and someone broke into her house while she was gone and tore up her house—all the doors, and she had money, and they took the money. They pulled the phone out of the wall. She came running down here. I think she went down the other way, but couldn't find anybody. But here she comes and she was just hysterical. She was speaking Italian, and I couldn't understand her. Finally, I told her, "Calm down, calm down." She told me what happened, so I called the police, but they never did find out who did it. She wanted me to call the telephone company to get the phone reconnected. The person at the company said they would come out tomorrow. The woman said, "No, no." She was petrified because she was there alone. So I begged this person at the company, telling her that this woman is an old woman and someone just broke in her house. She needs the phone, please. So they sent someone out. That woman was so grateful. Every time I looked at her, she said, "Kitchen." After that incident, many times she cooked and brought Italian dishes for my family. But it took an incident like that. Slowly, they came around. We were good enough to live with them in the Bush, but the Italians did not want us here.

One Italian woman lived around the corner and if you wanted to know what's going on, you talked to her. She knew everybody's business and she got in everybody's house. I had a bunch of kids in my house, my own kids and neighbors' kids, and she just couldn't believe that I had a clean house. I let her have it. We had an East Indian couple that lived in the neighborhood. They had some type of weaving business in their basement.

They sold these gorgeous sweaters on Langdon Street in front of the Union, nicest people. They didn't bother anybody. She went downtown and told somebody that they had this business in their home in a residential area. She made so much trouble for those people that they left.

I want to talk about Charles and I in school. We lived on Bram Street, so we attended Badger School, which was across from the Badger Bowl. In my day, the right side of Bram Street was in the town of Madison and [the] left was in the city. The city had the water system, and we had a well. It was just a mess. So, we moved from Bram Street and lived for a short time over off Sherman Avenue and had to attend Sherman School. We lived up the hill, across Northport. So the first day, Daddy took us to school. The kids said, "Look look. Here come the n——s. Here come the n——s." And Daddy said, "Come on, come on." He took us into the principal's office and said, "Now, I know you heard those children calling my children names. Now, I'm leaving my children here with you and I expect for you to take care of my children. I don't want any harm to come to my children." Those kids were so nasty to Daddy. They didn't call him n—— or anything, but you know. Daddy said, "I don't want you to walk home, I'm coming back to get you." For at least two months, Charles and I had to physically fight on that playground. I used to tell my mama that I didn't want to go to school. Mama didn't want us fighting. She was like Martin Luther King—just no violence. But we couldn't just stand there and let them hit us or call us names. We fought. They finally learned that we weren't going to eat them or kill them. They would throw things, take our lunch, wouldn't sit next to us. They were awful. Those teachers and that principal didn't say a word. Not a word. I went through this in Madison, Wisconsin.

By the time we left Sherman, we had a lot of good friends, but it was awful at first. Mama used to say, and I hope I can say this without crying because she was such a sweet woman, but she would say to us, "You tell them that your face might be black, but your heart is white, and their face might be white, but their heart is black, because you would never call them those names to hurt them, and that name-calling hurts you. Tell them that we're all God's children, and God wants us to love one another." We tried that, and I believe it really helped. We said all of that because when Mama tells you something, you had to do it. But we still had to fight.

When Charles joined the labor union as a carpenter, they told him it was mostly Italian, that they didn't want him. They wouldn't sit next to him. They were awful to Charles and he could not get a job. Charles had the certification from [Madison Area Technical College]. He went to all the large construction companies that were here at the time, filling out applications, but nobody would hire him. Finally, my mother, bless her heart, went to Marshall Erdman. He remembered my mother. He came to her funeral. She came to him and said, "I'm just asking you to give him a chance. He's good. Put him on probation. If he doesn't hold up to your expectations or whatever you think he should do, then you let him go. But just give him a chance." He hired Charles. Charles would go on the job, but the fellows wouldn't talk to him. He had to eat lunch by himself. They would not socialize with him. The foreman would give the instructions and Charles did his work, working ten times harder than the others. It was bad. Marshall Erdman called my mother and said that Charles was the best carpenter he had. Charles learned so much from him. Charles stayed with Marshall Erdman Company until Charles and Calvin went into business for themselves, calling it the Harris Construction Company. Donald helped out part-time, because he owned a cleaning business. Each one, though, built his own home. I think they built a total of twenty-seven homes in Madison. Later, Calvin got a job with the state as a building supervisor. By the way, Donald and Cal were in World War II. Donald was in the navy and went to the Pacific, and Cal was in the army and went to Germany.

Mama would say that you don't have to socialize with them, but you have to work with them; they own everything, so you have to work for them. You get your education, she preached education, and then you can buy a business, and you can be your own boss. Daddy would say that you look a man in the eye. If you owe a man, you pay that man. You don't let them walk over you. They didn't want us to fight, but they said that you have to get your education. The only way you can be successful is to have your education so you will know what they're talking about. So you can pick up the newspaper and know what you're reading, or if you go to the job and they give you a job order, you can read that job order and do that job.

My mother belonged to the NAACP, along with Mrs. [Dimetra] Shivers, Mrs. [David] Simms, and all the others. At that time, they really were about something. They would take on causes and work together to improve the lives of Black people. They stuck together. Reverend Washington would go to the Capitol and speak before the legislature. It was just so different. They cared. I can remember as a kid that the Montgomery Bus Company only came out as far as Bowman Dairy on Park Street. Calvin and the NAACP and the churches led the fight on that. They went to the city council and didn't rest until the city did something about it. And they were small in numbers. Finally, the bus came out to the St. Martin House. My mother was a member of the Mary Bethune Club, which was kind of a social club.

I told somebody a few years ago that Genevieve Trotter, Eddy Mae Champion, and Leona Collins, all native Madisonians, were three of several Black women to graduate from college with teaching degrees. But they couldn't get jobs here. Genevieve was my cousin and Zach Trotter's daughter. She had to go to New Jersey to get a job. Leona went to St. Louis. Eddy Mae went down south to get a job. But the mothers of these women cooked and scrubbed floors and worked for churches in Maple Bluff and in Nakoma, the White areas, but their children could not get jobs here in Madison.

My mother made quilts and crocheted. She loved to cook, and I think she was a fantastic cook. She made cakes and biscuits from scratch, knowing just how much flour and sugar. We had biscuits every day. Mary Hargrove could cook like that, too. Oh, I miss those women and how they could cook. Charles didn't like it, but we all had to take piano lessons. Our piano teacher was Miss Treelow. I took tap-dancing lessons. My folks would come to the recitals and Daddy would be so proud. Mama would straighten and curl my hair and put a big white ribbon in it. Daddy would say, "That's my girl up there." Folks don't see their kids do anything these days. I took violin lessons for a while, too. I loved it. Mama just felt that we should know all of those things. We should know good music. We had Halloween parties, went on picnics, hayrides, and skating and skiing parties in the winter. We took advantage of the winter.

Ownership was very important to us. Several families owned cars. Most Black families owned their own home, or shortly did. They didn't rent, at least not for very long. They took pride in that. Education and ownership. They worked for things, and no one owed us anything. That's what was taught in my house. We used to call him tight when we were growing up, but Uncle Bud would go to the Cadillac dealer and pay cash. Uncle Bud said he would never owe any man, and he didn't. And Daddy used to say if you ever go to jail, you must have had a plan to get you up there so you better come up with a plan to get yourself out, because we will not come to the jail. We knew he meant it. Daddy's word was gospel. When George Harris said something, he meant it. We'd go out to play, and Daddy would say to be in the house before the sun goes down. You talk about running to get home. We had chores and didn't grumble about doing them or talk back to him about those chores. We had respect for each other, too. When you passed a Black person on the street, you had to speak to that person. Even in church, some people don't want to speak. We have lost something so valuable.

Geraldine Hopkins Clarke,
Jean Hopkins Redwood, and
Hannah Hopkins Christian

The three Hopkins sisters attended the Madison public schools. After graduating, Geraldine attended Bennett College in Greensboro, North Carolina. She was a loyal and devoted member of the Order of the Eastern Star for more than fifty years. Jean received a bachelor's degree in sociology from the University of Wisconsin–Madison and moved to Chicago, where she taught for twenty-five years. As the oldest of the three sisters, she took on the responsibility of helping her sisters to develop self-respect, self-discipline, and good character. Hannah was a grade school teacher on army bases in Japan and Germany. While living in Germany, she traveled extensively throughout Europe and Africa. When she returned to Chicago, she taught grade school until she retired.

GERALDINE: Our parents, William China Hopkins and Georgia Ankrim Hopkins, came to Madison in 1913 from Richmond, Texas, and Dayton, Texas, respectively, looking for employment.

HANNAH: As a teenager, our dad was in the army. But neither of our parents completed high school. They were obligated to begin work at an early age. They soon realized the importance of education and sacrificed for many years to make certain their children received the education they had been deprived of.

GERALDINE: When they arrived in Madison, the city was very different from what they had been accustomed to. Only a very few Blacks lived in Madison at that time. The Black families who were there then were the Millers, Abramses, and Hendersons, who owned a farm on the south side of Madison and raised pigs, cattle, and chickens. Also, there were the Hills, Mosleys, Weavers, and Glovers.

JEAN: Our parents settled in the Greenbush or the Bush, with more of a melting pot of immigrants. I remember that many Blacks were settling

A Hopkins family photo with Anthony and Claude in the back row and Charles, Hannah, and Jean Hopkins seated in front. COURTESY OF MICHELE THURMAN

in this area. As more and more Blacks arrived, the earlier arrivals found themselves targets of these new arrivals—much bickering, jealousy, and name-calling.

HANNAH: I remember that the groups were compatible and friendly but did not intermingle. Each group had its churches, businesses, activities, and social affairs. It was during the Depression and none of the groups were well off economically, but all were hardworking and helpful to one another. In our immediate neighborhood, there were three grocery and meat markets. One store sold only kosher meat. There were about four restaurants with bars. Two were owned by Italians, and two by African Americans: a billiard hall owned by Mr. Dixon and a barbershop.

JEAN: Where men from the community and university students would come to have their hair groomed. Mr. Jimmie Evans operated a cleaning establishment, and Mr. Trotter operated a tavern and lunch counter.

HANNAH: One Italian man allowed our parents to sell hot tamales in his restaurant for a while. This special recipe was quite popular among his customers.

GERALDINE: Hop [our father] sold tamales in the Italian restaurant on our street. Each day after getting home from school, we had to help our mother make tamales, until I got tired of it and decided to join after-school sports, leaving Jean and Hannah, and my mother to struggle with them. Our parents brought this tamale recipe from Texas. Even though my family did not start a business of their own, they were instrumental in helping Mr. Mosley start his tamale business. Mr. Mosley was having trouble securing enough money from his restaurant to provide for his family. Knowing our father had a recipe for tamales, he asked Father to sell it to him. Our father first said no, but our mother talked him into selling it to Mr. Mosley for twenty-five dollars. Mr. Mosley made quite a business with the tamales and became known as the Tamale Man.

JEAN: We remember that the Allen Hendersons owned a farm which was quite productive. One morning while milking cows in the barn, Mr. Henderson and his younger son were shot to death by a Caucasian. He tried to push his way into the house, and Mrs. Henderson told him she was not dressed and not to come in. He asked for the older son and was told he had gone to town. When Mrs. Henderson went to the barn, she found the bodies of her husband and son.

GERALDINE: Our father's first job in Madison was doing menial work for Judge Lewis's family. Our brothers, the firstborn, Anthony and Claude, received hand-me-down clothes from the Lewis family. Our father worked for the New Park Hotel for a few years. Then he heard that a new hotel in Milwaukee was hiring European waiters. After hearing this, he moved the family there. He applied for the waiter's job at the hotel. Arriving at the hotel, the manager said to our father, noticing that he was Black, "I didn't ask for you to come," and Hop, as he was called, said, "You didn't ask me not to come." Father was eventually hired and spent three years in Milwaukee where Jean, the first daughter, was born.

After working for several years at the hotel, rumors were circulating that the hotel was about to close. At that point, the family moved back to Madison, where we—Hannah, Charles, and I, the last three children—were born. Our father hoped to get employment as a waiter in one of the hotels in Madison. It turned out they were not hiring African Americans. So he was fortunate to find work at the St. Paul/Milwaukee Road railroad station, doing duties such as redcap, porter, janitor, and whatever else had to be done. The pay at that time was sixty dollars a month.

HANNAH: While working for the railroad, he was entitled to receive free passes for the family. Our mother took advantage of this and traveled to Texas to visit her relatives every summer. She took us with her and we would spend a month or two in Houston. During these vacations, we experienced firsthand the devastating racial segregation prevalent at that time in the south. Our father remained on that railroad job until his retirement in 1956.

JEAN: As we said, there were not too many jobs available to African Americans except for janitors, maids, and cooks. They took jobs that would keep a roof over their heads and food on the table. A few men had applied to become postmen but were not hired. There was one Black city bus driver and only Blacks knew this. There was a Black lady anesthetist from Harvey, Illinois, who worked at Madison General Hospital, which was one of the few places that would hire Blacks.

HANNAH: I worked there during the summers as a nurse's aide. Jean and Geraldine worked at Baron's Department Store; one worked in the kitchen of the restaurant and one worked as a helper in the beauty shop. Our two older brothers worked at the railroad station as redcaps during the holidays. After a while, they went into the military. Sometimes we would receive baskets of food from charitable organizations. Our parents never owned a telephone or a car during these years. We were without many basic things, but they saw that we were properly educated and instilled the right values in us. Some summers our parents would rent a room to a graduate student attending the university. These students would come from the south to work on an advanced degree. They were professionals, seeking to continue progressing their fields. They became role models for us and helped us to realize even more the importance of education. They encouraged us to succeed.

GERALDINE: There was not a lot of visiting in the homes. This in part was due to families trying to provide for their families and not having adequate resources to participate in many community activities. Simply stated: they did not have money for other things that would take away from the "well-being" of their families. Also, the families were separated from each other—some living on the east side of town and others on the west side. People did not become close with each other, and the two sides usually stayed with their respective groups.

HANNAH: The center of activity for the younger children was the Neighborhood House, which was attended by children from all the ethnic groups. It was operated by two Caucasian ladies, Miss [Mary Lee] Griggs and Miss [Gay] Braxton, who lived on the premises. They held classes in sewing, crafts, and dancing; we played games and saw movies.

JEAN: Five or six blocks from there was Brittingham beach, enjoyed by many during the summer months. Often, we went fishing with my mother or hiking with some university students.

GERALDINE: In high school, Anthony and Claude were members of the school band. Anthony became friendly with the drum major in the band, and since he was graduating that year, he wanted Anthony to take over as drum major. He often tossed the baton to Anthony when they marched. The two decided to ask Mr. Klosey, the band director, if Anthony could take over. They got a resounding "No." Mr. Klosey stated he would not have a job if that happened, because the Whites would protest a Black leading an all-White band. Rosemary Sanders and Geraldine were the top women athletes in the school and always brought home the "bacon." Anthony and Claude ran track and won many ribbons for the school. Charles was into boxing, but lost as many as he won. The National Honor Society had never had a Black member, so my home economics teacher mentioned to Rosemary and me that she was going to submit both of our names before the group and see what happened. She said she didn't feel we would be accepted, even though we were honor students. She was right; we were both rejected.

Just being nominated was a big thrill for Rosemary and me, as no Blacks had ever been nominated before or after until several years later, when Dolores Simms was nominated and accepted into the Honor Society as a member. I remember some of our Black schoolmates:

George Dockery, an outstanding athlete who won many games at the school. He considered quitting school in the tenth grade because of grades. He was exempt from sports until he could raise his grades. He decided to quit school. What a loss.

Calvin Harris had a lovely baritone voice and sang for many of the school functions. He was in great demand for school and holiday programs.

LeRoy Banks was a very reserved and quiet individual and a man of few words. He married Ollie Mae Mathews and had two children, LeRoy (Butch) and Eugene Banks.

Leona Collins was very quiet, stayed to herself mostly. Very smart in school. Went to the University of Wisconsin and became a teacher in St. Louis.

Junior Dunn. I don't remember too much about Junior except his being an outstanding dancer. Before we realized it, Junior had all the young men swinging out.

Rosemary Sanders. Her father was the minister at Mt. Zion Baptist church. She and I were great friends and both honor students in school. She had a brother, Paschall (Sonny) Sanders, cute too! Rosemary moved to Texas before graduation.

Marion Eugene Banks enrolled in school in the tenth grade. After graduation, he moved to Washington, DC. I lost track of him.

I had my own experiences working in Madison. My first job was at the Wisconsin Telephone Company. As no Blacks had worked at the telephone company prior to my hiring, I was quite a spectacle. I do believe work ceased on that day as there was so much talking back and forth around my desk. Nevertheless, I made it through the day successfully. I remember only one occasion where one lady didn't want to associate with me. Of course, those who know me know I didn't take that sitting down. I confronted her. There were words exchanged and I was called into the "Big Boss's" office, Mr. Armfield. After several hours of talking with him and after he talked with her, an agreement was reached. We decided to stay clear of each other and have as little contact as possible. Her excuse was that her husband was from Georgia and he did not want her to associate with Blacks. When we came out of Mr. Armfield's office, two of the other girls in the office were busy getting my work together so it could go out in the mail. To this day, we are close friends and they also attended my wedding to Frank Marques, Ricky and Miguel's father. Those two women were Betty Dolan and Betty Grant.

My next place of employment was at St. Mary's Hospital in the medical records department. This was an enjoyable workplace. There were five girls in the office plus me. Again, I was the only Black. After having worked for St. Mary's and knowing most of the doctors, I decided to apply for work at the Dean Clinic. During my interview, the interviewer asked me if I was Indian, and I said no. He proceeded to question me about race until he finally said, "You're Indian. That's what I'm going to put on

your application." He further stated, "If they knew you
were Black, you would not be
hired." So I said, "Thanks, but
no thanks." That ended my interview with the Dean Clinic.
I was truly amazed because I
worked with the doctors at St.
Mary's and my children were
patients of two of the doctors
at the clinic. I then went to
University Hospitals, where
I worked several years before
transferring to the [state of
Wisconsin] Probation and Pa-

Geraldine Hopkins with her son, Miguel
Marques. COURTESY OF MICHELE THURMAN

role Department. The supervisor went around to each secretary and asked
if they had any objections to working with me. From what I gathered later
in my stay there was that as long as I worked and did my share, they did not
mind working with me. It seemed they had an impression Blacks did not
work, but just slid by—doing nothing or very little. I had no more trouble
from my coworkers except for a stolen fan. While I was on vacation, the
girl in the front office had taken my fan and refused to give it back to me
upon my return. This was an enjoyable experience and as usual, I was the
only Black, until Lorraine Davis came on board as a social worker.

I now understand why my father refused to let me apply for different
jobs at different companies as the NAACP had requested. They wanted to
send me to different companies applying for work, and if they didn't pan
out, the NAACP would step in and take it from there. My father said no.
Ah, to be Black in early "lily White" Madison. One never knows what to
expect.

Like most of the Black families in Madison, our parents stressed high
moral standards and a good education. I went to Bennett College and became an administrative assistant at Tuskegee University; Jean and Hannah
received teaching degrees from the University of Wisconsin and earned
their living as teachers; Anthony began college at the University of Wisconsin but finished at Temple, and also became a teacher; Claude went to

Wilberforce and Chicago College and became a US postal inspector; and Charles attended electronics school in Chicago. Charles's job was controlling the master computer system for the state of Wisconsin. When computers were down or out of order, it was relayed to Charles so repairs could be made through the main system.

HANNAH: I was born in Madison and spent my formative years there during the 1930s and 1940s. I left Madison when I was in my early twenties to seek employment that I felt would not be available to me as an African American in Madison. These formative years influenced the remaining years of my life in a positive way. Having the opportunity to attend the public schools in Madison and the University of Wisconsin provided me with a solid education and the chance to progress economically and socially. Our parents taught us that we would encounter many hardships, but to "stick to the task and eventually things would work out"—and they did. We say bravo to those parents who sacrificed so much so that their children would not be left behind and could become a part of the American dream. Many Black Madisonian children attended elementary, high school, and the university but had to find employment elsewhere. Shame on Madison!

JAMES LINCOLN GREENE

James is a descendant of the Shepard and Green families that originally settled in Lancaster, Wisconsin, in the 1850s. James worked for the Gisholt Machinery Shop in Madison and was a fireman for the Milwaukee Fire Department, a computer specialist for the Milwaukee County Library, and finally the 911 emergency coordinator for the state of Wisconsin. He also was a licensed private pilot and a United States Professional Tennis Association tennis instructor.

My father, George Greene, lived in Birmingham, Alabama, and graduated from Tuskegee Institute in Tuskegee, Alabama. Then he moved to Chicago and then to Madison to start a dry-cleaning business. He came to Madison, too, because he thought he could get a better job and he didn't like the big city. He was a haberdasher; he was a maker of clothes; he cleaned and pressed them. He liked the small community of Black people who were here. Because of being from the south, I don't think he patronized or fraternized with any White people at first. However, he was good at what he did, making, pressing, and cleaning clothes.

Through the efforts of several organizations, including the church and the Masons and other Black people in town, he was introduced to certain people who helped him. Someone found an opening for him at the Loraine Hotel. Not finding work for which he was qualified, he took the job at the Loraine shining shoes. Finally, he worked his way up to pressing and cleaning and then designing and making suits and clothing for the people who came to stay at the hotel. He became known around the city for his clothes-making skills that he learned at Tuskegee. Sometimes he was called "shoeshine boy," even though he was older than any of them. Several times, he was replaced by somebody higher up the chain, a White person, so he did feel like they wanted somebody else. In the end, it proved to be that they [Whites] couldn't take that kind of working environment, and the management would have to call my dad back. None of the replacements worked at those jobs for long because they considered the pressing and cleaning business beneath them. He was considered self-employed under the hotel's general manager, which meant he had to work very long hours. He worked from seven in the morning to six or seven at night, every day of the week, and half a day on Sunday. They let him off to go to church. He kept that job there for the rest of his life. We helped him after school, weekends, and on vacations or whenever we could. It wasn't anything we could get excited about.

In spite of the difficulty, he made a living. He saved his money from working at the Loraine Hotel to buy two cleaning businesses. One was called Victory Cleaners on Carroll Street off of the Square. Then he started Four Lakes Cleaners near the corner of Park and Erin Streets. He hired a few White workers and a few Black military personnel, who were mostly from the south. Keeping these businesses open was also difficult because the White landlords and managers would raise the rent, which made it seem like they were trying to force my dad out of business. Eventually, they did drive him out of business and he had to go back to the hotel.

My mother lived in Pleasant Ridge outside of Lancaster, Wisconsin. She grew up there. Her ancestors were both slaves and freed Blacks who settled there as farmers from Missouri. My great-great-grandfather, John Green, came there to sell apples and when the slave owner asked him to come back to Virginia, he stayed in Lancaster and bought a farm outside of Lancaster called Slabtown. He was considered a runaway because, although he was to help the master to sell apples, he stayed in Wisconsin and wouldn't go back and he knew the slave owner couldn't take him back. My mother, Mildred, left the family farm in Pleasant Ridge near Lancaster, Wisconsin. However, back then, my great-aunt Mamie Davis, formerly Mamie Green from Pleasant Ridge, owned a successful restaurant business called Davis's Road House, located across from a private airport, which later became South Towne shopping center in Monona. They helped my dad get started and get established in Madison. As it happened my ma's name was Green. She married my dad, who spelled his name Greene with an *e* on the end.

My ma graduated from high school in Lancaster to attend nursing school, which she found to be a financially impossible path for her. The only job she could find was at a department store managing the stock and ironing the clothes before they were displayed. Sometimes the management

Jim Greene (right) is pictured with his siblings, George Jr. and Catherine. COURTESY OF DOLORES SIMMS GREENE

asked Ma to work after hours to serve guests. On occasion, when they had a salesperson come in, a guy who traveled, my mother would have to come back, not knowing anything about it, and serve at parties. That was part of the job. They had to do this in order to hold on to their jobs.

We lived out on the south side. At that time they called it Hell's Half Acre. I think White upper-class people from the west side dreamed up that name because it was made up of mostly poor Blacks and poor Whites, some Norwegians, German Jews, Italians, Irish. It didn't have water or electricity; streets weren't paved, no curbs or gutters; it flooded. When we had a storm or some environmental crisis, we were the last to get serviced. I imagine that would lead to a name that forewarned people that this was not the best place to live. Of course, the houses were small and were not in the best of condition.

In spite of the difficulties, my family helped others by opening our small home on Fisher Street to the needy, even Whites, and the new arrivals to Madison. Blacks who were already living in Madison were kind to any other Blacks who came. Sometimes, we directed these new folks to members of the Eastern Star, the Masons, and to the Allison House for help. Typically, we gave help and did not reveal the help we gave. We did not talk publicly about it. For example, we had to loan, give up space, rooms, and clothes for various periods of time to the families my parents helped. We never looked down on each other. When the southerners first came after the war, plenty of them were of school age. I know I volunteered to walk them to school, anything I could do to give them help. Charles Hargrove was one. I walked him to school. We had differences of opinions, but

Jim Greene, pictured in his Navy uniform, served in the Korean War. COURTESY OF DOLORES SIMMS GREENE

we tried to be helpful, talking to them about fighting and calling names. I took Freddie and showed him the ropes, talked to him, interactions with good intentions.

If Ma was cookin' at one of the fraternities and the fraternity was going to have a dance, then Ma would recommend somebody else to come and help do the job, or if somebody got sick and couldn't work, Ma was asked to come and cook or if she couldn't do the job, then she would get somebody else that could. Another example was Dolores and how she got her first job. When Charlene Hill, who worked at the Darling Shop, needed help, she recommended Dolores.

Established organizations, such as the American Federation of Colored Women's Club, did not have helping people find housing and jobs as their goals. They followed either national or state goals and focused on providing social events. We would picnic with each other whenever we could. We would go to Black people's homes. Our folks had house parties and played cards. Trotter's was a bar and lounge Black adults frequented. There was a big restaurant called the Pines on top of the hill on South Park Street that Blacks went to and a club called Autumn Leaf where folks also ate and drank. Some of the clubs helped their members with etiquette and manners, how to sit and dress, and write poetry. They discussed whatever they could bring in from Chicago or Philadelphia. Old Man Stewart peddled the *Philadelphia Courier* all over town, and that was the only news anybody got from what Blacks were doing elsewhere in the country.

We had trouble with various teachers. Teachers discriminated against Blacks in art, music, and gym. I didn't get the awards the White kids got for the same level of participation. At Franklin, we had a new principal. Fred Banks and I and several other Black kids were in gym class. We played soccer. Someone kicked the soccer ball and it went high into the net. No one could get the ball except Mr. Gibson, the principal, and he was tall and skinny. Fred said, "Let Gibson get it." Mr. Gibson got so mad at Fred that he came over and grabbed him on the shoulder and lifted him right up off of the floor and shook him. Gibson threw him down on the floor. Gibson said, "You don't ever use my last name. You say mister." We were all shook up. We didn't know what to do. Fred was crying, but I don't think he had to go to the hospital. Mr. Banks and Annie Rogers had to come to school to talk to Gibson. That was one incident, but there were several like that.

Jim Greene (right) with friend Fred Banks. COURTESY OF DOLORES SIMMS GREENE

The parents got together and got Mr. Gibson transferred out of Franklin School. It was a different Black-White type of atmosphere thereafter.

The word "n——" came up quite often then. We had to fight after school. We chased them, and they chased us. We'd never know when we were going to hear n——. We had such a diverse neighborhood that we couldn't concentrate on it. However, more Blacks came to the neighborhood. They weren't Blacks that were established in the community. They came from places in the south. They had a fighting culture and wouldn't stand for a lot of things we would slough off. We couldn't get involved in fighting. They would start things, take something away from somebody, like a bike, and beat them up. We couldn't do that because we would get punished. I don't know if they would get punished or not. They would take whatever they wanted. It was a different culture. We wouldn't make that kind of an enemy out of a White kid unless we really had to. This was quite a shock to us, at least to me and to other settled Blacks. They did this mostly to White kids and sometimes to Black kids, but not that much. Our parents dealt with problems. At times, the authorities set things straight. Some families were known to pick fights. These fights were seldom long-lasting and not violent in today's terms, that is, no knives, no guns, no gang activity. The older Jewish and Italian kids usually quelled any disruptions in the Bush, mainly because there were more of them and they were rooted the longest in the neighborhood.

We had hobbies and created our own clubs. We formed a group called the Black Eagles. The group members were Burt Rogers, [my brother] George Jr., Freddie Banks, and me. We built model airplanes from kits we bought for ten to fifteen cents a box. Each box contained twenty to twenty-five planes. My aunt Mamie Davis heard about how badly we wanted to fly those planes, especially since African Americans were not allowed to fly at the time. She tried to contact a famous writer who would write a poem or story about us boys and our love of planes. In addition to the plane-building club, we had a boat-building club called the Rafters. The members of this club were Bert Rogers, Tom Rich, Harvey Williams, Clarence Brown, the Harris brothers, the Elvord brothers, and me. We started out building rafters and then began to build boats and float them up and down Murphy's Creek, now known as Wingra Creek, on the south side of Madison. We also went from Vilas Park to the bottom of Fisher Street out to Lake Monona.

The values that my parents tried to teach my brother, sister, and me were to behave, be respectful, and be religious. My dad was always at church. My dad's mother, Grandma Hawkins, was a schoolteacher, but she taught us what those values were. Because my ma and dad needed help taking care of us, she lived with us and took care of us. We were disciplined. There were many times when we'd be out playing and we'd say, "Oh, here comes ole' grandma," and zoom, we'd take off.

RALPH LEE JR.

Ralph is a descendent of the Allisons, one of Madison's earliest African American families. While growing up in Madison he attended Longfellow Elementary School and Madison West High School. He lettered in track and field. In 1950, Ralph moved to Milwaukee, Wisconsin, where he became an officer in the Milwaukee Police Department. After his tenure there, he applied for and was accepted as a deputy in the Milwaukee County Sheriff's Department. He retired from there in 1983 at the rank of sergeant. Ralph loved jazz, all sports, automobiles, and poker. He was a history buff and a member of the Polar Bear Club, taking many of those subzero dips. He was also a licensed pilot and owned two Cessna airplanes, one of which he built himself.

I am a descendent of the Denning/Allison families. My great-grandfather Charles Denning was originally from Marshalltown, Iowa. During the Civil War, he joined the army, where he became a drummer boy. He was discharged from the army in 1865 at Camp Randall, after which he moved to Lake Mills. Great-Grandfather Denning married my great-grandmother, from which came five children: Maude, Millie, Myrtle, Myron, and Myra, all born in Madison. In fact, Myra lived on Fair Oaks Avenue, which was a woods back then. Myra Denning married Harry Allison Sr., my grandparents on the Allison side. Those grandparents were born in West Virginia. Harry Sr. migrated to Kansas City, Missouri, by working on the railroad as a porter. Eventually, he settled in Chicago, where my grandmother Myra had also settled. They married and moved to Lake Mills. From this marriage came my mother, Margaret, born in Lake Mills in 1911, and four other siblings, Harry Jr., William, Connie, and Ellen. Actually, there was another one, Marian, but she died at birth. My ma, Margaret, married Ralph Lee Sr., who attended the UW–Madison and graduated with a master's degree in English. They moved to Stanton, West Virginia, where I was born. However, my ma decided that she and I (I was nine months old) would go back to Madison to be near family.

Ralph Lee's grandparents, Harry and Myra Allison, at his wedding in 1953. COURTESY OF RALPH LEE III

My grandfather, Harry Allison Sr., worked as a janitor all his life. All he did was janitorial work. He did plenty of that and he never missed a day's work in his life. However, after World War II, a few jobs opened up in Madison. Blacks worked at Badger Ordnance, Oscar Mayer, and Truax Field. Granddad got hired out there at Truax Field. He was a maintenance man, making a dollar an hour, and boy, he thought that was gettin' rich at eight dollars a day. My grandmother, Myra, cooked at fraternity houses and washed dishes in the tearoom. My grandmother also integrated a Kresge's dime store and diner on the Square. She went up there and they called the police to put her out, but the police couldn't do anything about it and that was the end of that. They said there was no beef. After that, Blacks could eat there.

Blacks had the sweeping jobs. We couldn't work on the city garbage and trash trucks doing the rubbish collection. Jim [Greene] was the first Black to work at Gisholt. He applied to these jobs and they said no. Duke Ellington used to stay at our house because he wouldn't stay at those second- and third-rate hotels—him and Billy Strayhorn. We would set him up a room

Ralph with his mother, Margaret. COURTESY OF RALPH LEE III

in one of the bedrooms upstairs—the rest of us were all crowded up—but he stayed there several times like that. And Dolores Greene, she graduated from the University of Wisconsin and couldn't get a job in the educational system under Falk. Not a Black person could teach in the city of Madison. She had to go to Milwaukee.

My grandparents bought a house on 628 South Park. The city had deemed the area commercial, so my grandfather could add on to the house they lived in. He also owned the lot next door. While we lived on Park Street, Granddad bought a house on 18 South Murray and rented it out to students and other Blacks who couldn't find a place to stay. I remember when the Stanfields and the Johnsons came up from Arkansas and they didn't have anything. My grandmother let them stay in the hall on Murray

Street until they could find suitable housing. They all stayed together in the hall. I took care of the furnace at that place every day. This was an apartment with three floors. It was something I had to do. I also collected the rent. The biggest rent was about sixty dollars a month for three rooms. The Office of Price Administration froze the rent so landlords wouldn't gouge the renters, but we didn't. This was during the war. We had community toilets, one on each floor. My grandmother and grandfather put a complete heating system in the whole thing, hot air heating system with a stoker, and I was the one that took care of that furnace for about five years. I cleaned the hall, too. I had to get up early every morning and fill the stoker up and take the clinkers out and then go to school. This meant that when the ashes from the coal didn't burn, I'd have to shovel them out and put more coal in. Then I'd have to come after school and fill up the stokers again. Sometimes, in the cold wintertime, I had to go down there in the middle of the night to put more coals in the stoker.

After some time, Grandfather Allison sold the lot on Park Street for eight hundred dollars to Mr. Price, who built a hardware store on the property. In 1940, after my great-grandmother Denning, who had come from West Virginia to live with them, had died, Allison sold the house on 628 South Park and bought Gertrude Harris's three-story house on 18 South Murray Street. Gert Harris, as she was called, used her home as a rooming house. However, I think she lost the house through foreclosure. Granddad remodeled it into four apartments and three single rooms. This house was once owned by the Troia family, who had a butcher shop and a dance hall. My friends and I went there to dance.

My first job was at Grand Brothers, a clothing store in downtown Madison. Although I was not allowed to sell clothes, I did other small jobs, like drive the trucks, stoke the furnace, mop floors, and deliver stock, for which I received twenty-seven dollars and fifty cents a week. At that time, a few Blacks could operate the elevators in the stores.

My grandfather was in the Masons. My grandmother was in the Utopia Club, an association club for Black women, which was affiliated with the Milwaukee branch named after Phyllis Wheatley. She was part of the NAACP, too. There were some efforts by the Communist Party to recruit Blacks in Madison into its organization. In those days, Blacks did not fear the Communist Party, even though White people had characterized

Ralph and his mother Margaret, pictured at his wedding in 1953. COURTESY OF RALPH LEE III

it as a dangerous political party and one that should be feared. I was just a teenager when I sneaked in to see what the meetings were about. I remember hearing that the motto was "any means to an end" and recruiting Blacks into the party was a means to an end. It was about integrating Black men with White women. The party used the White women to recruit Black men into the organization. I remember when I was at one meeting. We were someplace on West Washington Avenue or Mifflin Street and were all sittin' on the floor with our legs crossed. They had a sing-along. One song they sang was "Ole Black Joe." This one White man got up and said that he would not sing this song again. He was mad. He was trying to show his outrage for singing a song like that. One time, Curtis Taliaferro Sr. and I went to a New Year's Eve party that the Communist Party was hosting on Vilas Avenue near the zoo, although we did not know who the hosts were at the time. We thought the party was just a party. They were making toasts. They had toasts to all these different people. Most of those people were White women making these toasts. They toasted the five Black men who had been killed in the south, the Scottsboro case. Actually, the toast was to salute freedom of the five who fought for their freedom, but at the same time, the toast was for freedom for the Communist Party. This scared me to death because you know Communists were subversive. I was there. The Communists were supposed to be real liberal and real understanding of the Black people's causes, but it was really furthering the Communist Party, that's what it was. My grandmother warned me several times to stay away from it because you'll get in trouble, but I didn't care about that.

Everybody knew everybody. You couldn't get in trouble because everybody knew what you were doing. There was no real animosity among Black people. When I lived on Park Street, I would park my bicycle in the middle of the sidewalk and it would stay there. Park Street was a busy street and my bike would stay there for three or four days. Weeds would grow up through the spokes and nobody would move it. We didn't have to worry about anybody stealing anything.

Word of mouth was how you found out about what was happening. The churches, like Mt. Zion, and the Holiness churches had services. The kids used to go down there. Connie and Sonny Cochran would go there to dance to the music at the sanctified church. The people were jumping and dancing and the music was really some kind of music. The church folks found out that they weren't there for the service, but were there just to dance, so the church people put them out. But they came back anyway. When I was coming up, I couldn't go to the show on Sundays. I had to sneak and go past the church. Sometimes, I would catch hell because they knew my friends and I had been away too long for us not to be at service. I remember when St. Paul's Church burned. I remember because my grandmother was on the stewardess board and the board had a hard time getting the money from the treasurer. My grandmother talked about it and argued about it and they had meetings about it for two years and finally he came up with money to repair the church. They couldn't pay for the repairs on account because they couldn't get the money from him.

I was a fair athlete. I used to run the 131.6 half-mile relay, but some guys ran 128.3. I tied the city record and I broke the record in the broad jump. That was junior high. And I won by one-tenth of a second in the two-hundred-yard dash. That was the best day I ever had in athletics. I never had a better day. Joe Washington and Charles Hopkins just killed them that day, and I anchored the relay team that year. I didn't do much braggin' about it. Outside of the sort of braggin' that was done about it, no other kind of celebration was done. I remember when we used to play football out on Burr Oaks. No equipment whatsoever and never broke a bone, and we used to play hard. We would play with no equipment, no helmets—nothing. These two White boys. I could not beat them in speed skating. They would get me every time. As athletes, my relationship with them was all right. They had no choice but to respect my ability. We played tricks on each other in the locker room. They did it to me, but we did it to them, too, like putting wintergreen in their jock straps and stuff like that. Wintergreen burns. I didn't have any trouble with them, but I know about two different incidences. One incidence was when Jim [Greene] was on the volleyball team. They made him flip a coin between another White boy to see who would take the place on the team. Jim lost. They always told him [Jim] that he couldn't play hockey because he was too rough. There were a few incidences like that. I never stayed over-night on trips. But back in 1946–1947, I was the only Black on the track team, and in Rockford, Illinois, you couldn't eat there, but I ate there, I had to eat with them. Blacks in the city couldn't eat in these places and I know they couldn't. But I did. Rockford and Beloit was just like being in Mississippi.

My uncle William was a good musician. He was a drummer. He had his own band for a while and worked at the Town Club on Sherman Avenue. The members of the band were Eddie Hudson, piano player, and Tommy Hates, who played the trumpet. They played six nights a week at the Town Club. They made good money, but they had to work. Uncle William worked at the plastics place called Celon Plastics on Johnson Street. [My aunt] Ellen was an excellent pianist. She could have had jobs with bands, but she did not want that kind of life, but she taught piano in the park.

CHARLES ANTHONY DENNING

Charles Matthews, a cousin of Ralph Lee, wrote this account of his great grandfather Charles Anthony Denning's journey to Wisconsin, which is used with permission of the Allison family.

When Charles Anthony Denning marched under the big stone arch at Camp Randall, I wonder if he had any idea what he was about to "commence"? Yet commence he did, one fine day in March of 1865; and here we are, almost in the exact same place where the man affectionately known as Charlie marched on this Wisconsin soil.

Born in Queensborno, New York, in 1837, Charlie was one of three children of William and Hannah Denning. William Denning was determined that his "mulatto" (or mixed-race) children would not be raised in slavery, so he sent his two daughters to his family in Ireland and enlisted Charles into the Union Army. After surviving the war, Charles came to Wisconsin with soldiers from Wisconsin's 31st Regiment Infantry, Company C.

Luckily, Charlie had acquired a vast knowledge of farming from his father while growing up. His knowledge of these farming techniques became the key to his survival in Wisconsin. For the first few years, he traveled back and forth between Madison and Lake Mills, managing farms for Reverend Miller and Reverend Updike, ministers for the First Congregation Church, located in Lake Mills.

In 1833, Charlie married Mildred Aaron Pruitt, affectionately known as Millie, from Lake Mills. While still a small child, Millie, her mother, and younger sister fled from slavery in Bolivar, Tennessee, to Cairo, Illinois. Shortly thereafter, however, her mother died. A Dr. Pruitt stationed in Cairo found little Millie and sent her north to live with his family in Lake Mills, while her five-year-old sister, Liya Ann, was sent to Fort Atkinson to live with the family of a Dr. Simeon Bicknell.

Shortly after their marriage, Charlie and Millie moved to Madison. Charles's knowledge of farming made him the instant choice of Reverend Miller to manage his large farm on the bank of Lake Monona and the

Yahara River. While there, they had five children: Maude, Myrtle, Myron, Myra, and Millie.

In 1891, Charlie moved his family back to Lake Mills, where he ran a large dairy farm for Reverend Updike. There, Charlie met Booker T. Washington, who came to Lake Mills for a brief respite from many years of directing and continuous building of his school (now known as Tuskegee University). Charlie and Dr. Washington became close friends, spending hours discussing Tuskegee and farming techniques. Myra Denning Allison could recall Dr. Washington and her father kneeling and designing Tuskegee in the muddy shores of Rock Lake. In Dr. Washington's memoirs, he pays high tribute to Charlie for his assistance.

Charlie succumbed to pneumonia. After the death of her father, Myra Denning (future matriarch of the Allison family) took a lead role in her family. Described as feisty and proud, she was also kind and gentle as a lamb. Myra learned early in life the joy of laughter as well as the seriousness of responsibility to her family.

MICHAEL SHIVERS

Mike Shivers worked at various jobs while going to UW–Madison. He found full-time work with the US Department of Agriculture in 1959, and he worked there until he retired. He served as alderperson from the Seventeenth District for twenty years. He has also served on many committees, subcommittees, and boards, including the Dane County Parks Commission for fourteen years, the East Madison Community Center board, the board of directors for the Cheyenne Settlers Heritage Society, and the Madison Jazz Society board. In 1989, Mike was nominated for the Dr. Martin Luther King Jr. Humanitarian Award. His mother, Dimetra, was the first recipient of that award.

Mike Shivers. MURIEL SIMMS

G randma Elsa, my dad's mother, when she was a little kid, came on a ship to Ellis Island in New York. She was a Neumann and lived in the Deerfield, Cottage Grove, Cambridge area. She met Grandpa Oscar. He was delivering in Maple Bluff. She was a maid over there, and that's how they started their family.

My mother's family's origins began in Tennessee. Her father, James, had two brothers, Proctor and Willie, and three sisters, Mildred, Euphrasia, and Ollie. James married Lela Evans, and they started having children. They moved from Brownsville to LaGrange or Maywood, Illinois. They were going to school there, and Grandpa got a job at the boiler works factory in Kewanee, Illinois. He and his family moved there and started raising the rest of the family in Kewanee. My mother, Dimetra, was born in Brownsville. She and Odell and Curtis came from Brownsville to Kewanee, where Grandpa had the job in the boiler factory. My ma had been quite an athlete in high school and interested in going to the UW and studying nursing. She decided that after Odell came to the university to study chemistry, she would come on up to Madison . . . beautiful views. After she graduated from high school in 1930, she moved to Madison. I don't know where she lived, maybe with Odell. Her sister, Mercedes, came with her after graduation or with Grandpa. In 1932, my ma met my dad. They got married in 1934 and had me in 1935. Grandma was a milliner in Kewanee. Ma's baby brother, Wayne, and little sister, Gail, came with Grandpa and Grandma to Madison and went to West High School or Central. I've been trying to get this information from the Board of Education but for some reason or another, it's a military secret to find out when relatives graduated from high school. Odell graduated with a degree in chemistry. It was in the forties that ma became active. She and Odell with the Hamiltons and Reverend Swan and Shorty Collins got active because there was so much discrimination.

One of her good friends was Lucile Miller. She and Lucile were tight, but they would become especially active if somebody was discriminating against somebody else, another family of color, not so much women's rights, but color, they would raise Cain about it. When they discovered that Black soldiers in the service were not allowed to come to the PX to get groceries and cigarettes, she and Lucile said, "You better start selling stuff to Black soldiers or we're going to start picketing this place." Somehow, they got results. They integrated the thing as far as selling to people of color. There was no dial phone. You had to pick up the phone and say, "Operator, operator. What number please? Badger 2011." That was our number back then. She and Lucile were on the phone all the time, talking about stuff, but she got active with Shorty Collins, [Harry and Velma] Hamilton, and her brother [Odell] and sister-in-law, Hazel. The other people in the family were not active; they had other things to do. So Ma, she was a stalwart.

We lived on Brooks Street and on Mound and also on Proudfit Street. From there, we found a house on Corry Street, just before you get to the railroad tracks. My dad and I painted that house three or four times while we lived there. People saw my dad, but they didn't know he was Black, but the Shivers name had been around since the early 1900s. When they saw my ma, they had a fit. Oh God, they did mean-spirited things. A guy had a dog down the street, a big black dog, almost like a Saint Bernard. He would bring him down and have him do his business on our lawn. And guess what the dog's name was . . . "N——." My dad said, "You better stop bringing that dog down here because I got a shotgun." So the guy stopped.

We were the first family of color to move east of the Yahara River. I was six years old. Dad had a chance to buy that house. The house was seventeen hundred dollars. Dad was working on two or three jobs, painting, tending bar, driving a bus, and a mechanic at the bus barns, and worked at Rayovac for a while to try to support the family, but it was too much money for him. So we stayed there, paying rent, until 1958, when we moved out. He got his draft notice in 1941. Dudley Montgomery, who owned the bus company back then, said, "No, you can't take Stan Shivers. He's the best driver we got, and he's the only good mechanic we got, and this is a public service, and we need Shivers to keep the buses running. You can't take him." So my dad didn't have to go. His brother, Nelson, was a super draftsman, intelligent. He got in the Convair Company, which made airplanes. Uncle Frank had a medical discharge, bad ear. My Uncle Duby was the youngest of my dad's brothers. They took him. He went into the segregated army. My dad was very light, Nelson was swarthy, almost like Hispanic, Frank was yellowish, and Duby was very dark. His given name was Algae D. Shivers, but they nicknamed him Duby. They made him a sergeant and let him give orders to the other Black soldiers. Duby was very smart. The other soldiers didn't respect him because he was lighter skinned. But he was a good soldier. My aunt Fay went to Texas where he was training to see him, but they would not let her on the base because she was White, and he was training with all-Black troops.

United States troops were fighting in World War II in northern Italy against the Germans. There were two units, one Black and one White, both fighting near each other, but separately. It was raining buckets of shells on the White and Black troops, but both units were ordered to go knock it out. The White soldiers refused to go up the hill; they were afraid. So Duby was ordered to lead twelve Black soldiers up the hill to knock out the German gun nest. According to Duby's daughter, who heard the story from her dad, Duby was never so scared in his life because there were machine guns. But the Black platoon knocked out the big gun and knocked out the German nest, and when Duby came back down the hill, he only had three men left. Uncle Duby should have gotten the Congressional Medal of Honor for his heroism, but supposedly the records of his achievements in World War II were "lost in a fire." Clinton or Obama should give him this honor for saving a lot of lives. When Duby came back from the service and was living

Four buttons from the US Army uniform of Mike's relative Alga Shivers who served in World War I. COURTESY OF S. MICHAEL SHIVERS

on Fisher Street in south Madison, he told his kids what happened as they grew up. Duby not getting a medal makes me so mad.

My ma got involved with other people in the forties and fifties: the march on the Capitol for fair housing, the march on Washington, she was part of that. We have a picture of Mom boarding a Greyhound bus at the Memorial Union to go to Washington. She was one hundred feet away from King when he made his "I Have a Dream" speech, and that was important to her.

My dad's great-uncle, Tom Shivers, came up through Illinois from Tennessee with his brother, Ashley Shivers, who is my great-grandfather. They walked and took barges or paddleboats and ended up in La Crosse County, and from there they came down to Vernon County. Tom Shivers became a very prominent farmer in the Hillsboro area—the first farmer to have electricity, the first farmer to have a gasoline tractor. He was respected by everybody in Vernon County. When you would see anybody in Vernon County who was seventy-five to eighty-five years old and ask them, "Did you ever hear about the Shivers family?" "Oh yes, they had a farm, and Algae Shivers, Tom's son, built the round barns in Vernon County." The Shiverses were very well known and very popular and very well accepted in Vernon County. The Shiverses' roots are up there. Thomas and his children, Herbert, Alga, and Mary, were some of the first Black settlers.

Great-uncle Ted Shivers barbered in Sparta [Wisconsin]. Great-grandfather Ashley barbered in La Crosse but later came to Madison because his son Oscar had met Grandma Elsa, and then they got married. Ashley possibly came to Madison in the early 1900s. Ashley had three children by his second wife: Oscar, Claude, and Nettie. We don't know details about when and why. In Hillsboro, it was like the people living in the Bush. There were Czechs, Whites, and Blacks, and when somebody died in that farming area, you took the kids and raised them regardless of whether they were Black or White.

Stan was born in 1911 in Madison. His siblings, Hazel, Nelson, Frank, Algae (Duby), and Adeline (Sally), were also born in Madison to Oscar and Elsa. The center of activity for our family was at Grandma Elsa's, 11 South

Members of the Shivers family pose in front of the family barbershop, circa 1900. From left to right are Claude Shivers, Rebecca Ann Shivers, Nettie Shivers, unknown, Ashley Shivers, unknown, unknown, and Oscar Shivers. WHI IMAGE ID 45964

Murray. As the Shivers children married, they moved to other areas of the city, but basically they stayed in the Bush for a while. My mother and dad lived on three or four different streets in the Bush. They lived on [the] corner of Milton and Murray Streets, the Amato house. Ashley lived at 610 Milton Street. Jackie and I moved in next door to my mother and father on 113 South Park Street and then we moved to the east side.

Another family moved on the east bank of the Yahara River near Marquette School, and that family was Leroy and Sadie Poole. My dad and Leroy became friends. Leroy was a crane operator at Gisholt. My mother had gone to the Board of Education and talked to somebody, saying, "We are moving to the east side. Which school should my son, Michael, go to?" This was 1941. Somebody at the Board of Education said, "Well, Mrs. Shivers, our records show that you are a Negro. If you were going to move there, it probably would be better for you to send your child to Longfellow School." Ma said, "Why?" The woman said, "Because there are other Black children there." Mom said, "No, I can't do that. He's going to go to Emerson or Lowell." It turned out that there was a lady teaching at Emerson who was from the Bush herself who my mother knew. The problem with Emerson was that I would have to cross busy East Washington Avenue to get to Emerson, and going to Lowell would mean I would have to cross two different sets of railroad tracks, four times a day. Mom chose Lowell so I would not have to cross East Washington Avenue. I went to Lowell and, of course, I heard the word "n——" so many times. I did well in school and I became popular. When it came time for me to graduate from Lowell and go to high school, the Board of Education told my ma I should not go to East. My ma said, "Well, why?" They said, "Because he should go to Central where there are other Negroes." I went to East, became a popular guy, and had a lot of friends.

When we first moved into Corry Street in 1941, the neighbors got a petition. It said, "We don't want those n——s in our neighborhood." A lot of people in the neighborhood signed, saying, "Get those n——s out of our neighborhood." They took the petition to our next-door neighbors, Joe and Verane Schumacher. Joe was just about ready to go into the service. We had swastikas painted on our sidewalk, eggs thrown against the house, and crosses put on our front yard. Joe and Verane said, "We're not going to sign that petition. Those are nice people that live next door to us. We're not going to sign that petition." Some neighbors across the street didn't sign the petition either, the Andersons. So that saved our family from getting evicted from the neighborhood by a petition. The Schumachers became very good friends of my folks. My dad had beers with Joe and shared stories. I had a lot of fights. I never got beat up, but I did a whole lot of beating. I learned how to take care of myself. Why should I be afraid of someone who wanted to call me a name? Within a few days after we moved in, Wayne Anderson, who lived across the street from me, came over. My ma cut up a bunch of carrots, and we sat at the table and ate carrots together. We both were about six years old.

My mother worked at the United States Air Force Institute, across from the YWCA, the old Belmont Hotel. She worked as an elevator operator at Hills department store, but got this job at USAFI in the late forties. She could type and write well. At USAFI, someone thought that because she was doing all this work on racial equality that she was a Communist. Every move she made, they investigated her because she was Black. We faced those barriers before these young people today are getting headlines for what they think is terrible discrimination. They talk the talk, and my mom and those who are gone walked the walk. She was investigated. She is Black. She must be a Communist. She didn't take anything from anybody. My ma did not walk quietly, and she carried a big stick. My dad walked quietly, but he carried a big stick. He wouldn't say much, but if he got mad, he'd let you have it. They did drop the charges.

Ma did not write letters to the editor like I do. She would just make a phone call. She would be in your office, in your face. That's why Lucile Miller and her were the same. They would fight with people and fight with each other. She and Lucile would be mad and wouldn't talk to each other for a month or two, and pretty soon the phone would ring and they would be talking to each other again. She was crazy about politicians who were for social justice. We have a picture of her standing with Congressman Bob Kastenmeier and Teddy Kennedy. She loved Bob. He wrote to her. They would send Christmas cards even when she was in the nursing home.

Back when Jackie and I had our son, Steve, we found this house on Morningside Drive, two blocks from the school, near shopping and the bus line. Nice house. We made arrangements to look at the house. The real estate person met us. We no sooner got in the house than the phone rang. The neighbors knew the seller's name and phone number. The realtor picked up the phone and said some words: "Oh, really. Okay," and hung up. He said to us, "The house is no longer for sale; someone else has bought it." It turns out that the person across the street said, "We don't want people like that living in our neighborhood," meaning me and Jackie. Jackie and I tried many times to buy houses at different places, and they would be already rented. Ma would call the rental people and say, "We are interested in this rental place." The person would say, "OK. Make an appointment." This was in the sixties. The things that we did. We walked the walk. We didn't just talk the talk like it seems today. We did what we said we would do.

My mother was discriminated against. She was the first person of color to sing with an all-White band—supposedly in America. Somebody said, "Well, Billie Holliday was the first Black singer to sing with an all-White band." Billie was a great singer, but Mother did some research and said that she was, because she was singing with local White bands in areas around southern Wisconsin. Al Averson's band was all-White. We've got pictures of Doc DeHaven and Ma standing up there with this big band as a singer. They sang at the Club Chandelier in Middleton.

The first time she went out to the Club Chandelier, they didn't want her to come through the front door. The band members said, "Well, this is our singer. If she doesn't sing, we can't play because she's part of our band." They stood up for her so the club said, "Well, OK." This was in the late thirties and forties. Ma talked about how she sang in southern Wisconsin. A big band would come to the Madison area. She and the guys would go to a tavern out near Fort Atkinson to jam with Jack Teagarden and well-known old players.

She was friends with Duke Ellington. Black musicians could not stay at the Loraine Hotel where my dad used to tend bar. They didn't know he was Black. The Black musicians would come to stay at Grandma Elsa's because she had lots of room, or they would stay at the Allison House, kitty-corner from Grandma Elsa's. Duke Ellington walked in and said, "Oh, D," because that's what she liked to be called—D. When my ma was pregnant with me, Duke put his hand on her belly and said, "You are going to have a healthy baby." Jackie, my wife, recalled her experience with Duke. She saw him when he came to the university in the early 1970s to do workshops and talk to people about music. They had classes and had performances at night with a big performance at the end. Dimetra and my wife were in the

Dimetra Shivers and Duke Ellington. COURTESY OF S. MICHAEL SHIVERS

chorus. Duke came and rehearsed with the chorus and then they did this big performance at the Union Theater. People danced down the aisles. I took my dad and the kids. Ma followed these musicians around.

The prejudice against my dad was like, he looks like us so let's not be too hard on him. He did experience discrimination on some jobs, but he was able to get good jobs in the forties. Freeman Brown, who worked in the cinematography and photo lab at the University of Wisconsin, hired my dad. He liked my dad because my dad could do anything, drive a truck, anything, and he was smart. Freeman Brown took my dad to New York to take moving pictures of something out there. For those big cameras they used to have in the old days, you needed a generator for the lights. They had this big truck at the photo lab. Brown said, "Stan, you can come with me, drive the truck, and help me with the lights." Dad drove the truck to New York and back, and didn't have a truck driver's license. Also, Mr. Garver was a very wealthy man who owned Garver's Feed there by Olbrich Gardens. My dad filmed lots of work for him. Dad worked for people like that because Dad was well-liked. Most of the discrimination was openly directed at my mother.

Ted Wilson was Black, Gene Krupa was Italian, Benny Goodman was Jewish. A lot of clubs would not want to hire them because Teddy Wilson was their Black piano player. Teddy Wilson was one of the best jazz pianists of all time, compared to Oscar Peterson and some of these other people. He was great. My mother loved Teddy Wilson. She would say, "I love the way he plays. I wish he could play for me so I could sing sometime. He was good at accompanying people. Just look at his eyes. I love his eyes." Teddy Wilson was playing at the Union Theater back in the late forties and early fifties. I went with her to a concert. After the concert we were outside the Union Theater on Langdon and Park Streets. Ma said, "Look. Here comes Teddy Wilson." She walked over to him and said, "You are such a good piano player. Meet my son." I shook hands with him. She looked google-eyed at him like she did at Kennedy and Kastenmeier. So I met Teddy Wilson. I played the piano from 1941 to 1984. I sat in with groups that played on State Street, like Doc DeHaven, but I was not that good of a group player.

What really broke up the family was the demolition of the Bush. Everybody had to move out. My mother was a Baptist. She spent a lot of time dealing with Shorty Collins and Reverend Swan working on political stuff. Grandma Lela was close to God. You never said a bad word in front of her. She was in front of the radio every Sunday. Grandpa and Grandma were very religious. My mother saw that a lot of people would go to church and listen to the gospel, but as soon as they left those church doors, they would forget about the gospel. So she would say, "Let's go deal with the politicians who are making the laws."

Uncle Algae, who was darker skinned, applied for police and fireman positions but was refused because he was Black. Uncle Algae was the only Black man who played for the Italian baseball team. George Fabian has a picture. Harry Stuhldrer recruited Blacks for the UW–Madison football team. He got Eddie Withers. I have a picture of my dad and his brother, Nelson, on the 1929 Central High football team.

Uncle Nelson was going up Regent Street to West High. Some White guys from West High—and West High had mostly kids from wealthy families—a couple of White guys were beating the hell out of Nelson—two or three of them. There were some Italians from the Bush who saw that and they ran across the street and beat the hell out of those White guys. Why? Because they were from the Bush. Guys from the Bush, regardless of race, stuck up for each other.

Grandma Elsa lived on 11 South Murray next door to the Pulara family. Pure Italian family. Anthony Pulara married Arlene, who taught all of our kids at Hawthorne School. Grandma Elsa and Mrs. Pulara would lean over this old raggedy wire fence between the two yards. Grandma told Mrs. Pulara a joke in German. Mrs. Pulara would laugh and tell my grandma something in Italian. Somehow, they understood each other. They talked about a lot of stuff we couldn't understand. We got a recipe for meatballs from Mrs. Pulara.

EDWIN HILL JR.

Ed Hill worked for AnchorBank for forty years, eventually becoming the vice president of property management there. During his career, he volunteered to be on health care–related boards, some of which he chaired, such as Madison General– Meriter Hospital and the Health Care Association. Other organizations in which he became involved included Wisconsin Physicians Service, American Red Cross, and Dane County Memorial Coliseum. In the early 1970s, he helped found Group Health

Edwin Hill Jr. MURIEL SIMMS

Cooperative. He was an alderman from 1970 to 1972, representing Madison's Fourteenth District. Ed was also a competitive pistol shooter, winning two state championships in the marksman class.

My grandfather and grandmother, John and Amanda Hill, owned a grocery store on the corner of Blount and Dayton Streets. They bought the store before World War I from Mr. Turner. My grandfather opened the store at seven a.m. and closed it at ten p.m. My grandmother would help out by staying in the store from two to four p.m. while my grandfather took a nap, which he did every afternoon. I worked in the store to pay off money I owed my grandfather. I did chores like cleaning the floors and windows, mowing the grass, and getting food from a local distribution agency down the street. My grandfather's grocery store, during the war and seeing how it was a neighborhood grocery store, was probably eighty-five percent White. And they'd come from all over because he had all the different groceries except for meats. He did not have a meat market, but he had cigarettes, and cigarettes were sort of rationed during the war. People would come because if you were a good customer you could get two or three packs of cigarettes. So he would have people come along and buy twenty-five, thirty, forty dollars' worth of groceries just to get cigarettes. I used to have to pick up groceries in my little wagon. There was a wholesale house called

ER Godfrey on the end of Blount Street where the Fauerbach Brewery used to be. I think the American Legion or the VFW is there now. My grandfather would run low on stuff and so he'd have me go down there to pick it up with my wagon. I'd pick up cigarettes, and I'm talking about cartons of cigarettes. I'd have to come by Kayser Ford and the people would see me go down the street with my wagon. I'd be coming back and they'd be standing there, "Have you got any cigarettes today?" I said, "Yes, he's going to have cigarettes today." These folks would follow you right back to the store. No one stole the cigarettes from my wagon, but today you probably couldn't do it. You'd have to have an armored car to do it, but back in those days and that's just [the] way people were. People were honest. We didn't have locks on our doors. You could go for weeks and no one would disturb you.

I used to go to Gardner's Bakery. It was down on East Washington Avenue. When he'd run out of bread, I'd go down there, and the foreman would always say, they all called me Junior, "How would you like to have some fresh doughnuts?" They'd take me back to the line where they were making the doughnuts and take a box and say, "What kind of doughnuts?" I'd say, "Just give me variety." He'd pick up these doughnuts, put them in a box, give them to me and say, "Okay, now take that with the bread." In the wintertime, I'd have my sled because the wagon couldn't make it through the snow—but I really enjoyed growing up in Madison. I enjoyed living on that block. It was a great place to live. For me, it was a great place to live because of the interaction, because of all the kids. We all got along and all the families got along. Across from my grandfather lived retired fire chief [John] Lahm. He and his wife were great customers at the store. My grandfather used to have charge accounts, and if you were a good customer, he'd let you charge. He had a book that he'd write down everything you bought. Once a week, people would come and pay up or once every two weeks—whatever their pay period was, they'd pay up. If you were a good customer, but not great customer, then he'd let you only charge for a week's worth. He used to have index cards where he'd write down what you bought and, within two or three days, you'd have to come back and pay that. He used to have this hanging on a little rack in the store. When I think back about it, the Lahms were in the book and the DuWaynes were in the book. There were five or six families that he trusted would be in the book. I thought it was a great system.

The church played a tremendous role in helping Blacks in the city of Madison. That's where everybody met. My grandfather owned the house that was on 114 North Blount Street. When Ben Parks came to town, that's where he lived. He used to tell folks when folks asked him, "Where do you live?" "I live over with Mr. Hill." Ben tells the story of when he was working at a barbershop at the Belmont. Mr. Piper owned the Belmont Hotel and the Piper Garden Cafeteria. Ben was cleaning the barbershop or cleaning something in that building, and Mr. Piper didn't know who he was. Ben said, "I live with Mr. Hill." Piper said, "Well, if you live with Mr. Hill, then you got to be all right." Ben still tells me that story. My grandfather did that for a lot of people.

Freddie Mae Hill, daughter of John and Amanda Hill.
WHI IMAGE ID 119528

The railroad used to have porters who would stay overnight in Madison because they couldn't stay at a hotel, so at that same house at 114 North Blount, there were rooms upstairs. I think there was one, two, or three. There might have been four beds up there. The railroad paid for those people to stay there at that house because hotels weren't allowing Blacks to stay there in the early forties. It was difficult to find housing. I know after Rosemary and I were married, we were living at 114. I got drafted and then I was deferred. We lived with her parents for a while and then we ended up living at 1842 Fisher Street, which is the house that Jim Greene grew up in. I bought the house eventually from Jim Greene's father, George. Back then when you tried to find a house to live in, it was very difficult. An Italian family lived on Fisher Street. The Cardarellas lived up on the corner, and I remember calling the Cardarellas. Mr. Cardarella and I talked all the time. I called him one day anonymously and wanted to know if his upstairs was still for rent. "Yep," he said. I said, "I'm Black." "Oops, it's already rented." Just like that. Then, I remember talking to him on the street, and I said, "You know I'm the person that called you the other day about your flat." He didn't know what to say to me. But then when we moved to 1842, we lived right across the street from him. Mrs. Stamps lived right around the corner, and he lived next door.

The relationships among Blacks were good because they depended on each other. They shared food. They spoke all the time; no animosity, not among us because there were so few of us. When I think about our block, the 600 block of Dayton Street, I think of my great-uncle and aunt, Otis and Fannie Mae Daniels. There was our family, then there was my grandfather and his wife and his two daughters, and then next door, there was Anna Mae Miller and Lucile Miller. Carolyn Johnson and her husband lived there for a while when they would come back in the summertime. They lived there and raised their kids there. Next to them were DuBois and Emily Miller and Mae Miller and Ernie Mitchell. Then next to them was, I think, the Caires who lived there for a while, and then [the] Hendersons lived there, and then the Buttses, and then the Weavers, and then, around the corner, Mr. Guy lived, and come back the other way were the Gothards. Those were the Black families on our block. There was another house that the Goldsbys lived in for a while, and a White family lived there, too. It was funny because we all played together, Black or White or whatever. When I went to Lincoln School, and all of my sisters went to Lincoln School, we were the only Black kids there, because all the other kids, for some reason, they all went to Lapham. When Scrammy and Billy came to the east side—they originally lived over on the west side and probably went to Longfellow—they didn't live with their grandmother until they went to Central High School. By the time Carolyn Mitchell and the Gothards came along, they had put a dividing line in there. But because I had started at Lincoln already, my sisters all got to go. The block was interesting.

My grandfather, on the Hill side, came from Atlanta, Georgia. My mother's folks came out of Hope, Arkansas. That would be on the Daniels side of the family. My grandfather's big thing was that he always wanted to go back to Atlanta. He was always saving his money to go back to Atlanta, and then when he got into his nineties, he got sick and then he couldn't go back. But he sent for a brother and two sisters to come up here from Atlanta. They came up here and spent a month. There was Sam Hill and Ethel and Tootie and they all came up here and you know what's crazy? I used to travel with the drum corps. I used to be a bus driver for the Madison Scouts. We went to Atlanta one time. I found out my great-aunt and uncle's address before I left Madison. I get down there and we were playing at the stadium where the Braves played. I go up to this policeman and

I said, "Where is this number on Peachtree Street?" He told me where it was. I knock on the door and my great-aunt Ethel comes to the door and wants to know who is there. They weren't about to open the door to anybody and I didn't know about the neighborhood. She's peeking through the screen. I said, "I'm Junior Hill, John Hill's grandson." I had a shirt that said Ed Hill. She must have seen Ed Hill on the shirt and so she said, "Sam, it's Junior, it's Junior." You could hear Sam running through the house. He gives me a big hug and everything so I stay there for about an hour talking to them. I told them that I had to get back and get ready to take these kids to wherever they're going on their next stop. The Black kids who were in the corps when my sons were in there were Dave Davenport, whose nickname was Couch, Jim Elvord, Phineas Horton, and a lot of Black kids.

I knew my great-grandmother on the Carmichaels' side. That was Ida Carmichael. Ida Carmichael was my grandmother's mother. She lived at 114 North Blount Street. We lived there, too, when Rosemary and I got married. We lived at 114 North Blount, and Mother and Dad at that time were living at 118. The grocery store was 649 East Dayton. We owned those three properties right there on the corner of Blount and Dayton Streets. Ida died in 1941, when I was about in the fourth grade. I think she and my great-uncle Josey were the first [family members] to come here. I have no idea why they came here, but my grandfather and my grandmother came here in 1910. My mother's father, who is Charles Daniels, lived close to the Simmses. He lived in the house behind the house on the corner of Frances and Dayton Streets. The Gentrys lived in the front house. Charles's wife, Myrtle Daniels, was my mother's stepmother because her biological mother was Salome, who died in Hope, Arkansas. I used to go over there because my grandpa used to cut my hair. Back in those days, you had no Black barbers in town. So you always called somebody to cut your hair. The Carmichaels came around the 1900s because they and the Millers got here pretty early, too. The Carmichaels lived off of State Street.

J. Anthony Josey started the first Black newspaper in the state of Wisconsin. The paper was called the *Blade*. There were always copies at my grandmother's and great-grandmother's house. We didn't know what they were, so, when we cleaned the house, we chucked them all out. If I'm not mistaken, he was buried here in Madison. I was reading the *Capital Times* and the columnist reported that he had been calling around to find out who Josey was. I called him up, and I told him that Josey was my great-uncle. As a result, my wife and I were invited to come to Milwaukee to honor him for publishing the first Black newspaper. He was a great Republican and my grandfather was a great Democrat. They used to argue all the time. At the Republican convention about 1948, Josey was a sergeant of arms. His chest swelled up so big because he got to be a Black sergeant of arms at the Republican convention. He was a good friend of Joe McCarthy. I have a picture of him and Joe McCarthy at some event, standing around shaking hands with all the other Black Republicans. They used to call him the mayor of Brownsville in Milwaukee, and there are a lot of people still in Milwaukee who still know who J. Anthony Josey is.

I don't know why my family came to Madison. Maybe it's because, when they got here, they probably thought you never heard anybody complain. I never heard my folks or my grandfather complain about anything that ever happened to them to make them come to Madison. I know when he came to Madison, the first business he had was a shoeshine stand. Then he bought the grocery store from a guy by the name of Mr. Turner. Then my grandfather was on his own. When the war came along, he got hired as a clerk for the federal government. He also worked for the state.

I remember when I went to Milwaukee to look for a job. Uncle Joe said he was going to get me a job. He was going to get me a job at the Heil Company because he knew the governor. I figured Uncle Joe was a big shot. People would drive him around because he didn't drive. So I figured he knew Governor [Julius] Heil. Well, I expected Uncle Joe to come walking through the door and say, "Here is my grandnephew. Give him a job." Heil takes me out there to the personnel office. I say to myself, "I could have done this myself." So I filled out all the paperwork. No one called me. I happened to be reading in the Milwaukee paper that the Trackston Company was hiring, so I went out to the Trackston Company and filled out my own application with nobody helping me. I got a job the next day. My Uncle Joe was that type of person, because when he'd come to Madison, he'd stand in the backyard and whistle for us kids to know that he was in town. He would be over visiting my grandfather at the store, his brother-in-law. He'd have a pocketful of pennies and give us kids two or three pennies, and boy, we'd think, "He's a rich man. He's got these pennies." Our Uncle Otis used to do the same thing when he'd come, but he'd give us dimes.

Truthfully, back in those days, there were no problems. There were no problems because my grandfather lived on the block. He owned the property, so my family always lived there. All the kids were treated the same at school. When I came along, my parents took us up to Lincoln School. You got enrolled. The kids who went to Lapham, they got enrolled. There were no problems. When I transferred from Lincoln to Central, you just went through school. When I went to the University of Wisconsin, there were no problems, as long as you had the money in hand. My first semester's tuition was fifty-five bucks. If you had the money, they didn't care.

I never heard name-calling. I saw a friend yesterday, Francis McMann. We graduated from high school together sixty-five years ago. But he and I have known each other since probably second or third grade. He was a kid I used to beat up every other month just to keep sharp, you know. When we graduated from high school, I was going to go down to the office to ask if I could walk across the stage with McMann. He got there before I did to ask if he could walk across the stage with me. We've been friends that long, but I ran into him one day at the Junior Fair. This person came up to me and said, "Are you Ed Hill? I bet you don't know who you're talking to, do you?" I'm looking at the person, and I said, "I'm sorry. I do not know who you are." "I'm Francis McMann." I played in his polka band in grade school and in high school. I played the accordion first and then the saxophone in his polka band. I had to learn all those old-time tunes. Francis McMann and the Shamrocks, that was the name of the band, but we didn't really have any problems.

The neighborhood. There was a tavern across the street. Everybody went to the tavern. Nobody had any problems in the tavern. They didn't break the glasses like they do if a Black person was there. There was one tavern out on Park Street. The owner didn't want any Black kids in there. We were always told that if you went in there to have a beer, he broke the glasses. But it didn't bother us. So we'd go in there a lot just for him to break glasses. We didn't have any problems. If someone told us there was a problem, we didn't aggravate it, but if he's breaking glasses, we'd say, "Let's go there all the time." Then the Golden Pheasant was down the street, run by Elisa Berget. She just told you up front, she didn't want any Black folks there, but later on she relented and most of her customers were Black. The Golden Pheasant was on Park and Dane or Park and Buick

Street. She was up front that she didn't want kids there, but eventually, she turned over a new leaf.

Paul Washington, Billy McDonald, and I, we were the three musketeers. We all graduated from the same high school. You know, when I look back growing up in Madison, when I was a kid, it was a great place to grow up because I didn't even know what discrimination was until I left here. I didn't know what was going on until I got into the workforce. I guess the thing I liked about growing up in Madison when I was a youngster was that as long as you had the money, you could go anyplace you wanted. You could go to any restaurant; no one ever kicked you out. You could take your girlfriend to any restaurant as long as you had the money.

The city barns were in the neighborhood. The city used to use horses to pick up the garbage and plow the sidewalk. I remember sitting on the Millers' steps when they ran all the horses out of the barns. They had like a roundup. The building that is still sitting on the corner of Blount and Dayton is the original horse barn. That is the building that Sol Levin had his office in and the offices are still in there for the people who run that portion of the program for the city of Madison.

My grandfather knew a lot of people and the police department because of the grocery store. Every time I would do something wrong, the police would say, if they found out I was John Hill's grandson, "We're going to tell John Hill. He'll get you straightened around. We don't need to worry you." Back in those days, the police used to pick up a lot of bums on the railroad. They used to have an arrangement with my grandfather where they would bring them by the store. He would make a sandwich for the bums, give them fruit, and either a pint of milk or a pop that came in the bottles, no cans. The police would pay my grandfather and then take the men out to the end of town and say, "Now look, get out of town. Here's this lunch. Take it with you and make sure you don't come back." He knew all the policemen, and even today, I'll run into folks who are old retired policemen who say to me, "Are you related to the guy that ran the grocery store?" "Yeah, he was my grandfather."

My parents didn't participate that much. They participated in the NAACP for a while. Mother used to try to go to the PTA meetings. That's what it was called back then. My mother participated in the church. Church was a big item. It seems like, for many Black people, the church was the most important thing because that's where all your friendships were. My father was a Mason. I'm still a Mason. I've been a Mason for fifty years. I was a third-degree Mason. My mom was an Eastern Star. I joined Zimbo Temple to be a Shriner because my mother wanted to be in the auxiliary of whatever they had. My father wasn't a joiner. My dad was a quiet person. He was comfortable just sitting there and let my mother do all the talking. I guess I've always felt that you have to get involved. I call it being civic-minded. I've always told people, I believe that no matter where you live in whatever community you are, you owe something to that community and you should get yourself involved. I call that paying your civic rent. I don't care what you do as long as you're doing something.

I mostly got involved because my kids were involved. I always believed that if your kids are involved in something, then you should be involved. It used to tick me off because the YMCA used to have these tours and they'd ask fathers to come along with their sons. Only two Black fathers were there, me and one other father. There would be all these Black kids, but no Black fathers. And even when my kids were in the drum corps, I started traveling with the drum corps because of the same thing. My kids are going. I'm going to be volunteering because these are my kids. When my kids got out, I looked around and there are these Black kids, but no fathers. So, I started driving the bus and I drove the bus for twenty-five years—coast to coast. I used to tell those kids, "I'm here for you. If you want to sit and talk about something, I'm here to talk." I used to see Juanita Goldsby. She'd come every now and again. But she was a female. Ed and Bea Elvord showed up occasionally. I did it for the Black kids. I used to be on a bus three or four weeks. I had a good employer. I worked for AnchorBank. Harold Scales, who was the president at the time, believed in community service, so I didn't have to take vacation time to go do this. Because that's the way he felt. The whole community spirit is different now.

I also got involved with the South Madison Neighborhood Center. We started a Southside Credit Union at the South Madison Neighborhood Center. A person by the name of Mr. Highland from CUNA Credit was involved. They used to call him Mr. Credit Union because all he did was go around setting up credit unions. I was the treasurer and I volunteered my time to be at the neighborhood center. We got a group of people to donate five hundred dollars in our account so we'd have money to loan out to people. It must have went on for about two or three years. And when I got elected to the city council, I couldn't find anybody who wanted to run it. Nobody wanted to donate the time. They didn't want to make a commitment and the next thing I knew it was out of business.

Seeing that I was the only boy in the family, I was expected to do all the chores. So come over here and do this and do that, shovel the sidewalk, cut the grass. Once you start cutting the grass, you have to cut from the store to all around over to the Carmichaels' house and then you cut the backyard. It didn't hurt you, but that's one of the things that says something about what values and ideas you get from your parents and grandparents—hard work doesn't hurt you. Be willing to do what it takes to get the job done. That's what my grandpa would always tell me. Another thing he used to always tell me, "Make sure you keep something in your back pocket. Always save something." Just before he died, he was always telling me, "Save, save, save, save, save." But it was a big thing to him, just do a good job. That's all he kept saying, "Just do a good job, do an honest job." That's all I ever heard. "Just do an honest eight hours of work. No matter who it is, what you're doing, do an honest eight hours of work. If you can't do that, then you're slacking." My grandfather didn't go for slacking. When you did your job, you were supposed to do it and get it done right. As long as I can remember every time I had a job, I did the best I could. It's just a part of my philosophy. But it's one of the things that really stuck with me.

I went to the university for a while and didn't like it. I went to trade school and said, "Ah, this is great." I found something that I really liked to do. Once you find something you really like to do, take it and run with it. If you want to get ahead in this world, then work. If you don't want to work, then you're not going to get there. But if you're willing to put forth the effort, and like I said, in my case, I was at the right place at the right time, and I was qualified to do the job, and that's the important part. You went to school and learned how to do these things. So that when the time came that you applied, they look at you and they look at your resume and they say you can do the job. I'll never forget Mr. Steinhauer, the first day that I went to work at Anchor. He said, "I got a little problem." I said, "What kind of problem do you have?" He said, "I'm takin' all this flak from people because I hired you, but don't worry about it. If anybody comes and gives you any kind of flak, you let me know that." When people found that

I knew what I was doing, and I didn't take any BS, there were no problems. I never once had to go to him.

My father would umpire the ball games. I don't think there were any family traditions except getting together for the holidays. My mother used to be good with the needles. Knitting and crocheting. She was always making doilies. My mother was working all the time and worked as long as I can remember. She worked at the Orpheum Theater as a maid. I remember she used to take me to work with her when the big bands would come to town, like Cab Calloway, Tommy Dorsey, and all those types of bands. I used to go and enjoy them and it didn't cost me anything. My mother would get me in free. Work was the most important part and taking care of the family. There were nine of us kids, and that made it tough to have nine kids back in those days because money wasn't very plentiful. Mother used to sew a lot. She made a lot of my sisters' clothes. My grandmother was always knitting and crocheting. I know my Aunt Chess and Auntie Josie were big in ceramics.

We sat on the porch. Grandfather Hill would sit on the porch and listen to the baseball games or listen with Mr. Okey. Mr. Okey was a White fella who lived up on the corner. Every night, they would sit on the porch and they would have two or three radios going, listening to two or three ball games all at the same time, sit there on the porch all summer long. If you were there when my grandfather had ice cream, then you got ice cream. It was great. To me, it was a great time to be a kid. I can't find anything wrong with it except we didn't have a lot of money.

When I got my first social security sheet, showing when you first paid into social security, I was cleaning the bakery, the Women's Exchange up on King Street. I don't know how many years I cleaned up there. Three or four dollars was taken out for social security. Before that I had a job working for a fella by the name of Pete Rortvedt. He's one reason I got started in the building trades. He paid me sixty cents an hour, a penny a minute for firing boilers and pulling clankers and cleaning hallways, cutting grass and shoveling snow. I know I'll never forget. He got sick. He had a hernia. I used to come every Saturday and work for him all day Saturday for sixty cents an hour. I came this one Saturday and his wife, Ann, said to me, "Pete's in the hospital and you'll have to do all the work yourself." "Yeah, I can do that." She said, "You'll have to come twice a day to do it." "No big deal."

I knew what to do. He used to always tell me, "I can set the clock by you coming on Saturday mornings." I had to be there at six o'clock on Saturday morning, but I'd be there before six o'clock. I'd come and I'd get started, and I'd fill all the hoppers, and pull all the clankers off, and get the rubbish out. At the end of the week, she handed me sixty dollars. I said, "What is this for, Ann?" She said, "That's what you get for doing the work all this entire time." I think I did it for two weeks. When he got out of the hospital, he was thankful that he had this kid. The only way Pete knew me was that I used to deliver newspapers for him when I was twelve or fourteen. I had a *Milwaukee Journal* paper route.

It all started when, one day, Pete needed someone to put the storm windows on. He said, "Kid, do you want to come back and help me put the storm windows on Saturday? What's your name?" "I'm Ed Hill." "Okay, Eddie, I'll see you on Saturday." Just like that. I show up on Saturday and we got the storm windows done, and then did the furnaces. He said, "Okay, do you want to come back next week and help me?" Every Saturday, I was there. Then we got so busy that he wanted to know if I knew somebody else, so I got Billy McDonald to help. In the meantime, he gave me a raise to eighty cents an hour. When he hired Billy, I had to go back to sixty cents an hour. He couldn't pay us both eighty cents, but he could pay us both sixty. But I thought, that's fine. Billy needed something to do, too. When he got done with Billy, I never went back to eighty cents; it was sixty cents, but it was another great experience. I just happened to be in the right place. I was an honest kid, willing to do what the guy needed to do. Pete and I remained friends forever. When he died, I went to his wake. Pete was one of those guys who'd give you the shirt off his back. He was one of those types of guys. He appreciated everything you did. And I appreciated it, too. That's the whole story. I've worked for tremendous people over all these years. I had some ups and downs because we don't get along with all folks. I think I only heard the N-word on the job once or twice.

I was working for Madison Steel, and we were doing a rod job out in Verona. I never did a rod job before, putting reinforcing rods in. I go to work and the boss said to me, "Here, you take these drawings. There's this job we got out there in Verona. There's going to be some ironworkers out there to meet you. You give them the drawings and you tell them, you are going to work with them." So I get out there and there were two southerners. I told them I had the drawings. The first thing they said to me was, "We don't work with n——s." I said, "Fine. You guys can go do what you want to do. I'll go back to the shop and I'll tell the boss." So I go back and tell Dick. He said, "No problem. I'll get a couple more tomorrow." So he did. So we both go out there and there are these two new guys, one guy lived behind my grandfather on Marion Street. Elsworth Swenson. He knew my grandfather, Charlie Daniels. When I show up there, Elsworth shows me how to do it. There was another guy there. He was an Irishman named Sullivan. He was always on my case, but I got along great with these guys.

I couldn't join the union. That got under my craw, but as long as they were paying me the wage, I didn't care. I think at that time, it cost one hundred dollars to join the union. I was paying one dollar a week to work, which the union called a permit fee. With that fee, I paid ninety-nine dollars of my money. They didn't want to take that last dollar because then I'd become a member. I remember Coleman telling me, "Hill, if you want to be in this union, go to Detroit. You're not going to make it here in Madison." All of this was going on because I was Black. This one person I worked for didn't care. He'd still send me out on the job. He'd still pay me whatever the ironworker salary was. He didn't complain. I ran a crane for him for like ten years. Same thing, I couldn't get in the union. I remember working for CUNA one time. There were four cranes on the job. Three guys that had the other machines were all nonunion. The business agent from the operating engineers, which is what you called them, came out and waved at me. I had been up to see him about getting a permit. He wouldn't give me a permit. He signs those three guys up. But no one ever complained. Here I am running these machines. I'm getting paid, get all the benefits, but I'm not paying union dues. I thought they would complain, but they didn't complain. They didn't want a Black in the union. That's what it was about. In fact, a guy by the name of Wallace, who was also an operating engineer, knew the problems I was having. I had already gone to work for Anchor then. He came up to me one night and said, "You can get in the union. We took a Black guy from Milwaukee." I said, "It's too bad now. I already have another job. And I like what I'm doing now." I don't need that. It always amazed me.

You go through all this. You served your apprenticeship more or less just to prove you can do it and you go on the road with the machines. You'd be on a union job and no one would say anything because they knew what was going on. You can't join. No one ever complained. The field agent for the ironworkers was on my back all the time because I'd be out on jobs and some White ironworkers would call and complain about this Black guy out here doing our work so out he'd come. And he'd get there and say, "It's you, Hill. Why don't you call me and let me know where you are so I can tell them it's okay when they call in?" I thought, "It's not my problem. It's your problem. As long as Dick sends me out to do the job and he doesn't have a problem with it, then I don't have a problem with it." We got a lot of iron up. When I was running the crane, I used to tease these guys and say to them, "I get paid by the ton, so we're going to swing a lot of iron today." These guys would look at me, and these are all White guys and they'd say, "You really get paid by the ton." "Yeah, I get paid by the ton and we're swinging a lot of iron today. And then I'd tell them, "No, I get paid by the hour just like you do." But it was funny.

You know, looking back on my life in Madison, Madison has been good to me and my family. I have worked hard, been in the right place at the right time, and I have paid my civic rent.

Paul Washington

Paul worked for the Gisholt Machine Shop, Madison Water Utility, the Madison Police Department, and as a supervisor in the Dane County Sheriff's Department. After his retirement from government work, he continued to work part-time as a driver for delivery service companies and to volunteer with Badger Honor Flight,

Paul Washington. MURIEL SIMMS

which flies veterans from Madison to Washington, DC, to visit monuments. Paul has been the State Commander of the Disabled American Veterans of Wisconsin, president of the Korean War Vets in Madison, and a member of the Veterans of Foreign Wars Post 1318 and the Dane County Veterans Commission.

Susan Dunkin from Kansas City, Kansas, and Reverend Joe Washington met somewhere along the line. They came to Madison around 1930–1935 from Iowa to pastor at Mt. Zion. Reverend did not talk about why he came to Madison. He made no mention of job opportunities in Madison as to why he came here. He worked for Rennebohm's drugstore, cleaned, and did maintenance work. They lived in the Bush on South Francis Street, then moved to Wilson Street. They knew the Gentrys, who lived on South Francis Street. Reverend was pastor of Mt. Zion when it was on Johnson Street across from where the Nitty Gritty is now. He raised three of us. There was Lucille and Joe, his sister's children, and me. I was the youngest. I was adopted as a young kid. The final adoption was about when I was five or six years old. Initially, I was raised in a boarding school, St. Bonaventure in Milwaukee. My biological mother is Francis Givens Thomas. Frankie, Howard, and Joe are my half-brothers. I called them my brothers, you know. I went to the old Marquette School. Then they built the new Marquette School on Livingston. I lived on Wilson Street down by the Gisholt. The Pooles lived on Main Street. Mrs. Poole's parents,

Joe Washington Placed on All-City Football Squad by Times and Journal

Nov. 21—Monroe at Central
Nov. 22—Central at Ripon
Nov. 28—Central at Horlick
Dec. 5—East at Central
Dec. 12—Central at West
Dec. 13—Central at Stevens Point
Dec. 19—Beloit at Central
Jan. 2—Central at Janesville
Jan. 9—Kenosha at Central
Jan. 16—Central at Park
Jan. 23—Horlick at Central
Jan. 30—Central at East
Jan. 31—Central at Kenosha
Feb. 6—West at Central
Feb. 7—Park at Central
Feb. 13—Central at Beloit
Feb. 20—Janesville at Central

Joe Washington, Central High School football guard, was honored by the Wisconsin State Journal, and the Capital Times on Nov. 12, when he was placed on their All-City squad. Joe was chosen because of his terrific play. He was shifted from fullback to guard last fall, and showed much improvement in his new position.

Walter Bigley, tackle, and John Jensen, fullback, were placed on the State Journal second team.

The Capital Times named the best sophomores in the city. Central players honored were Bill Mischke, halfback, Jim Waters, center, and Bob Lee, guard.

Receiving honorable mention in the Capital Times were Clem DiLoreto, end; Walter Bigley, tackle; LaVerne Gasser, halfback; and John Jensen, fullback.

Other boys mentioned in the State Journal for their good play were Clem DiLoreto, end; George Guzzetta, tackle; Jim Waters, center; George Barry, center; Don Gasser, fullback; and Bill Mischke, halfback.

Sophomore Basketball Squad Members Open Season With Horlick

The sophomore basketball team, under the coaching of Harold "Gus" Pollock, will play their first game this season when they meet Racine Horlick at Horlick on Nov. 28. The boys started practice on Nov. 10, and have been practicing since.

Last year's sophomores came in in second place in the Big Eight basketball league. As to this year's prospects, Coach Pollock states that if the boys will get their fundamentals down pat, they will have a chance for a good season, for the

Two Central Football Boys Receive Mention In Big Eight Listing

Jim Waters, Central center, and Joe Washington, guard, were given honorable mention in the choices of

Paul Washington's brother Joe played football for Central High School and was selected for the all-city squad his sophomore year, according to this article from the *Madison Mirror*.
DANE COUNTY HISTORICAL SOCIETY

Mr. and Mrs. Bostick, lived on Wilson near Dewey Court—when they used to call that area the Isthmus back then—by Badger Welding behind where the old Red Dot Potato Chip Company used to be. I went to Marquette, then transferred to Lapham and then from there to Central High. My brother Joe, who was crazy about Dolores Simms, went to East until they redrew the boundary lines. Everybody on the south side of the line went to Central and on the north side went to East. We lived on the south side of the line, so we went to Central. He liked Dolores, but then Jimmy came into the picture. I got to know my biological mother after I came back from the service. I was in Korea for two years and got injured. My mother lived a couple of doors from the Hills on Blount Street. Back then, Blacks didn't talk much about families and where they came from. They just accepted us as we were. I hung out with Ed Hill, Billy McDonald, and Charles Harris. They called us the four musketeers.

Reverend Washington didn't talk about any barriers. He was welcomed with open arms from what I remember. He would have prayer services in the home. White people would come on Sunday afternoon after church service. His home was looked at as a place to stay. People knew they could stay at his house until they found a place. As an example, Roger Parks's children, Eugene and Erma, the twins, were born in Reverend Washington's house. Roger could not find a place; they stayed at our place. He was working at Oscar Mayer. They finally found a place on Regent Street,

The congregation of Mt. Zion Baptist Church in 1948, when Reverend Joseph Washington was pastor. WHI IMAGE ID 52695

so they moved from Reverend Washington's house to Regent Street. The house on Wilson Street had four bedrooms, so there was plenty of room for people to stay.

My parents, and even myself, didn't experience any discrimination while growing up. Reverend Washington was invited to this place and that place. He was involved in things that the White people invited him to. He was the chaplain at the Capitol, in the legislature. Everybody knew him. All you have to do is say "Reverend Washington" and everybody knew who he was. Susan didn't work; she was a homemaker. People were at the house all the time. You'd think we were running a boardinghouse. Different people would come to visit, some needing a place to stay. Reverend Washington was a Wisconsin Republican. He was invited and got his way paid to Republican conventions. He had contact with the right people to do whatever he wanted to do. I don't know how, but he did. No problems with the neighbors. We were the only two Black families on Wilson Street, us and Virgil Woods. They lived two houses down. They were members of St. Paul. Reverend Washington was involved in a lot of organizations, including the NAACP. There were two areas I didn't argue with him about; they were politics and church. Even though he was not a Mason, he was invited to attend their functions to give the invocation. People liked the way he gave an invocation. Reverend Richard Pritchett and Reverend Washington were good buddies. Several White ministers came to the house. Some people would come to the house just to receive prayer. They liked the way he prayed. He had a way of making them feel relaxed with a prayer. He would go to the hospital to minister to Blacks and Whites, not only those from Mt. Zion but those who belonged to other churches, too. Reverend Joe Dawson took over in the fifties when the church was still on Johnson Street.

I started going to St. Paul because of Ed Hill and Billy McDonald, even though I had been raised in the Catholic Church. My brother Joe was a member of St. Paul, too. Joe wanted to get involved in St. Paul because Dolores was there. I never associated much with Blacks on the south side. However, the Washington family used to go to Deacon Harris's house all the time on Sunday. The Reverend would get invited to other places to eat Sunday dinner, but we went to the Harrises' most of the time. Mrs. Harris would cook. Mother Benjamin was there, too. She was mother of the church when Mt. Zion was on West Johnson Street. There would be other members of the church there, too. They had a big farmyard. That was country out there. They had chickens and all kinds of animals. The Elvords lived down there on Bram Street, too.

My mother was up in the morning on school days making biscuits, fried eggs, oatmeal, and hoecakes. My mother would make hoecakes and put them in the oven to bake. You'd eat these hoecakes with jelly and syrup. Most of the Black mothers cooked breakfast for the kids. I used to walk from my house to Lapham School and walk back home for lunch, and then walk back to school. I had to cross East Washington Avenue. Kids today don't know what that's like. They won't go to school unless they have a ride.

The values were "behave yourself" and religion. I started working at about seven or eight years old. I had a paper route. My parents said, "If you want it, you earn it. You get the money. We'll help you." I bought my first bike by delivering newspapers; I had two paper routes. That's the way I earned my money. I shined shoes at the barbershop—the barbershop at the old Washington Building where the bank is now. I'd get good tips. Joe used to shine shoes on Saturday and clean up at the barbershop. I used to help him. When he went off to college, he turned it over to me. I did maintenance work or whatever I could do. I never turned down a job.

I didn't know much about discrimination. I heard people talk about it. As far as I was concerned, it was all down south. I never had any problems. There might have been some words said, but I ignored them. They went in one ear and out the other. I let it go. Nobody physically bothered me. Sure, I heard the word "n——" periodically. Kids I hung around with were mostly White, other than the Hills and the Mitchells. Most of the White kids I hung with were German and Irish—those kids who lived near Willy Street.

I was a little terror. Mrs. Washington would send me to the store on Saturday mornings, up to Kroger on the square to get some stuff for her cooking. I would fall in with the kids and wind up going to the movies. I would take the money and go to the movies. If we didn't have the money, we would sneak in. We went to the Majestic, the Strand, and the Parkway to see the Western movies. I didn't come back, so Mrs. Washington would have to go to the store herself. When I would come home later that evening, she would say, "Where have you been? It didn't take that long to go to the store." That got to be part of a habit. I was a little devil. We used to go to the Gisholt Machine Company parking lot. That's how I learned how to drive. Back then, people left the keys in their cars. We used to get in the cars and drive them around the parking lot. I taught Ed how to drive. I cracked up his car somewhere near Lapham School. I borrowed his car and had this accident—rear-ended a guy taking the car back to Ed. It was an old Plymouth. He was a bit upset, but I repaired it.

As time went on, I went to high school, the Centralites controlled State Street and Coney Island, which was a restaurant on State Street near Johnson Street. We used to hang out at Coney Island. We chased all the West and Wisconsin Heights kids away after the games at Breese Stevens Field, telling them that this was our territory. But we were always home by curfew—eleven on Saturday. The Jewish, Black, and Italian kids—we'd say, "Keep movin'. This is our territory." We had a little riot down there one time. We all wound up getting locked up. Mr. Washington had to come get me from detention. Mr. Amborn was the probation officer who handled juvenile cases. This was at the old courthouse where the ramp is across from St. Raphael's. We wound up having to go to the courthouse once a week. A bunch of us had to do this—Whites, Blacks, and Italians. It was kids' stuff, ya know. We also had our cars to drive around in, especially at graduation time, up and down State Street and around the Square. We didn't hurt anyone. We'd get into little fights sometimes. We were little toughies.

I was involved in the Boy Scouts and Drum and Bugle Corps as were Charles, Calvin, and Donald Harris, and E. B. Matthews. Other than playing baseball and wrestling, I didn't play other sports. I never cared for fishing. I wrestled when I went to Central and received the typical awards they give you. I played football a little bit, but was not that good like Charles Harris was. Ed Hill was in the band. My mother had me take piano lessons. I played for a while. Even though she played piano, she sent me to get lessons from a lady she knew. I worked a lot to get the things I needed because ministers didn't get a lot of money back then. While in high school, Roosevelt Harden and I were the first two to enroll in Madison Area Technical College's cooking class. I didn't get along with ol' lady Smith. Rosy didn't get along with the chef. I took the final exam for the course while still in the service. I graduated from Central and went into the service, Charles Harris and I. We went through boot camp together. I went to school for explosives and wound up in Korea because they needed people who had knowledge about explosives. Charles was a vehicle mechanic.

I met Shirley Alexander after I came back from the service. She was a good friend of the Hill family. Shirley has three brothers and two sisters. St. Paul Church is where I met her. Her guardians were the Gardners. Ira Gardner was in maintenance at Madison General. They came in the fifties. After we got married, we rented a house next door to Cordio's store. I bought my first house on Bram Street, sold that, and then moved into my second house on Milton Street. When redevelopment came along, Paul Jenna and I were the first two to buy the new houses.

Black people cared for each other and lived reasonably well. Everybody worked, went to school. There were big families. Roosevelt Harden came from a big family and was a good friend of mine. Everybody got along. Everybody took care of each other, a lot different than now. We watched out for other people's kids. If you were seen doing something you shouldn't, they would say something. We didn't talk back to the elders when they disciplined us. We didn't have to worry about somebody shooting you. We used to leave our front door unlocked. We had a lot of social events, not fights.

I went to Milwaukee to study mortuary work. I was talked into it by Connie Ryan. Connie was already down there. He talked to me about it. I got interested in it because my dad was having a lot of funerals at the old Fitch Lawrence on University Avenue. Dad didn't drive, so I used to drive him around with things like that. I got interested in mortuary work and worked part-time for Ryan's ambulance service. They had the hearses, too. Their first funeral home was on King Street and Wilson Street. Connie's dad opened that funeral home there. I did my apprenticeship at Obie's Funeral Home in Milwaukee. Sometimes I'd have to pick up bodies in Milwaukee and bring them to Madison to the Veterans Hospital. One day I dropped by Travis McCoy's house to visit, and I had a body in the hearse. I pulled up in the driveway and Travis said, "What are you doing driving a hearse up in my driveway with a body?" He was so outdone. I said, "Don't worry. He isn't going to bother ya." Since I was doing my apprenticeship in Milwaukee, I had to move my family down there. We lived on Twenty-Seventh Street. Shirley didn't like the Milwaukee school system, so we moved back to Madison to Vera Court. Since we were Catholic, we went to St. Mary's on the Lake because St. Peter's wasn't built then. Later, after St. Peter's was built, the bishop came up with the borderline. Those people who lived on the north side of Northport were assigned to St. Peter's and those living on the south side of Northport would go to St. Mary's on the Lake. Since we went to St. Peter's Catholic Church, I bought my first house on Barby Lane and then we moved to School Road. Shirley was on the church board and I used to usher and take care of the maintenance in the church. I didn't go back into the mortuary field because I saw some things I didn't like, so I lost interest.

As far as I can remember, the families that lived on the east side were Virgil Woods, Bosticks, Pooles, Pierces, Shepards, Washingtons, and Braxtons—all lived around Willy Street. The Shiverses lived further out east. Joe is still alive and living in Pennsylvania.

SARA DAVIS WELLS

Sara Davis Wells is proud to say that she lived in the Greenbush neighborhood, attended Mt. Zion Baptist Church on Johnson Street where Reverend Washington was the pastor, and was baptized at Brittingham Beach. She recalls going to the Neighborhood House when it was located on West Washington Avenue. She worked at Carmen's and Yost's women's clothing stores, where she stocked merchandise, dressed the mannequins, and operated the elevator. She also operated the elevator at Madison General Hospital. She held a job in the pediatric ward at the University of Wisconsin's Children's Hospital.

Sara Wells. COURTESY OF
MARY WELLS

My roots began in Salem and Youngstown, Ohio. I have ten siblings (Christine, James, Bertha, Bill, Ralph, Dorothy, Mary, Leroy, Oliver, and Ruby). My mother, Alice, and I came to Madison in 1948 because Ralph and Ruby were here and because my mother's brothers, Carl and Ed Elvord, were here. I had no problems enrolling in school or getting a job because my mom was a cook. She worked on the campus on Langdon Street. Ruby, Mama, and me lived on Langdon. My mama cooked for a fraternity for girls. That didn't last long because the house mother, Mrs. Halprin, who was shorter than me, even with her spike heels, had something to say to my mom. One day Uncle Ed came to visit Mom, and after he left, Mrs. Halprin knocked on the door and hollered at her, "Alice!" She was very rude. "Don't you ever have anybody down here eatin' my food." Mom knocked the woman down to the floor. This was the first time I ever heard Mama raise her voice or hit anyone. She called Ralph, who lived on the corner with the Porters, an elderly couple, and said, "Get somebody now with a truck because I am getting out of here." Bill Adams and Ralph came and picked us up. So we lived on Mound Street. We lived there quite a while, in the Bush, near Trotter's on West Washington Avenue. It wasn't prejudice, but she just did not want anybody eating the food. We lived with Mildred and George Greene, too. Mrs. Greene had dinners. Mom was working for them. Ma could always get work because she was a cook. Maggie and John Davis were pillars of the community. Mrs. Davis was a cook for a number of years at a fraternity house. She helped Mom get a job.

I went to Central. I had to quit because I was overly tired. I used to be an A and B student when I lived in Youngstown. When I came here, I had to work in sorority houses helping to set the table and prepare the meals. I couldn't do both. When I got to study hall, I fell asleep.

[The] Elvords had a restaurant, a barbeque restaurant. Aunt Christine cooked at the barbeque restaurant. I wrote my brother Ollie and said, "I'm going to find you a job." Emily and Dubois lived on the corner of Murray Street, where Emily had her beauty shop. I went to see Dubois about getting Ollie a job. He said, "Ollie can come out there to Verona," where his [Dubois's] business was in salvage and cars. Then from there, Ollie worked at Nob Hill. A lot of Black men worked there; some cooked and some cleaned, and that is where he got a second job. And from there, he went to Oscar Mayer's, where he retired.

My father was a preacher and in a discussion with my family members about preaching, he had to defend what preaching was like in the early years. Preachers could not go to school in those days, and although my father was a jackleg [amateur] preacher, he still could preach. The churches in Madison did not help my family, but they did play a role in helping other Blacks. I cooked dinners for Second Baptist for the needy. Mt. Zion bought a house for a family whose house had burned down. Before the firemen came, my Uncle Clyde tried to climb the side of the house to see if anyone needed help.

My mother's side of the family, the Elvords, had settled in Wisconsin many years ago. I was going to go to the music concerts on the Square, but I didn't have transportation. I went with this friend and a young couple. On the way back home, someone on the radio was talking about Hillsboro, Wisconsin. I said, "Oh, that is where my aunt and uncles used to live when they came to Madison." The woman who invited me to go to the music event said, "Oh, you're lyin'!" I looked at her and said, "What is wrong with you? My aunt and uncle lived there. In fact, I've been there." And she couldn't get over that, thinking no Blacks lived up there. The woman

Sara Wells (right) with her daughters Mary (left) and Alice. MURIEL SIMMS

in the front had to laugh. I said, "I don't know where you came from, but I know good and well that my relatives are Black and sure came from up there. My cousin, Ed, took me there. I picked up dirt; it was just like sand." Ed and Alice Elvord lived there. Ed, Clyde, Charles, and Ralph Elvord lived in Hillsboro at one point in time, in Adams County or Vernon County.

Ralph loved to play the piano. Dorothy had a beautiful voice, out of sight. Ralph sent her to the School of Music here in Madison, but she never developed her voice in any way.

Living in Madison was a good experience. Madison is a good place. You can make it better for yourself, but you have to work, and get along with people. If anybody needs help, then you help them, if you can, because in the long run, life is beautiful. You are always going to find good people, I don't care who you are. Be truthful and kind to people, and share.

Marie "Patsy" Caire Thomas

Marie was born in Madison, the third daughter of Edgar and Mary Caire. She worked for the city of Madison in the mayor's office and in the Planning Unit of the Planning Department. She was on the board of the South Madison Neighborhood Center, a member of the city of Madison's Minority Affairs Committee, and a member of the Wisconsin Women of Color Network. She served as president of the regional branch of this group.

Marie Caire Thomas.
MURIEL SIMMS

W hen my dad came here, he said that the only families he knew who were here were the Millers, Allisons, and his uncle Sam Pierce. Other people came, but they did not stay. I know he went to Central High School. His grade school was on the east side, although he might have gone to Longfellow because they used to live on West Washington Avenue. He graduated from Central and had gone to the University of Wisconsin for two or three years and was going to be an electrical engineer. However, he didn't continue because he married my mom and they raised her younger siblings. He would often become frustrated with his job because he knew he was smarter than the people he worked for.

The things he would do were clean taverns, be a janitor or a yard person, or a redcap for the Greyhound bus company. After Greyhound stopped hiring redcaps, he got a job at University Hospital, and he worked there until he retired.

My grandparents on the Caire side left New Orleans, Louisiana, because the family split. One side was going to pass for White and the other was not. My grandfather Edgar Sr., wife Mattie, and children [Edgar Jr., Alice, and Edwin] did not want to pass for White, so they went to Chicago and then from Chicago, they came here in 1919. Edgar Sr. worked for Zimbrick Buick, but it was called something else before then, but he was a mechanic for Buick. Edgar Sr. came here because his relatives, the Pierce family, lived in Madison. These relatives were Sam Pierce, his mother, Hettie, and Sam's nephew Ted. Sam was working as a messenger for Governor La Follette.

My mother, Mary Beulah Thomas, came from Gurdon, Arkansas. My mother and her five siblings had their own home. Their father, Alfred, was a carpenter and a shoemaker and built their house. Alfred died in the 1920s during the time of the big flu epidemic that killed so many people in the United States. He died from the flu, so mother Jessie had six children to take care of. My uncle Frank was the oldest child. He left school when he was in ninth grade. He worked at the chicken factory, killing and plucking chickens. My mother went as far as the tenth grade. She had to help her mother do laundry for White people once a week for money for the family. After Alfred died, Jessie's family was treated badly. Jessie's sisters would come in and take all the nice things she had in her house and use them and never give them back. Jessie said she wanted to get her children a thousand miles away from Gurdon. Her friend, Mrs. Gentry, Joe Gentry's mother, would write her letters all the time and told her she found a nice man for her to marry. Jessie started writing him. Mrs. Gentry said the children could go to Central High School and the younger children would be able to go to Washington School. Mr. Kenneth Newville had a truck and he went down to pick up my grandmother and the family. Jessie and the two younger kids sat inside the truck with Kenneth Newville. The older children sat in the bed or back of the truck. They came one thousand miles. They rode like that to come to Madison because Madison is exactly one thousand miles away from Gurdon, Arkansas. And we didn't know that until I drove Mama down there one year and I said to her, "This is exactly one thousand miles."

The man Jessie married was A. T. Stewart. He used to sell the *Jet* magazine and Black newspapers in Madison. When my mother came here, they thought they were all going to go to school. My mother always wanted to go to college. When they got here, A. T. Stewart had jobs for all of them. Uncle Frank worked for the fruit and vegetable produce company that was on the lake. My mother and her sister, Annie Laurie, did day work for White people and Jews. They thought they were going to go to school. Jessie was very sick when she got here. She had been sick for a long time, but they didn't know what was wrong with her. She died of cervical or ovarian cancer at forty-six. My mother had been dating Edgar Jr. So when her mother, Jessie, died, he said, "I am marrying you and we will take care of your brothers and sisters." They [the county] had sent them to foster homes. They sent Uncle Arthur to some school because they said he was mentally disturbed. There was nothing wrong with him. When Edgar and my mother got married, they got the kids back, and they raised Uncle Arthur, Uncle Bennie, and Aunt Christine for a little while. Uncle Bennie told me, he said, "I will always love and respect your father because he was so good to us, because we would have been in foster homes if it wasn't for Edgar."

My father never said anything and my mother never said anything. Uncle Bennie and Uncle Arthur stayed with them until they were old enough to go into the service. Uncle Arthur went into the merchant marines, and Uncle Bennie went into the army toward the end of the Second World War. Uncle Bennie was sent to pack up all the equipment that was in the Philippines. He used to sing, and his voice used to sound like Nat King Cole. He would sing, and all the Filipino women would just flock all around him. He said that one night some Filipino men shot poison darts at him. They did not like the way the women were flocking after him, supposedly because he could sing so good. After he came back from the service, he was shell-shocked and went into the VA hospital. In a year, he died in a halfway house outside of Madison.

We lived in the Bush. No Italian people would rent to you. They wouldn't even talk to you, but the Jews would rent to you and would sell you food. The Italians didn't even want you in their store. My dad said he remembered the gunshots when the Mafia would kill a man in the street. One time my dad and another little boy saw it, and they had to run and hide. They knew somebody had seen it. They thought it was two White boys because my dad was light skinned. They had to hide him out for a while. Madison was kind of rip-roaring. When people would ask, "Where do you live?" and you said, "In the Bush," they would say, "You lived in the Bush!" I used to think it was because we were Black, but it was mainly because of the Italians.

We lived on 805 Mound Street in Mrs. Freeman's house. We lived in the apartment upstairs. Then we lived at 813 Mound Street, and that was Bob Jones's house. He had four apartments. We lived in the back apartment, next to Agnes Johnson's house. Then we moved back to 805 Mound, then to 621½ East Dayton, but that house burned down. Then we stayed in the apartment above the St. Paul A.M.E. Church because they had bought a parsonage for the minister. Then we moved to 728 West Johnson, above my Aunt Frances and Uncle Frank's house. Now, that house was Aunt Frances's mother's house, Mrs. Givens. So we lived up there until I was in the second grade. Then my mother bought a house on 1703 Fisher Street. If you rented from Black homeowners, then you had no trouble finding housing. When we lived at 728 West Johnson, the neighborhood was very much mixed. There were East Indians and Chinese because they were students at the university. We didn't have many problems there from White people, except we would steal the grapes from their grapevine, and then they would get mad at us, but that was about kids' stuff. When we lived there, we used to play in the cars at the car dealership on University Avenue. They would let us play in the car. We would pretend we were driving to Chicago or driving someplace. After playing there, we would go to the back door of the Three Bells Tavern, and the man would give us those big sixteen-ounce Cokes—ice-cold Cokes. He would give us those every day. Then, we would come back home and Aunt Frances would have made doughnuts. She was a baker; she made the best doughnuts and sweets.

Then after we left 728 West Johnson Street, we moved on the south side. Mama said it was hard to find an apartment that would take four kids. I remember, she would talk about this one lady who said we could come live there, but she didn't want us using the toilet after a certain time at night. We would have to go to the bathroom in a slop jar. That's when my mother talked to the Sinaikos. They told Mama to get two hundred or three hundred dollars down for the down payment for one of those prefab houses on Fisher Street. She borrowed the money from Margaret Straub, who worked at the St. Martin House. She gave my mom the money and that's how we moved into 1703 Fisher Street. We were so happy. I was in fourth grade, and it was like a palace. Gretchen and I shared a bedroom, and Corinne and Dolores shared a bedroom.

My mother worked at day work for this one Sinaiko family for over twenty-five years. They were very nice to us. They gave us a turkey at Christmas and Thanksgiving, and a ham at Easter. Mama did other day work for other families. She would get so mad because she was always away from us. She stayed at home until we hit sixth or seventh grade. When I was in ninth grade, she got a job at the university. She took some classes because they were starting to hire Black folks in offices. She got a job at the Department of Transportation. What she did was renew drivers' licenses. Everything was done by hand then. She worked at UW Hospital, where she took trays around to people and did the day work. While we were little, she worked in the middle of the day when we were at school so when we got home there was always good hot food. You didn't have trouble getting a job because it was whatever they let you have. The only reason she got into the university was because of the Civil Rights Act. In order to get that federal money, they had to hire.

My mother was a charter member of the Eastern Star that started in Madison, the NAACP, and she helped start the S. S. Morris [Church]. She belonged to the Community A.M.E. Church, the colored women's clubs, Les Joyeaux, Mary McLeod Bethune, and the Bram's Addition Neighborhood Association. She and Percy Brown, the city's neighborhood planner, helped start the neighborhood association, and she was involved in the South Madison Neighborhood Center. She was on the board for South Madison Neighborhood Center, but she was on the board for Neighborhood House, too, years ago. She was always involved with the Neighborhood House and St. Martin House. We always went to all those meetings. My dad did not do anything like that. All he did was work.

They helped each other through the church because when new people came to Madison, they would come to the church and then the church would send them to the people they knew who would rent to them or send them places where they knew would hire Black people at that time. Mainly, it was like janitorial, maids, cooks, and gardeners. Mr. and Mrs. Gardner came here and worked for the Oscar Mayer family. She was a cook and her husband was the chauffeur. Most of the cooks at sororities and fraternities were Black, I think. They would send food from their kitchens to people who didn't have food.

My mother was into community and neighborhood. When Sam and I got married, she said, "You all need to get on the Center board and help get that place straightened out." So I was on the Neighborhood Center board, but then the Center burned down. Mayor Paul Soglin called me. I worked in the mayor's office at that time. He said, "If you guys want to build a new center, I'll give you the money, but you have to commit to be on the board." So that's how we got the money to build a new center. Anything to make the neighborhood better. She was always making people feel better about themselves, letting them know, "Yes, you can do this." I tried to be like that, too.

I was on the city of Madison's Minority Affairs Committee, which is made up of minority employees. Mainly Black employees joined that one. There weren't very many Hispanic people, Chinese, and Asians. They never came. We did things for schools. We adopted a class and helped with getting kids tissue and paper, and pencils. We'd have a picnic or donate money. Then we would put up Black History Month displays in the cases in the post office. We did one on the buffalo soldiers and on African culture.

But mainly, help came through the churches then. Mount Zion, St. Paul, Second Baptist, people who were going to those churches, those are the people who would get together to help people. I think the church doesn't do so much of that anymore. Mount Zion does a little, but not like it used to be. Everything came out of the churches. If there was any kind of network, it was from the churches. They were the social, cultural, economic, everything. All the programs were held at the churches . . . potlucks to raise money were held at the churches. The churches knew White people or White organizations that would help Black people.

They helped each other back then. They supported . . . like when the beauty shop and barbershop came in, even though people did hair in their homes, people still supported and went to the barbershop and got their hair cut and the beauty shop and got their hair done. Now, people don't want to do that. I don't know what happened when people don't support Black businesses. Back then, you supported Mr. Mosley and Mr. P's. If you were trying to create something, we were your cheerleaders, saying to them, "Yeah, that's great. I don't like that ole man, but I still think he should get his business started, go ahead." People did that. When you try to do that now, it's like, "Who do you think you are?"

Do you know how I got started? I used to type for a lady named Dori Brown at the Neighborhood Center. I did all the typing—all the programs, any of the papers the kids were going to use, the flyers that went out into the neighborhood. She was friends with the woman who was the civilian personnel director at Truax. When they passed the [civil rights] bill in 1964, that's when I graduated. At the beginning of 1965, Dori Brown said, "I'm going to have this woman talk to you about working at the base because they're looking for someone who's Black to work at the base." I said, "I have no way to get out there." We didn't have a car. My dad and mother never drove. They sent an airman to pick me up in the morning. I went out there, interviewed, and took the tests, and they brought me back home. That night, the airman came back and dropped off my test results. I was to work in a SAGE [Semiautomatic Ground Environment air defense system] building, and I had to have security clearance. I was one below top secret. We had to keypunch to all the bases in the US and tell them how to fix stuff and ship stuff out to them. And once we got to work in the War Room. That was something. So that's how I got hired at the base, to be a keypunch operator. And that's when they really wanted you. I had such a good time out there with all those young guys. I would talk to them and they said they would be missing home. I'd tell Mom and she said, "Tell them to come to dinner on Sunday." So my two friends, one named Brown and one named McGhee, two airmen that worked in my unit, would come in their uniforms. They said, "Thank you for doing this. We really miss being at home." Mama would say, "This is your home away from home."

When we first moved on Fisher Street, it was all White people. We were the first Black family to live in the 1700 block on Fisher Street. These people across the street from us—there were three brothers—they had houses next to each other. Then, there was this Irish guy, Mr. Ryan; he was next to them, and then the Maloneys on the corner, and then on my side, there was the Williams family. The White folks across the street from us didn't want us living there. We were going to church. When we woke up in the morning, our yard was full of beer cans, and our mailbox was full of cigarette butts and ashes, chuck full. We were so mad. We had to clean it up before we went to church. I said, "Mama, this is a lot of stuff." She said, "We can't leave the yard looking like this." We had to hurry. We didn't have garbage bags, so we had to put them in garbage cans. Some of those kids were laughing, so Dolores said, "We're going to get them." We went over there, and we whipped their behinds. We fought on the ground and in the dirt. Corinne ran into the people's house and snatched one girl. She tried to run away, but Corinne dragged her back outside in the yard and beat her. We were fightin' like cats and dogs. We fought the kids because they were the ones laughing and making fun of us. My mother didn't say anything except to make sure we were okay. We had some scratches and stuff, but not like they had. They used to call us n——s all the time, but after that they never said anything to us and finally and slowly they moved, those three brothers. They were the instigators. They were a big construction family, and finally they moved. Each built a house and moved off. One of the brothers-in-law lived there, and he got to be nice.

We used to cut through this one woman's yard. I put my foot on her fence to tie my shoelaces. She told me, "You got more guts than Oscar Mayer's." I fell out laughing. She thought I was going to get mad, and they finally moved, too. But I think they moved because she got Alzheimer's or something like that. Yeah, they didn't want us out there because that block was the only block that didn't have Black people on it.

My dad had one of the Bartholomew sisters for a math teacher. I had her for a math teacher, too. She told me, "You are just as stupid as Edgar." I said, "My dad is not stupid." She said, "Even he couldn't get this." I think it was algebra. I said, "You know, my dad went to school to be an electrical engineer. He couldn't be too stupid." Oh, she got mad then. She made it hard for me to pass algebra. Kids from Maple Bluff came to Central. This one guy said, "I'll help you so you can pass this class." He gave me little things to show me how to do stuff. When I finally learned that, I realized that those teachers didn't teach Black kids like they should have. They weren't giving us everything, unless you had someone who was a decent person. Sometimes there are decent White people. He sat and helped me. She was mad because I passed. She couldn't flunk me. She had told me, "You're gonna flunk out of this class." I got a D minus. The guy said, "You probably should have gotten a C. But that's all right; you passed the class."

Oh, when I was in high school, Mama wanted us to learn how to type. Miss Juniver was the business education teacher. She told me, "Marie, I don't know why your mother has you in this class. You will never be able to get a job. So, why should you learn how to type and do shorthand and run business machines?" So that made me think, "I'll show you." I remember when I got my first job with the state taxation department. I wrote her a note: "I'm working in the office. I guess I did get something out of the class." But she didn't pay much attention to me. I was the only Black in the class. Mother said, "You are going to learn it." They used to give us these cards that had the keyboard. I would bring it home to learn how to type. You learn how to type by memorizing the keys. I had to take a typing test for the city. I had done keypunching, which is different than typing because the keyboard is different, so I had to learn how to type again. But I passed the test; I got sixty-eight words a minute. I worked in the word processing pool. We used to type everything for the city. This other woman and I did all that typing. When I applied for the job as secretary in the Planning Department, they said, "You have to take another typing test. We have to make sure you can type." I typed over sixty-eight words a minute.

My mother took us to the St. Martin House to learn how to sew and make our own clothes. I always made my own clothes all through high school. Back then, there were no stores like Lane Bryant stores for big women. You had to go to Milwaukee or Chicago or order through the catalog. My mother sewed and embroidered. Corinne and Dolores crocheted. I did ceramics and scrapbooking. Gretchen does make jewelry. My dad liked horse racing. He would sit on his bed in the bedroom, lay across the bed with his racing form and his loose-leaf notebook, and would work on this thing for hours. He would go with his racing forms every week to check all the horses and tell us who was going to do what. When I got old enough, I said, "Daddy, who is going to win the Derby?" He said, "It's going to be so and so." I would give him ten dollars to put on that horse. He would go down with his Italian buddies, and they would be all dressed up with their big hats and overcoats. They'd sit in the clubhouse with their big cigars. This one guy said that he wanted this notebook. Mama would say, "I don't know if I should sell this." I said, "Mama, give it to the man, sell it to him." After my dad died, he bought it from my mother for a lot of money. It probably was worth ten times that. It had all these horses, all handicapped, horses they sired, what was their last speed, and time. My dad would bet on the horses a lot. Whenever he won, it was like Christmas. He would fill the house full of food, and buy us whatever, give us money to buy dresses, and toys. Because when he won, he won big.

Growing up in Madison had its ups and downs, but overall, I got a good education and was able to raise a loving and supportive family.

EDITH LAWRENCE HILLIARD

Edith retired from Alliant Energy in 2000 after thirty years of service and went on to work for MPI Products in Deerfield, Wisconsin. She has served on the boards of various organizations such as the American Cancer Society, Elder Care of Dane County, Madison Scouts Drum & Bugle Corps, Blackhawk Council of Girl Scouts, and the YWCA. She has also been a member of the Wisconsin Women of Color Network, Olbrich Botanical Gardens board, and Women in Focus, Inc., has been active in her church, and has served as a tour guide for the Monona Terrace Convention Center. She has re-

Edith Lawrence Hilliard. MURIEL SIMMS

ceived a number of awards, including the Martin Luther King Jr. Humanitarian Award and the YWCA's Women of Distinction Award.

I think it was because there was such a strong concentration of African Americans living in the Bush. I can remember my great-aunts saying that it was like just one big family because there were a lot of Italians, African Americans, and everybody. It was a family unit. I know they helped start St. Paul A.M.E. Church. My grandmother was in the Mary Bethune Club. She was active in the NAACP and the Federated Women's Club. She was the recording secretary for the Mary Bethune Club. They talked about how well they got along with each other. Again, it was like a family atmosphere. I remember when I was twelve. Everybody was everybody's family. George Rogers and I decided we were going to go on the other side of town to smoke a cigarette. We took a bus to the other side of town to smoke this cigarette where nobody would find us. We were sitting there getting ready to light up and a hand reached and grabbed me. It was Maggie Davis. She said, "What do you think you're doing?" She gave us a spanking and threw us in her car and took me to my grandmother's house and told my grandmother and said, "Grace, let me tell you what George and Edith were doing, and don't worry, I took care of them, right on the spot." My grandmother thanked her for taking care of us. She took George home and the same thing happened there. Then my grandmother took care of me again. You couldn't go anywhere without somebody knowing you or taking care of you or taking ownership of who you were. Everybody looked out for everybody else's children. That was such a wonderful atmosphere.

I spent a lot of time at Betty Banks's house. I remember her father used to cook all the time. Again, it was like family. If you were there at dinnertime, then you sat down and ate. When I think about growing up here as a child, it was wonderful. Everybody got along. You didn't hear about fights or guns or gangs, none of that. You [didn't] call adults by their first name.

My great-great-grandfather, Nathaniel Owens, came from Shreveport, Louisiana, to Baraboo, Wisconsin, around 1865 when he was twelve years old. When he got to Baraboo, he lived with a White family called the Hacketts. They taught him a trade, and then later he worked for the railroad. He met Cynthia Roberts, an African American Indian woman, and married her. They had twelve children, six girls and six boys (Sadie, Mamie, Minnie, Emma, Fannie, Maude, Fred, Baylus, Jessie, Merton, Clarence, and the baby who died at birth). The girls worked in the home. They had a beauty parlor in the house. They were the only African Americans in Baraboo for over eighty years. Some of the boys worked with their father on the railroad, and some of them—Minnie, Baylus, and Clarence—worked in vaudeville in the Ringling Barnum and Bailey Circus. I have an original poster from their traveling around in vaudeville. When the kids got older, two went to Chicago, and the rest of them came to Madison. One of the twelve children was my great-grandmother, and that was Sadie [Owens], and she married a Hickman. My great-grandmother had one child who was my grandmother and her name was Grace. And then Grace had three children, of which one was my father. His name was Alexander Lawrence, and then came me. So, that is five generations to me, and then my children would be six generations, and then my grandchildren would be seven, and now I have two great-grandchildren, so there are eight generations of our family who have been in Wisconsin and seven generations in Madison.

Letting them know about the history of your family; keeping a family unit. I have three adult children and eleven grandchildren. Out of the eleven grandchildren, five are in college, one is in the service, and

Edith's great-aunt was Minnie Owens, a musician who performed with the Ringling Bros. and Barnum & Baily Circus. WHI IMAGE ID 45966

I have smaller ones. In 1996, one of my granddaughters said that she never gets to see her cousins except on Christmas or Easter. I decided to start Cousins' Day. I told my children what I was going to do. Every third Saturday of every month from noon to four p.m., I wanted them to bring all the kids to my house for Cousins' Day. There were certain things we were going to do. We kept a journal, made leaf forts in the backyard, and had pumpkin-carving contests. We had Bible study, reading time, and I told family history. Depending on the weather, we went on field trips or we made something.

PIA KINNEY JAMES

Pia has lived in Madison all of her life. In 1975, she became the first woman of color to be hired as a police officer in the Madison Police Department, serving twenty-nine years. She worked in most units there, but her proudest and hardest job was the crime scene investigator position, which she held for thirteen years. After retiring, she volunteered to be a member of several boards of community service organizations and professional associations that support women and children.

Pia K. James in her Madison Police Department uniform, circa 1975. COURTESY OF THE MADISON POLICE DEPARTMENT

My ancestral family history goes back to early Wisconsin. Although my mother, Doris Buskirk-Barlow, was born in Minneapolis, Minnesota, she arrived in Wisconsin at age one with her parents, John and Esther Barlow, who later died. Doris and her brothers, John and Joe, were placed in an orphanage about 1937 in Sparta, Wisconsin, because, after their father died, the state of Wisconsin said that a White mother should not raise Black children. Then they were sent to a foster home in Beloit, Wisconsin. In 1940, my mother was placed with Harry and Myra Allison, the African American family that took in children and rented to families that had no place to go. Her brother, Joe, was sent to Racine, Wisconsin, and her brother, John, was sent to Lancaster, Wisconsin, where he lived on a farm with the Greenes, who were one of the first African American families in Wisconsin. As teenagers, the brothers joined the military, and later reunited again in Madison in 1949. My father, Herman, was born in Michigan, moved to Indiana and then Beloit, Wisconsin, approximately in 1933. My dad served in the US

Army in England during World War II from 1943 to 1945. He was a supply truck driver in a segregated unit with a White commander. Dad did not talk much about World War II until he was in his mid-eighties. When discharged, he was told by the military, "Go home and start your life. Don't talk about this war." After leaving service, he came to Madison, [and] met and married my mom in 1949. They had six children and helped us to continue our education past high school.

My mom taught me to sew, knit, crochet, iron. Mom and I made many of our clothes, mainly because we could not afford new clothes all the time. Going to St. Vincent de Paul, the used-clothing store, was often an adventure. We played many board games. As a family, we did crossword puzzles and played the game Scrabble. My dad taught us to garden, fish, and fix things. Most of our vacation time was spent camping, fishing, and clam digging. We always had family meals together. To this day, although our parents are now deceased, we get together for birthday parties, graduations, baby births, and other celebrations. Hard work was the main value. Grandma Kinney made everything from scratch and canned many garden items. On Saturdays, my dad cooked homemade pancakes and his special syrup. Our holidays were abundant with love, food, and small gifts, although we were financially poor. My parents and grandparents expressed how lucky we were to be in Madison, as opposed to living in the south, even with the problems of racism, living at a low income level, and not having much. Madison has been a beautiful city for a long time. There is great scenery with our lakes and green parks.

We had new people stay over at our house until they could get housing. Sometimes we provided dinners or canned goods. Churches provided support and camaraderie. The Allison family boardinghouse helped many newcomers, especially Blacks who were not allowed at the local hotels because of racism. We had a couple of private food vendors and personal talents, such as barbers, tailors, and caretakers. We had a couple of small family-owned grocery stores. Sometimes networking was house-to-house. If you did not have a food item, you could have it. We bartered for exchanges, like tend a garden for produce or other items. The South Madison Neighborhood Center was very helpful with employment training, a library, cooking, and dance lessons. Although my family belonged to the east side church, St. Paul A.M.E., there were also churches on the south side. Those were Mt. Zion (Baptist), St. Paul (Sanctified), and Second Baptist (Baptist). The churches were places to gather. I remember inviting other churches for dinners. They offered counseling and resources. We were a real community. The young respected the elders, and they watched out for us. We felt safe in the neighborhood, not locking the house or car doors. We welcomed in other African Americans new to Madison—those who were airmen at the Truax air base, and those who found work at Oscar Mayer, the Gisholt Machine Company, and the University of Wisconsin.

Most barriers dealt with racism. Most Blacks who lived happily for years in the Greenbush area were pushed out from there to south Madison by the government, claiming revitalization of the Triangle. Buying a home in south Madison was difficult—working with realtors and the banks. Housing was substandard, often built with low-grade materials, and which needed replacing later. I remember how my parents spoke of the misleading dealings, and how they would have to get another job or two to afford the house. My mom started her at-home office business to add income, as she was a stay-at-home mother. We all helped to stuff and lick envelopes for her. The difficulty was getting a job without a college degree. Mom taught herself to use a computer and do research through the library's resources. Schooling was not difficult to get into until high school or college. I wanted to take college-prep classes in high school. I was told I needed to take vocational classes. My parents had to go with me to the school and talk to the guidance counselor and principal. They were very reluctant to place me in the college-bound classes.

My parents always told us to "be careful" when going into certain areas of town—anywhere west, past Breese Terrace near the UW Field House, and north of the viaduct on North Park Street. Police in our south Madison neighborhood treated us differently than they treated the Whites. Usually, harassment occurred whether you did something wrong or not. Arrests were much higher for Blacks than for Whites for the same charge. The city "redlined" our neighborhood. This affected the higher prices in insurance policies greatly. The streetlight colors showed police and fire they were entering "Hell's Half Acre." This was their name for south Madison, not ours. But in spite of all we had to go through, we still actively participated in organizations like the Loft, Alpha Sorority, South Madison Neighbor-hood Center, Capital City Lodge, Eastern Stars and Junior Eastern Stars, Mary Bethune Club, Brownies, Girl Scouts, Boy Scouts, and the Madison Urban League.

My mother lost contact with many other family members after being placed in the orphanage. She hand-wrote letters and used the old-fashioned typewriter to correspond to state agencies to look for them. She convinced me to start doing genealogy, when she asked that I continue to locate the rest of her family.

PEACHES MOSLEY LACEY

Peaches Mosley Lacey worked for Oscar Mayer and several nonprofit agencies for forty years. She also was a Soft Sheen product merchandiser. While working for Soft Sheen, she and others began a project called Project Concern, advising African American inmates at one of Wisconsin's correctional institutions on how to manage Peaches Mosley Lacey. MURIEL SIMMS *their hair. Peaches earned her cosmetology license, allowing her to manage a salon. She belonged to the Allied Cosmetologists, Inc., of Illinois. While a member of this organization, she designed a logo for a membership watch for fellow members and their families. However, her volunteer work was just as important to her as her work life. She has been a volunteer at WORT Community Radio for twenty years. She became known as Lady P, host of the Dusties Storm Saturday morning radio show, and has volunteered for most of the activities and fund-raising events involving WORT.*

My grandparents were Luberta and John Scott Mosley, who came to Madison in the early 1900s from Pine Bluff, Arkansas. They both came to Madison to get a better life. They had four children (Geraldine, Jean, Jewel, and Arthur). I developed my love for music from my mother, Geraldine, because her mother spent many days listening to and patronizing Chicago's Club DeLisa, where popular artists performed.

My grandparents came to Madison in the early 1900s. My mother, aunts, and uncles were all born in Madison in 1914 through 1924. I don't recall exactly how they were able to obtain the pool hall and barbershop businesses, but I'm sure there had to be some struggles and barriers they had to go through. My understanding from listening and talking to my mother, is that they were one of the groups of families that was able to pick up and make a way for themselves. The pool hall and barbershop were located in the 600 block of West Washington Avenue in the Greenbush area. My grandfather was a master barber and my grandmother had a teaching certificate from Pine Bluff. They used those kinds of connections when they first came here and, luckily, they found an area, and I don't know how this happened, but they found the area that was really conducive to a lot of people, and that was the Greenbush area, which was Milton, Mound, and Charter Streets in the Bush.

It was something to grow up and go to school with Italian immigrants and African Americans and Polish immigrants who were all there because they all were seeking a better life for themselves and their families. This is where they happened to come and things prospered from there. Even though the times would not permit my grandmother to teach in Madison, she did help out cooking hot tamales and chili at the pool hall. My grandparents sold food at the pool hall and the barbershop, and my grandfather sold food on the Square from a cart, especially if patronage at the other two businesses was slow. From time to time, I would run into some of the older people who remembered buying the food from my grandfather's cart. The tamale recipe was handed down to my aunt Jewel Mosley Anderson, who made them during her life in Madison in the restaurant that my grandfather Mosley opened. You know they never talked about how difficult it was to go into business, not around me, anyway. It seemed like it was a better time. They talked to the people and they knew what they wanted. It wasn't the struggles like African Americans have to do now to get a business because they did pretty well.

I think Grandma and Annie Golder made the tamales. Annie Golder is Grandma's twin sister. They were identical twins. I think the recipe died with Mamma and Aunt Jewel. I don't know how much input my cousin, John Guy, might have had, because we just really didn't get that involved as kids and then they really didn't write that down. Well, Jewel said she wasn't going to. I remember asking her, "Why you don't write this down." I used to [try to] get her to write it down and then she said she wouldn't do it. And that was the policy with the family. They didn't want it written down because they didn't want anybody digging it up. I used to help, but I didn't

The tamale cart owned by John Mosley is shown in 1941. WHI IMAGE ID 18326

know what was in the meat. I don't know what the seasoning was. People ask me and get a little upset almost, but we weren't really that interested in the generation we were coming up in.

I'm sure there probably [was] some talk about discrimination, but my family didn't focus around on it. They talked about their struggles, I'm sure. At the time, I don't remember Mamma talking about it when she was in high school. It was encouraging for them to finish and get a high school diploma and that kind of thing, but I think that was a basic issue for all of the few Blacks that were here. She graduated from Central in 1938, so I'm sure there were issues like name-calling, but because of them growing up the way they did and being the color they were, I think that kind of had something to do with it. I can remember them talking about some of the Italians that were darker than my mother, so, you know, it just worked out to a degree.

I think when Grandpa got the business and people started patronizing, then he just became one of the people. Definitely the Italian population patronized. I run into some of the older men that used to come and get their hair cut at the barbershop, and that's what they remember. They remember Grandpa being up on the Square with his little hot tamale cart, like in between times, like when the hair cutting was slow or when the pool hall was slow. He would be up around the Square or in the community close to the Greenbush. He had tamales and chili on his little cart. So they got to know him and talk with him, and found out that he had some education. I think that kind of said, "Okay, we can talk with 'Mos.'" We can get correct answers. He knows about his lineage and where he comes from. I talk to some of the old Italian ladies and they were like, "Oh yes, we remember them and yes, you're Geraldine's daughter." So evidently, it must have worked out okay as far as them living and growing together.

Well, my grandma and her twin sister living in the south were like southern belles. They were really high-yellow. Blond hair, gray eyes, green eyes, greenish blue, very pretty women. They could pass for White, and they did to get their education. They went to college. They got teacher certificates, but that was about all they could do at that time. They took advantage of the fact that they were very light skinned in order to get their education, but they knew what they were. It wasn't like they were trying to pass after they came here. They were African American. They were Black people, so they were going to carry that to the hilt, and they could still do what they could do in spite of the struggles. They had to do what they had to do. They just didn't make a big issue of race unless someone brought it to them, and then they stood their ground. My understanding, too, is that they were nice and properly brought up and did not want to lose their identity. I know Grandma and Annie Golder just didn't want to lose that identity at all, so just before they came north, they really got involved in whatever they wanted to get involved in, like the A.M.E. church.

My grandmother and grandfather were a part of the original St. Paul A.M.E church. All the kids went to St. Paul A.M.E church. I know when my family came here, that was the first place they went. Church was all that Ma talked about. Grandma was also an Eastern Star. She became a Worthy Matron. She had a lifetime membership. Jewel and Mamma didn't involve themselves in the Eastern Star. My grandmother, Jewel, and Aunt Mayme were part of the NAACP. I just remember Mrs. Caire and Grandma being members of the Mary Bethune Club. I believe at that time the church was really a foundation for Blacks that came here, and then when they started the NAACP and the Urban League, then that was another something that drew people together to organize for any type of community strength. See, my mother was not that active in things. She was kind of a sit-back kind of person. Jewel got involved in some of everything. She was the one that more or less became the activist. She was feisty. She would see things that were wrong. She talked about it. And she didn't care who liked it or didn't like it. She was going to give her point of view. Mamma was a little bit quieter. She may talk about it, but she didn't take a stand. However, if an organization needed financial support, she would try to do that. But she really didn't get that involved. She was in no organizations. She was not in the Eastern Star. She didn't look to be involved in those fraternal-type things because they became too cliquish, and she really didn't want to get involved in that. She felt that taking care of family was more important.

My mom, Geraldine, married Booker T. Coggs Lacey in Madison. My father is a full brother to Isaac Coggs, who married Marcia Coggs, the state senator representing Milwaukee. My father was in the navy. He contracted diabetes while he was in the navy at the Great Lakes Naval Academy. He ended up back to Madison because the Vet hospital here was the best hospital to treat diabetes.

I know Mamma used to talk about when Blacks would come to Madison either for church programs or for shows. My family would take them into the house because there were not hotels for them to stay. I remember that because that's how Mom met a lot of people and that's how the whole family met a lot of people, the stars, singers like Sarah Vaughan. My mom and Jewel met Sarah Vaughan. Jewel was a jet-setter. Jewel and mamma met Rock Hudson, Della Reese, and Koko Taylor. Mama and Jewel used to go to the Club DeLisa in Chicago a lot. My mom lived in Chicago for a while. Club DeLisa was the hot spot. The music thing. That's how I developed my interest in music. Mamma and Aunt Jewel used to be around some of everybody, especially some of the Black artists, like Louis Armstrong. She loved to dance; she loved music. When Jewel and Uncle Brod moved to Altadena, California, before they moved to Las Vegas, they lived down the street from movie stars.

Grandma Mosley moved to Verona, Wisconsin, and bought property near Apex Orchard in Verona. Apex Orchard was just an orchard that supplied apples and apple juice. Aunt Jewel, Uncle Brod, and their son,

John Guy, lived in Verona, too. Jewel had a big house. When Mamma, Daddy, and I lived in Chicago, and I was out of school for the summer, I would come to visit them in Verona. Now, John Guy, being so much older than me, would catch a ride from the truckers and come into Madison with his friends and D'Etta, another cousin, because they were all around the same age. I would have to stay home. I can remember a lot of times just wondering, "Why does he get to go into Madison and I can't go?" Back then, Madison and Verona seemed so far apart. That's when I met DuBois and Emily Miller and their adopted daughter, Karen. They were friends of Mamma's and Jewel's and they just lived down the road a little piece. That's where I learned about this thing called party lines on the telephone. In Chicago, we had straight lines. I never grew up with party lines. When I would pick up the phone at Grandma's to make a call and there'd be some-body on the line, I'm like, "Who is this on my grandma's phone? Where are you, ya know?" But that's where I learned about the party line. Karen was the only one I played with because she was a member of the only Black family in the area. Then we moved back to Madison from Chicago, which would have been around 1964. Grandma bought a house and Mamma and Daddy bought the house right next door on Olin Avenue. We lived at 617 West Olin and Grandma lived at 623 West Olin.

My uncle Brod might have done some carpentry, but my daddy had been too sick to do anything and then he passed. My father died in 1966. Aunt Jewel was a socialite and worked. She worked out to the Oregon School for Girls and Uncle Brod worked at the post office. Mamma worked at the University School of Genetics. She was like a lab assistant helping to test mice for diseases. My mother was in nursing. She was a nurse at Cook County Hospital in Chicago in the early days. I've got pictures of her stand-ing out in front of the county hospital and that's basically what she was into and then she went into genetics. My father was an electrician. He was really into the stereo equipment. I still have an electronics book with his certificate in it. My parents didn't have major degrees, but they got good salaries. I used to get quite amazed how Mamma could walk into one of these stores and open a credit account just by signing her name. She could get anything and it was no problem for her and Daddy to get the houses.

My mother and father were definitely about education. I have been spoiled. We lived a middle-class life in Chicago. So that's all I ever knew.

If something happened to my dress, got torn or whatever, my mother would just walk me back to the store and get another one—the same thing with socks and shoes—and everything matched. We had what we needed to have, but education was always a really big thing. My mom was into reading. I know that when I first started school in Madison, the teachers asked me how I learned to talk so proper coming from Chicago. One of my teachers asked me that. That's the way I was taught to talk. It was different because of my foundation growing up in Chicago, where I was taught by Black teachers. There were mostly Blacks and Puerto Ricans in the schools that I went to from kindergarten until fifth grade. All I knew were Black teachers and Puerto Rican women teachers. They taught you how to stand properly, talk correctly, and pronounce words the way you're supposed to. Just because you live on the west side of Chicago didn't mean that you didn't have any education. Education was the thing that we always thought was important. That was one of [the] things that my family had been taught, even if they didn't take the roads to become big academically.

The one thing about my ancestors I guess I really would like for it to be known is that my ancestors, the Mosleys and the Andersons, were some of the first organizers and founders of this town. Our family was quite known, and it's almost as though people don't even know the connections. My mother and father met when they were teenagers through church. It was like a love at first sight. That was the only person she was with, and when she got twenty-one, she married my father. The Mosley and Anderson families set up activities in Milwaukee and in Madison, in Black communities. I really want the people to know because I realize that the strengths that I have and the struggles I've had came from their strengths. My mother came up in the Depression, so she knew what it was like to get a loaf of bread for five cents, and she talked about that. I never knew of that and her working so hard. My mother also got rheumatic fever when she was fifteen and was in Madison General for almost a year, which, I think, later progressed into the arthritis and congestive heart failure that she had, but she still went on. They did what they could within their groups, the community, and lived their lives and got what they could. Because that's the way they were being brought up—to be good citizens. It was different in my generation. When I came up, some of the things we did, my mother and others would have never done.

But let me explain about generations and the way things are now. When my youngest son was ten or eleven years old, the school system started changing and saying that when a kid felt like he or she was being abused at home, they could tell the social worker at school and then you couldn't touch your kids. When they took that control from parents, that's when things started changing. It probably started a little bit before then, but I really can remember around that time because I had issues with some of the teachers and how they were trained. They felt that you're not supposed to chastise your child. You're supposed to sit down and talk with them and explain it, and they're supposed to explain to you, and then everything was supposed to be just grand. It always doesn't work like that, so when you take control from the parent to be the disciplinarian, the kids feel they can do most anything. And that's when I had to start pinnin' my boys up against the wall, and tell their instructors that that's not the way it is. Also hearing some of the kids talk to their parents the way they do with no kind of respect. We respected our parents. You might go around the corner somewhere and call them whatever you wanted to call them, but you better not do it right there because you might be toothless. At that time, people did not see that as abuse, and those children grew up the way they were supposed to grow up. They grew up being citizens that could work within the whole range of the so-called American dream. That is when I started realizing that this is really different. When you take discipline away from parents and give it to this other person—no, no, I'm the one that had you. I'm the only person. I think that really caused a problem for me. Because the way I see things now in reading the various papers, that's what they're trying to get back to, giving control back to the parents. They want the parents to be involved. They want the parents to show up at the PTA, PTO. That's like thirty years later. I was really very staunch about it and expressed myself about that. I said, "You all are doin' wrong." When you take the control from the parents, then the children feel they can get away with anything. Then they always have somebody else they can run to. I don't care who you are. You can't run to anybody from me. From the way I hear from talking to people, my sons are really quite mannerly, and that makes me feel good, but also we know the trials and tribulations we had to go through.

Margaret Hall Studesville

Originally from Illinois, Margaret came to Madison in 1948 from St. Louis to join her husband, Alfonso Studesville. They made Madison their permanent home. Margaret worked at University Hospital until retiring in 1987. She and Alfonso raised four sons.

Margaret Studesville.
COURTESY OF THE
STUDESVILLE FAMILY

I met my husband, Alfonso, in St. Louis. Mr. Studesville died in 1979. In 1947, we came to Madison from St. Louis, Missouri, that is, with our two children, Alfonso Jr. and Larry. My sister, Vivian Hall Williams, and her husband, Sherman, were already living [in] Madison. My sister begged me to come. My husband had been working, but got laid off, so I told my husband, "I'll get you a job, if you come." Now, when my sister and Sherman first came here, they rented from the Simmses on Lake Street. Then, they found another place to live, and when we came, we lived with Vivian and Sherman. After that, we found an apartment in the Allison building, where the other two kids, Donald and Orlando, were born. We lived there until 1951.

When we came to Madison, it was a very small and quiet place. At first, I didn't like it, but I found out that Madison had good schooling for kids. That's my reason for staying. That was the most important, because in St. Louis, the schooling was very poor. I did not want to go back to St. Louis to raise my boys there. I didn't have any problems enrolling my children in school. The children were much better than they are today. I enrolled them in preschool, Miss [Mary Lee] Griggs's class, at the Neighborhood Center. Miss Griggs was a very nice lady. She would come by and talk to you, so pleasant. Everybody thought the world of her.

We found out that they were building these little houses in south Madison. So we bought a house on 1809 Baird, lived there for ten years, sold the house, and bought a house on 102 Ardmore Drive on the south side, where we lived for forty years. When we moved into the house on Ardmore, a

White family welcomed us to the neighborhood, but then, three months later, the same White family moved. But we felt good about the South Madison Neighborhood Center and about the schools.

I worked at UW Hospital for about ten years and didn't have a problem getting a job there. I took a break from working at the hospital. When I decided to come back, I called and they said, "Come on back. Do you still have your uniform?" I said yes, they said, "Then come on back." Alfonso's first job was with the Milwaukee Road, and his second job he worked for Oscar Mayer for twenty years. He would ask for things, like to get promoted, but they wouldn't let him. Even I went out there to try to get a job. I filled out an application and took exams and everything. It was me, another Black lady, and two White ladies; we all went up there for positions. When we got upstairs, they said they didn't have anything, but kept the White ladies. Alfonso didn't have any trouble getting a job, but he did complain that they were putting too much work on him and not the Whites.

We didn't participate in any organizations. Working and raising four children was about all we could do. Alfonso was a Mason. We were Methodists when we came here, but I joined Second Baptist Church. I sang in the choir and helped with dinners. Alfonso was an usher and attended St. Paul. I thought Blacks got along much better back then than they do now. I can remember when the kids were little. Every Sunday afternoon in the summer, everybody gathered in Brittingham Park, and talked in a friendly way; we had a nice time, swimming, playing ball, and having barbeques. Also, in the park were other folks like the Jews and the Italians, all those who lived in the Bush. People enjoyed sitting out there on a Sunday evening, Black and White, being so friendly. Kids would be friends with one another. Some are still friends with my kids. They mixed more back then than they do now. Everybody associated with one another. But after they put us all out, there was no more of that.

I took sewing lessons and embroidery. I didn't care for it. But my mother could do those things. We used to talk about that. None of us took after her. I had four brothers and five sisters. Our parents didn't push us too much toward getting an education. They made sure that everybody worked to have food on the table, because it was during the Depression. My family was born in Tennessee. They moved to southern Illinois, and then St. Louis, Missouri. My husband's family was born in Mississippi. They moved to Arkansas, and then St. Louis, Missouri.

Addrena Matthews Squires

Addrena worked for more than forty years at the old University Hospital and the Dane County Nursing Home (now Badger Prairie). She has been a valued community volunteer for more than seventy years. She served on many boards, including Independent Living, Madison School and Community Recreation, NAACP's Madison chapter, Urban League of Greater Madison Guild, Boys and Girls Club of Dane County, and the Wisconsin Women of Color Network. She has been recognized locally and nationally for her volunteer work.

Addrena Matthews Squires.
MONA ADAMS WINSTON

My mother's brothers would sell fruits and vegetables in the north. But my brother, William, brought my mother, Mamie Taylor, with him to Madison from Memphis, Tennessee, around 1926. Originally, my family came from Byhalia, Mississippi, and then moved to Memphis. They heard about Madison, and William brought her here to live because the family wanted her to do better. Some of the family found work available at the nearby Badger army ammunition plant in Baraboo, Wisconsin, and at the Oscar Mayer processing plant in Madison. Some of the family moved to Gary, Indiana, because of the jobs in the steel mills. Shipyard and manufacturing work was the draw for some of the family who settled in Benton Harbor, Michigan.

My brothers and sisters are Willie Jo Withers Walker, F. C. Boxley, Walter Boxley, Charles Boxley, Beauty B. Boxley, Edward (E. B.) Matthews, Ollie Mae Matthews Banks, Rose Lee Matthews Abernathy, and one who was killed by a car as a child. Willie Jo was born in 1912, E. B. was born in 1923, Ollie Mae was born in 1924, I was born in 1927 at Madison General Hospital, and Rose Lee was born in 1930.

The first house we lived in was on Mound Street, 809 Mound Street. We lived in an apartment near the synagogue on Mound Street. Mr. Hickman

Rose Lee, Ollie Mae, and Addrena Matthews posing by their garden, near the front steps of their house at 617 Milton Street. WHI IMAGE ID 95703

lived on the first floor and we lived on the second floor. Mr. Hickman was related to Mamie Owens. He was also the uncle of Betty Lawrence. I think we rented the house from a Jewish family. My mother, Mamie, did house-work. She had done housework for the Montgomerys ever since we were born. Dudley Montgomery was vice president of the bus company. She did that up until she couldn't work anymore. My mother passed in 1979 when she was ninety-five years old. I went to Longfellow School and I had no problems enrolling in school or problems with White people at all.

My brother E. B. played sports. He played football and basketball. That's when he went to Central. He never had any problems. The N-word never came up. We all stuck up for each other. If we had any problems, it was when the east siders came to the west side. There was no name-calling. They'd just come and think they were tough. No matter who the group was, Black or White or Jewish, we stuck together as a west side group. Ollie Mae and E. B. stayed in the neighborhood quite a bit. I would venture out into other areas, mainly past Regent Street and the campus, that is, after I got out of grade school. But Ollie Mae and E. B. hung around in the Bush. Ollie Mae was mouthy about everything. She even told the Italians how to make their sauce. She'd say, "You're doing this wrong, you're doing that wrong." She learned some Italian. She would come home and say how she told them to make this and make that. She did all the roaming around in the neighborhood.

My family was connected to Mt. Zion Church on 548 West Johnson Street. It was across the street from where the Nitty Gritty is right now. My mother and I compiled a book of old pictures about the church. I let other members of my family have the book. You should never let anything like that out because you never know when you want to get back that information. My mother stayed involved with the church. She was on the Mothers Board and in the choir. I'm sure the church did something to help people, but I don't remember anything in particular. I remember Reverend Cunningham and Reverend Washington. People didn't come to church asking for help back then like they do now. You'd be surprised how many come in wanting money for the electric bill and rent. Of course, everything was a lot cheaper back then, too. I think everybody tended to mind their own business. I suppose that if someone asked for my mother's help, she'd probably help them, but with her brother helping her get established here in Madison, I think that was enough for her to face. By the time I was twelve or thirteen, we had moved to Milton Street, 617 Milton Street. Imogene Skenadore and her mother, Margaret, lived on Milton Street, too, right around the corner.

My mother did not belong to the Eastern Star. There was the Mary Bethune Club. Mrs. Owens was president of the club. Mrs. Anna Hines, Blossom Maiden, Mrs. Buckner, and Gertrude Harris belonged, too. There were a lot of Black businesses like Trotter's on West Washington Avenue and Mosley's tamale place and Bertha Parker. She had a restaurant that was on the corner of West Washington and Park Streets.

We had house parties. Ollie Mae and E. B. would go, but I didn't go to those house parties. They enjoyed them, but you don't hear about house parties anymore now like you used to, not at all. We always liked to go to the Dells, the movies, not too much TV. We listened to the radio, "The Shadow," and we did a lot of walking. We walked to school. We walked downtown. My mother did a lot of quilting, all by hand. We held on to quite a few of them until I ended up giving them away after she passed. I wish I hadn't. She would make them for other people, too. Ollie Mae was always biking. She went up to the Dells. I don't know how many times. She would ride her bike all the way up to the Dells with several other people that she knew. Ollie Mae did not like to shop. Willie Jo asked her to go grocery shopping for her. Ollie Mae did it one time, but after that, she didn't speak to Willie Jo for I don't know how long. My mother's sister, Sally Dockery, was in Madison. She lived upstairs over us on Milton Street. That's Al, George, and Anna Mae Dockery's mother. She kind of made us mad sometimes. She would ask me and one of my sisters to go window shopping downtown with her. We'd walk around. This is something we did not want to do. She could have asked her kids to do that. So those were our little disagreements.

My family always believed in getting that education. We all went to Longfellow and graduated from Central. I graduated in 1947. I played the clarinet in high school and wanted to keep that up, but I took voice instead. I went on to the Wisconsin School of Music, where I was featured as a soloist in recitals. The song in *Porgy and Bess* called "Summertime" was my trademark song. I acted in many presentations of the Madison Theater Guild. I had to take music off and on, though, because I waited for Rose Lee to go through nurse's training. I took care of her kids. But I'm not too disappointed. Now, I can't sing. In the morning, I'd sing low, but then toward the afternoon my voice might go up. That's why I don't like to sing anymore. I also was the first Black cheerleader at Central High School.

We had our different interests. Willie Jo Withers Walker had an excellent work ethic. She cleaned her house every Saturday morning with a toothbrush along the floor baseboards. In her free time she enjoyed movies at the Orpheum and Capitol Theaters in downtown Madison. Ollie Mae spent her time with the Italians. Ollie Mae Matthews Banks was the family comedian, always keeping everyone entertained with her jokes. She went on the road cooking for the Madison Scouts and had notorious card parties. She dreamed of becoming a mortician, but wasn't able to find a school that would accept her. She went on to work at Oscar Mayer for thirty-seven years. E. B. was interested in horses. Every once in a while somebody would tell me that they saw him at the Coliseum. He liked horses a lot and was around them before he graduated from high school, but he didn't get seriously interested in that until after he graduated from high school. He participated in rodeos all around the country, winning many trophies and ribbons. In 1977, he bought a farm in Fall River near Columbus, Wisconsin, where he trained and boarded horses, living out a lifelong dream. In 1938, he became the first Black drum major of the Madison Scouts. Rose Lee Matthews played basketball and volleyball at Central High School. She graduated from Madison General Hospital School of Nursing with her degree as a licensed practical nurse (LPN) in 1958. She also embroidered, sewed, sang at weddings, and read a lot. So all in all, our family traditions and hobbies were waterskiing, photography, canning fruit and vegetables, making sausage, hunting, quilting, sewing, and singing.

There is one racial incident that I remember that led to good fortune for us. The house at 15 Lakeshore Court on Lake Monona was purchased by my mother, Mamie Matthews, my brother, E. B. Matthews, and my husband, Lawrence, and me in January 1951. The sale of this house was part of a feud between two White neighbors, a firefighter and a police officer. The policeman owned this house and decided to get back at his neighbor by selling the house to the first Negro who could afford it. E. B. heard about the house through word of mouth. He talked the family into putting their funds together to buy the house. It has remained in the family for almost sixty-five years. At one time during renovation, they found old KKK fliers in the walls. It was the basement apartment of this house that served as the place for many family and friends, and friends of friends to find shelter when they first came to Madison. My mother stressed that if anybody needed help, always help them, so that's why I stayed doing volunteer work as long as I have.

MARY HANNA

Mary received her bachelor of arts in sociology from Beloit College, a master's in urban planning from New York University, and her juris doctorate from University of Miami. After starting her career at the Community Welfare Council in Madison, she worked as a city planner in New York City, and later as an attorney in Newburgh, New York, and Philadelphia, Pennsylvania, where she provided legal help to low-income persons. She also served on economic development and planning boards and volunteered for organizations providing assistance and advocacy for domestic abuse victims.

Mary Hanna.
COURTESY OF MARY HANNA

My father [Hilton] was born on Acklins Island in the Bahamas. His father went to work on construction of the Panama Canal when my dad was about four years old. His mother died a year or so later, and he was raised by one of his mother's sisters and her husband on the island of Inagua. In 1921, the family immigrated to Florida as a result of the depression caused by World War I. The family found whatever work they could, primarily as fieldworkers in Florida. My father also had experience working a linotype machine and drove day laborers to construction sites along Miami Beach.

While attending a church young people's group in Opa Locka, a small community outside of Miami, he learned about Tuskegee Institute from a successful Miami real estate broker who had attended the institute. He wrote to the principal of the school requesting permission to attend and was informed he should present himself there. He did that, and after his accomplishments in the British school system in the Bahamas had been evaluated, he was admitted to the institute. He graduated from Tuskegee in 1928, having distinguished himself on the debate team. He worked as an orderly for the Veterans Administration hospital in Tuskegee to earn money for college, and then attended Talladega College, graduating in 1933 with a degree in English and a minor in journalism.

Although he had a job as a cub reporter and advertising person for the *Atlanta World*, he needed additional income to support himself and therefore also worked as an interviewer at the YMCA for the National Youth Administration Program. In his spare time, he did volunteer work at the Auburn Avenue Public Library. It was through the librarian at that library that he learned of a possible job in labor education. In Atlanta, the Works Progress Administration (WPA) workers' education program was recruiting people for that program. Although my father knew nothing about economics or labor history, he met with the recruiter the next day. After discussion of some of the issues involved, he was told he was hired. Orientation and training were done by a White woman. However, because she was White, they had to devise a way for her to instruct my father without violating the strict rules of segregation that existed at that time in the south. That way was solved when my father put on a chauffeur's cap and she sat in the backseat instructing him while he drove around Atlanta for two weeks! Through one person or another, he learned of the School for Workers at the University of Wisconsin. With the assistance of faculty from Talladega, he was able to obtain a partial scholarship in journalism at the university in Madison. Thus began another new chapter in his life—perhaps somewhat similar to that of leaving the Bahamas for Florida or making the trip from Florida to Alabama ten years earlier—not knowing what the future would hold.

After having been trained in workers' education in Atlanta, Georgia, and getting his naturalization papers, my dad came to Madison in 1934. Now that he was attending the UW–Madison on his partial scholarship, Dad wrote for the *Daily Cardinal*, a student newspaper, and joined the debate team. He and James Fleming from Jamaica became the first two West Indians who had achieved the honor of becoming inducted into Delta Sigma Rho, the national forensics fraternity. However, the only jobs he could get in Madison were cook, dishwasher, and waiter. In addition, no one would rent a room to him. My dad initially stayed with the Allisons when he arrived in Madison. However, he moved on to live with "Ma" Shivers, who he described as a German woman who had married a Black man during World War I. Ma Shivers rented rooms in her home to university students. Dad's roommate was a White man, Walter Uphoff, who was from a farm family in Sheboygan County. They both were interested in workers' education and became lifelong friends. While staying there, he cooked for four or five of the other students in exchange for his meals.

My dad made himself known by attending the Congregational church—which had its share of university and state government officials in the congregation. He was a naturally gregarious person and not hesitant to introduce himself to whomever, so he became known to many of the people in that congregation. He was also active in an interdenominational group, KOINOS, where he met a wider range of individuals in the community. In addition to writing for the *Daily Cardinal* at the university, where his articles were published as editorials under the heading "Roamin' Around," and because of his activities on the varsity debating team, my dad came into contact with a wide range of people.

He also brought with him a strong religious belief, having been raised as Anglican and Baptist during his younger years in the Bahamas. He also brought with him a very strong belief in pacifism that, again, started when he was in the Bahamas but became reinforced after he was introduced to Gandhi and the concept of passive resistance. He was a member of the Young Socialist organization, having seen and heard Norman Thomas, a socialist and pacifist, when he was in Atlanta. Add to these the need to earn enough money to survive, he also recited Negro poetry for church groups and civic organizations, he worked as a masseuse at the YMCA, had a newspaper route, just did anything to keep body and soul together.

Dad and some others organized two credit unions in the Madison area. One was for members of St. Paul's A.M.E and Mt. Zion churches. The other was for students affiliated with the Baptist Student Center on campus. It was through this effort that he learned of a tour of Europe that was going to be led by the Baptist student minister. The purpose was to study credit unions, labor issues, and cooperative housing. He and his roommate both went on that trip. One of the other members of the group was my mother. She was working as an industrial secretary for the YWCA in Wilmington, Delaware. But as a recent graduate of the University of Wisconsin, and a Wisconsin farm girl, she was familiar with the minister who had organized and was leading the group. And that is how my parents met!

An article in the November 23, 1934, issue of the *Daily Cardinal*—likely written by my father!— had the heading "Hilton Hanna Does Anything to Work Way through School." He was quoted as saying that he did oral interpretations of Negro poetry as one method of earning money. He declared that Langston Hughes and Sterling Brown were the *best* in the field. In the summer of 1935, he was invited to be counselor at the Congregational church camp at Green Lake, near Ripon. He also attended a five-and-a-half-week training course for teachers of Workers Education classes that was sponsored by the Federal Emergency Relief Administration for the purpose of training teachers who could be used in worker's education programs during the 1935–1936 year. One person he met there, a Farmers Union person, invited him to speak to a church group in Menominee later that year about the history of the Negro in America and to recite poems by Negro writers. He did so, and as he waited for his time in the front of the group, he noticed a young boy who was seated several rows in front of him staring at him. He waved to the child, who got down and walked back to where my father was seated. The boy then climbed on his lap and felt his arms and legs, then finally rubbed his hand over my father's face and looked at it. When he saw that nothing rubbed off, he asked if my father was okay. When my father told him yes, he returned to his seat with his parents. My father said that he used the child's actions at the beginning of his presentation to say the child had not "jumped to conclusions" that a Black person was different in makeup merely because of the color of his skin. This was one of the stories he repeated frequently to talk about race.

He joined a group of other students and ministers—all pacifists—who picketed one of the movie theaters because it was showing *The Red Salute*, a pro-war movie. This was at the end of October 1935. He was also in a university play, *Yellow Jack* (written by the same playwright who did the screenplay for *Gone with the Wind*) that had a theme of service to humanity rather than conquest.

After spending two years in the School of Journalism, he switched to economics, believing it was more consistent with his interest in workers' education and the labor movement. It was not until 1937 that he obtained a regular job through the WPA and began teaching in the university's Rural Workers Education Program. He also taught UW–Madison Extension

Division courses as well as developed the radio program *Labor Speaks* that aired weekly on WHA, and also for a while on WIBA. At the end of November 1937, he was invited to Appleton to speak with several church groups. He stayed at the home of the minister who had invited him overnight. In the morning, after he purchased his bus ticket to return to Madison, he went to a coffee shop for toast and coffee. He was refused service by the hostess, who told him, "We don't serve your people here." He told her that "his people" were not with him, that only he was ordering coffee and toast. Other customers laughed, the hostess made it very clear that she didn't like him or his comments, so he left without eating anything. He called the minister who had invited him and described the situation. A week later, a letter was published in the *Appleton-Post Crescent* newspaper from a woman who protested the "bigoted and unjust discrimination . . . when a gentleman was refused service because of his color." By the way, Jim Zwerg, a White man, and one of the early Freedom Riders in the 1960s, received a worse beating when he returned to Appleton, Wisconsin, than the one he experienced sitting at lunch counters in the south. Some things never seem to change.

My parents had kept up a healthy exchange of correspondence since their European trip ended in 1936. Since he finally had a regular income, they began making plans to get married. My father wanted to ask for my mother's hand properly and so he and his roommate drove down to the farm where she had grown up in Walworth County while she was visiting her mother. Walter, Dad's roommate, was shown into the parlor while my father was directed to the kitchen. Her mother thought he was the chauffeur. When she returned with the tray of sandwiches for her daughter and Walter, my father told her that he was the one who intended to marry her daughter— not a pretty scene. The men left directly and returned to Madison. However, my father looked at it as his having had a face-to-face meeting with his intended's mother and an opportunity to see the farm where she grew up! Obviously, they didn't let that stop them. Regrettably, it was almost twenty years later before her mother again had conversations with my mother. None of my mother's relatives ever visited us.

My father's pacifism really came into focus as the US prepared for and then entered World War II. He registered as a conscientious objector with the national Congregational Church and filed his appeal when he received

Hilton Hanna, holding daughter Mary, with his wife,
Lillian, and daughter Betty in 1948.
COURTESY OF MARY HANNA

his draft card. The appeal took over two years before a decision was made. The federal funding of the programs he'd been with evaporated as war making took top priority. Daddy worked as a freelance radio script writer for organizations including the Dane County Humane Society, the USO, and the Madison Federation of Labor. In October 1942, he began working at the Madison YMCA administering the Health Service Department, which meant he was a team of one doing everything from giving massages to cleaning the facility. My sister was born during that time. He had to pass up employment with the state because the appeal was pending and he had to be available for whatever the decision might be. However, ultimately, he did prevail in obtaining conscientious objector status. But as a condition of that, he was to work in an industry of national importance to the war effort, which is how he ended up working at Oscar Mayer. He spent fifteen months there working in the casing department, which required him to pull the small intestines of the hogs from the large intestines. It was there that he joined the meat-cutters' local union as a shop steward. One of his professors at the university suggested that he use the time he was at Oscar Mayer to gather information about how the labor union really worked in such a factory and put it together for his master's thesis. And that is what he did, even though it took him several years afterward to write it and get his master's degree.

My dad also was an active member and officer of the local branch of the NAACP, helped found and became president of the Madison Urban League, and fought for the city's equal opportunities ordinance in the 1960s. In addition, my parents had substantial difficulty buying a house when we had to move from the Baptist Student Center, on North Park across from Bascom Hall. We ended up living with one of my father's professors and his family for about six months. No problems there.

I attended Washington Elementary School. When I was in second grade, one of the boys who I walked to and from school with asked me, "Did your mother paint you brown?" That was a real shocker for me. I had no answer. Looking back on the situation, it made sense. My mother was the one who handled all of the weekday activities, such as going to school for parent-teacher conferences, and being the Brownie troop leader. In third grade, one day I fell on the playground and scraped my elbow. Miss Washburn, the teacher, was washing the blood and dirt off my elbow, when she suddenly stopped and said, "Oh, I'm sorry, I didn't realize your skin was darker."

I went to Wisconsin High School—which was from the seventh through the twelfth grades. Seventh grade was when my classmates, rather than their parents, decided who to invite to their birthday parties. There was an instantaneous drop-off in such invitations because that was when boys and girls started dancing together, usually in the basement recreation rooms of their homes with the lights turned down low. I understood that I was not on the "preferred" list of partners because of my racial background. Also in seventh grade, one of the most popular boys in the class asked me if I was "an Inkspot." I had heard of the singing group, and immediately understood what he was asking me. Again, I did not respond.

In high school, I was very active in the youth group at the First Congregational Church. The advisor to the group, Norris Tibbetts, was a remarkable man who various students sought out as a confidant. I was one of them. In my freshman year, a White boy had invited me to go to the movies with him on a Saturday afternoon. We were going to meet someplace near the theater. I went and waited until after the show was scheduled to begin. When I realized that he was not going to appear, I felt humiliated. I didn't want to go home, and I didn't know how to explain to my parents. So I went to the Tibbetts home. With great difficulty, I told them about being "stood up," and cried. When I calmed down, I went home, and my parents were none the wiser about what had happened. Somehow, I felt that I needed to "protect" them.

I reconnected with a White boy who had gone to the same elementary school as I did for two or three years. He went to West High. We started dating, and continued pretty much through high school. However, I learned from his best friend, who went to Wisconsin High, that he was getting beaten up by boys at West High because he was dating me. I felt responsible and didn't know what to do. We broke up.

One other incident at Wisconsin High: In eleventh grade, I had a speech class in which we were given the assignment of preparing a five-minute talk for the class that told something special about our families. One person told about a retarded sibling, someone else talked about a senile grandparent who lived with them, and I talked about what it was like to grow up in a biracial family. After each of the other students' presentations, there had been applause, and comments from the students. After mine, there was dead silence. No one said anything, and the teacher rushed to call on the next student. I was, once again, dumbfounded. I felt humiliated and embarrassed. Perhaps what this incident told me more than anything was that race was a taboo subject.

ODELL TALIAFERRO AND
DIMETRA TALIAFERRO SHIVERS

Odell Taliaferro and his sister, Dimetra Taliaferro Shivers, had been outstanding and outspoken advocates for civil rights. The following is an interview conducted in the early 2000s by Betty Banks, Muriel Simms, and videographer Terry Jackson.

DIMETRA: We always ranted and raved about everything that was happening to Blacks. We used to tell stories about office work. I was the first Black office worker. I worked for Mrs. Troy, who was head of the YWCA. She wanted me to be seen. The NAACP was first organized in the 1920s. Back then, it was called the Madison Negro Civic League. It was revived in 1943. Velma Hamilton was the first president and Harry Hamilton was the second president. Odell was the treasurer. We used the second floor of the YWCA for NAACP meetings at 122 State Street. About thirty to fifty people came to the first meeting, which was about office help. Blacks and Whites attending the University of Wisconsin came. Hiring, renting, or selling homes to Blacks was also discussed. Civil-minded White people, like Gretchen Pfankuchen, were eager to join. The NAACP set and regulated fees.

My husband, Stan, first wrote "Colored" on an application to be a bus driver, but changed it to "White." That's how he got the bus driver job. Stan had light blond hair. Stan had graduated from Central High School, and it got around that he was Black. Dudley Montgomery, manager of the bus company, said that he knew Stan's father, and that Stan came from a nice family. We will keep him, but if he has an accident or any excuse, we will let him go. His high school friends told Stan this. Stan was the only one who did not have

Dimetra Shivers.
BRENT NICASTRO
PHOTOGRAPHY

an accident in training. People began calling about how good and pleasant a driver he was. He drove until ill health. He was put in the office training other drivers.

ODELL: I was a chemist at the Badger Ordnance [plant] at Baraboo, but also became a leader of the NAACP. A small number of African Americans started the NAACP in the 1920s. I give Mr. and Mrs. William Miller much of the credit for organizing it. The Ku Klux Klan set up camp in Madison but found that Madison was not a fertile field, so it left. The NAACP could not sustain itself at that time, so racially charged incidents still occurred. Restaurants did not want to serve Blacks, the University of Wisconsin system was troublesome, and Madison housing practices created problems for Blacks. Argyle Stout was the first Black man to enroll in the UW Medical School. He was not allowed to give a White female a physical exam. Stout College at the time wanted Black students interested in studying science to enroll there. I made an effort to get some Black students enrolled, but failed. A Black minister formed the NAACP in Stout in an effort to get some

Members of the Madison chapter of the NAACP plan the annual Freedom Fund benefit at Central High School in 1961. Shown are Mrs. L. E. Pfankuchen, Odell Taliaferro, Mrs. Emery Styles, and Dr. Samuel Williams. WHI IMAGE ID 113671

Black students to attend Stout. Assistant Dean Walter Meek of the UW Medical School said that Black students could not enroll. I spoke with Meek man-to-man about the hiring practices at the UW Medical School. Meek said Blacks were uneducated. I reported my conversation with Meek to the NAACP. Twenty years later the medical school begged for Black students because the federal government gave money to colleges and universities that accepted Blacks. Well, I guess money solves everything.

As president of the NAACP, I and the members concocted a plan to accrue evidence that discrimination in University of Wisconsin housing occurred, using recordings and pictures. The plan was this: a willing Black student filled out an application for an apartment. The landlord refused the application. Then a willing White student applied for the same apartment. The landlord accepted him. The president of the university became aware of the ruse and was upset, calling me for a meeting. I accused University of Wisconsin–Madison of breaking a law. After this incident, Blacks could live in off-campus housing, but they still could not live in the residence halls. During my time in the NAACP, more Whites than Blacks were at sit-ins, and more Whites than Blacks were members of the NAACP. I remember when White students interfered with a class taught by a White chemistry professor, accusing him of holding me down because I had a bachelor of science degree in chemistry and should be teaching. I talked to the students, telling them I appreciated their efforts, but I was okay doing the work I was doing.

The NAACP fought the United Service Organizations (USO), which segregated Black soldiers. I gave a sermon about this problem at my church, but in 1946, even Blacks wanted a segregated USO. Entertainers came to Madison but could not stay in the hotels. Baseball players and musical artists, like Paul Robeson, came to Madison and stayed in Black and White private homes. The NAACP began to attack hotels for their practices. When my wife, Hazel, who could pass as White, wanted to attend concerts, she passed as White so she could sit where she wanted. My sister and I, who were darker skinned, sat elsewhere.

I had difficulties living in my neighborhood after 1950, especially the time when I bought my house in 1962. After my wife and I moved into our house, the neighbors threatened to burn the house down. There were three groups in my neighborhood: one group welcomed Blacks, one was hostile, and one did not pay any attention to them. A few moved out.

Members of the USO Service Club meet in Madison in 1945, at a time when the organization was debating segregation of its members. WHI IMAGE ID 34453

I talked to groups in Dane County about race relations. In the 1960s, I went to Milwaukee to speak, but at that time, militant Blacks did not want me around. I talked to a group of nurses in northern Wisconsin who were angry about what their instructor was telling them about Blacks. The prejudiced instructor told the nurses to keep Blacks in their places. I told the nurses to keep letting the prejudiced instructor talk because eventually that instructor would hurt himself.

BEATRICE RUSSEY GULLEY

Beatrice moved to Madison in 1930 to join her husband, Carson, who served as head chef at UW–Madison from 1927 to 1954. The couple were married on July 26, 1930. Beatrice worked as a seamstress and also sometimes appeared on his weekly show on WMTV, What's Cookin'. *Angela Whitmal interviewed Beatrice on January 6, 1979, for the Wisconsin Historical Society's* Coming to Madison *project. The following is an abridged version of the original tape.*

I came to Madison on July 22, 1930. Carson lived here, but I didn't. I lived in Arkansas. He came down there to visit his folks. He asked my mother to let me come up here to get married. I went to school 'cause I was more interested in my schoolwork than I was in gettin' married. I did get married, but I didn't know I was gettin' married. I thought I was goin' for a ride. My sister was married to his brother. Carson was much older than I was. I didn't know that Carson had been married before. He had been married and had a wife and some kids, but I didn't know that. I guess he had twin boys and a girl and another boy. There were four of them, I think. Everyone wanted me to marry him. And when he said let's go for a ride, I just thought I was goin' for a ride. When he got to Reverend Washington's house, he stopped and opened the car and he said, "Let's go in here." I didn't know any different. So I went in the house. I looked around for a place to sit down. Reverend Washington said, "Sister, you have to stand up for what you're goin' to do." That's the first I knew I was goin' to get married. I was staying with Mrs. Shepard. That's where Carson took me to get a room, at Mrs. Shepard's. Back in those days, I don't think you had to buy a license. He had been up here in Wisconsin. He was smarter than I was. Carson was ten years older than I was, and naturally he would know more than I did.

I went to Mt. Zion Baptist Church. Reverend Washington was pastor of the church when I married Carson. Then Reverend Anderson came there afterward to be the pastor of the church. That's one thing about the Baptist

Bea and Carson Gulley's Christmas card promoting their catering service. WHI IMAGE ID 46871

church. They let the preacher go whenever they want to. I think the Methodist church is different. The Baptist church does whatever it wants to do.

I did teach school. I went to Arkansas Baptist College and then I went to Tuskegee Institute. I spent four years at Arkansas Baptist College. Then I went to Tuskegee. When I married Carson, I was at Tuskegee Institute. They picked chapters of what you could study. I told them I was going to be a seamstress. That's what my father had said he wanted me to be. The first day I went to school, the teacher said to me, "You go back and read your guide sheet. Don't run up here asking me questions." So I went back and picked up the guide sheet and I read it, and I never asked her how to do nothin' any more after that. I just did what was necessary to be done. I didn't ask her anything else. I bought the pattern. I read the guide sheet like she told me and I knew what to do.

When I first came to Madison, I worked at Carmen's Store. The owner had another alterations lady. She did the suits and I did all the coats. Every coat that went out of the store, I hemmed it. I put buttons on it. That was my job. They had it fixed so that two women did the alterations. My job was to put on all the buttons and put the hem in. Mrs. Uphoff did all the takin' in. A girl came in there one day to buy something. This is when the dresses first got short. I looked at her length. I said, "I don't think you want that dress up there." She said, "Yes, I do. I know what I want." I said, "But I'm lookin' at you and I don't think you should put that dress up there." Sure enough, I put the dress where she kept on insisting on me putting it. Finally, she came back. When she went home and put that dress on, her husband didn't like it. She brought it back. Al was very nice to me. He said, "I know you did what she wanted you to do. We'll just give her another coat." That's the way we got around that. He was the boss of the store. He was willing to give her another coat to get her satisfied.

I think when you buy coats, you buy at a price you can afford. When you buy a coat, they have doubled the price before you buy it. When the coat comes in the store, it costs ten dollars. When you get ready to buy it, you have to pay twenty dollars for it. However, that's the way I made my salary. Usually, when people come in to buy something, Al had already doubled the price. You wouldn't have seen the price because he already marked it like he wanted so he could make money. It was like that. You didn't face any embarrassment. The manager did all the embarrassment. He went to work and priced the things and we just sold it at what he had it priced for. You followed your boss's orders. If he told you to do something, you do that. That was the rule back then. They started out with nothing but coats but then they finally started selling everything, suits and things like that. The only thing that used to make me so disgusted is that Al would turn around and mark them down to the original price. I told him, "You made me pay more for something and yet you marked it down. A person comes along to buy a coat doesn't have to pay as much as I paid for it." I figure he was smooth. He knew what he was doin'. Because when you operate a store, you have to make a profit. You have to pay for the building, for the help, and everything.

One thing about Carson is that he worked with food, and I worked with clothing. We had different occupations. I didn't bother with the food and he didn't bother with the clothing. That's the way we went. When I married him, I decided that if he was interested in food, I was not. I was interested in clothing. That is the way I figured it. You don't do the same thing as your husband did because you wouldn't do like he would do. So, I didn't tell him what to do and he didn't tell me what to do. He was the cook. I was the seamstress. We didn't have a conflict. People cook from just tryin' things out. And no doubt, that's how he learned how to cook, by tryin' out recipes. He worked for the university and I cooked for myself because I was by myself all the time. I picked what I wanted to eat. So we never came in conflict with each other. That's the way we got along. We had twenty-two some odd years. That's the way we were.

We had a cookin' television show. We were on there until Carson died. When he died, I quit. I was so used to standin' up there with him when he was doin' something. He always did the cookin'. I did the handin' in of what he needed. One day one girl said to Carson, "How is it that every time you want something, she hands it to you?" He never realized that was what I was doin'. It struck him as funny. He said to me, "From now on, don't give me nothing until I ask for it." When you know what the recipes are, you get all the stuff together and you make them handy for him. I know that one day I didn't go with him. He was standin' up there and needed something and this girl didn't know what to bring him. She wasn't used to it. So, after that, he found out what a big mistake he had made. This woman knew how to cook, but she didn't know what he wanted and when he wanted it. I suppose she had the recipe knowledge in her head. When I worked with him, I always would see what had to be done. That way I kept up with the recipes. By me having to work with the food all along, I knew what came next and what didn't come next. That's the way we worked it. The show was on for one half hour every day on Channel 15, WMTV. I think it's disgusting when you put on a food show and you don't know what you're doing. I think that's terrible. We always rehearsed the program beforehand and we knew what we were goin' to do. We did just like we had planned to do it. We never had a mix-up.

We catered every day. In fact, the boss always told us what he wanted us to make that day because he was pushing something that he liked. He'd tell us what to do. We did what he wanted us to do. But my husband was one of those people who'd tell him, "I just can't do that. We have to do it this way." He would conflict with the boss when it would come to doing somethin'. He owned the station, but he would let Carson do what he wanted. Milwaukee had a cooking show. One day, Carson was the guest. And that's when the boss decided to have a cooking show in Madison. He had seen Carson do this cooking show in Milwaukee. Then he wanted it done in Madison. So we started the cooking show in Madison.

We did catering for people. Like if you were going to have special guests, and I asked you what you want to have, you'd tell me what you want to have. We fixed what you wanted. That's the way we did things. If you wanted to have chicken, okay. If you wanted to have roast beef, okay. Whatever you decided you wanted, we'd cook it for you. Back in those days, Friday was the only day we cooked fish. Other days, you could cook what you wanted to cook. Dessert was one thing that you could have choices. It didn't mess with the religion. I worked for a Catholic family. On Friday they always had fish, but on the other days, they could have anything they wanted. I worked for this Catholic family for a long time so I got used to what they liked. That was easy. There were four sisters and they had certain days they would eat this and that. They would suggest what I should fix and I had to fix what they suggested. I made so much tapioca pudding. I got so tired of cooking tapioca pudding. Carson quit working for the university and that's when we started the catering business. I didn't do any of the cooking for the catering business. I did the pastry. He couldn't do pastry because he was allergic to flour. He couldn't handle the flour, but he could handle the meat, basic things like that.

I did like to golf. I was very good at golf. Carson liked golf. That's one thing we did together. He would drive the ball as far as he could and I would drive the ball as far as I could drive it. We had no disagreement about that because after all, you only hit the golf ball to go where you wanted it to go. You could hook. Sometimes I would fuss about my golf balls because there are some golf balls you can't drive far. The covers are too heavy or somethin'. I don't know what it is. I know Emery Styles. His wife played golf. She would cut up the balls so badly that he quit buying her golf balls that would cut so easy. Mabel would hit the ball and it wouldn't go far. I played with a different type of ball and my ball would go a long way because Carson knew I wasn't going to cut it up. Mabel would chop down on the ball. Emery decided he would buy her tough covered balls. When she finally found out what was going on, she gave Emery a good goin' over. He started buying her decent balls so she could play golf. It was real funny that she got on him. When he would do something she didn't like, she would tell him off. At least she got her mind cleared up. He finally got to the point where he told her, "You're supposed to hit under the ball, not on the ball." He took her out to practice. He taught her how to hit the ball, which was very nice for him to do that. After all, that's one thing that my husband didn't tell me. We played golf together all the time. He couldn't outdrive me. I could outdrive him. He didn't have to come to me and tell me that I was doing wrong because I knew what I was doing. Playing golf, you do have to know your ball. The only game I never tried is tennis. I think tennis is too fast for me. Golf is as slow as you want or as fast as you want. I used to always shoot my ball far enough to stay out of a person's reach so they could shoot their ball and wouldn't hit me. By the time I walked out to where it was, it was safe because I knew there wasn't too many people who could play golf who could shoot a ball that far. I never was afraid of people hitting me with a ball because most people drove their ball too short, but I drove my ball a long ways. I tried to walk where I wouldn't get hit. I didn't have any other hobbies. I'm getting too old and too lazy. I quit sewing, too.

CARSON GULLEY

Carson Gulley had an impact on members of the Black community in the 1940s and on the University of Wisconsin campus. Carson was born in 1897 near Camden, Arkansas, to sharecropper parents. At the age of six, Carson began picking cotton, but his father, a former slave, made sure he received some education by apprenticing him to a teacher in a nearby community. After graduating from high school, he returned to his local school to teach. After becoming discouraged with low teaching wages, Carson set out to find a career in the culinary arts. He traveled to different cities practicing this trade and developing his skills as a chef.

In 1926, Carson met Don Halverson, who was the director of University Housing, at the Essex Lodge in Tomahawk, Wisconsin. Halverson offered him a chef's job at the University of Wisconsin in December 1926, where, at age twenty-nine, Carson began distinguishing himself in the culinary field. In 1936, the president of Tuskegee Institute in Alabama invited Carson to teach a dietetics training course. While there, Dr. George

Carson Gulley. WHI IMAGE ID 48994

Washington Carver became his most influential mentor. Learning from his Tuskegee teaching experiences, Carson developed a Cooks and Bakers School for the US Navy, and then developed a professional cooks training school at UW–Madison, becoming one of the earliest African American teachers on campus. He published his first cookbook, *Seasoning Secrets,* in 1949, which allowed him to travel around the state speaking to towns that had no African Americans. In 1953, Carson and Beatrice were invited to host cooking programs on local radio stations, and then on WMTV television. As the host of *What's Cookin',* Carson was one of the first Blacks to have a TV program, and the show was the only show in the 1950s to feature a Black couple.

While achieving professional success and celebrity, Carson became discouraged by the continued discrimination and segregation he and other Blacks faced in Madison, where Blacks were not allowed to teach in schools, eat in some restaurants, rent rooms in hotels, and were excluded from Dane County jury lists. Landlords and real estate agents used restrictive deeds and covenants to restrict Blacks to housing in small sections of the city. When the Gulleys rented a house on West Johnson Street in 1932, neighbors circulated a petition in protest until the Gulleys' landlord forced them to relocate. After being evicted from another apartment in 1935, though, Carson considered accepting a job outside of Madison. To persuade Carson to stay, the university built the Gulleys an apartment in the basement of Tripp Commons Hall. Carson continued to challenge the city's segregation laws by attempting to buy property, and after many years of obstacles, he finally succeeded in buying a home in 1954. The fair housing movement did not gain wider traction until the 1960s, after Carson's death.

After twenty-seven years of service and being continually overlooked for the position of director of dormitory food services—which went to younger and White candidates—Carson retired from the university. He devoted the rest of his life to his catering, TV and radio appearances, and speaking ventures. The Gulleys expanded their catering business into a restaurant in 1962, which opened just six weeks before Carson's death on November 2. Beatrice continued to operate the restaurant until 1965, during which time she struggled with the city's refusal to grant a liquor license and racial harassment directed at the business. In 1966, a building—Carson Gulley Commons, where he spent his UW–Madison career—was named in his honor. This building was the first UW–Madison building to be named after an African American.

The information for this sidebar came from a pamphlet for the Carson Gulley Center Dedication (University of Wisconsin–Madison, Division of University Housing, 2013) and from Scott Seyforth's "The Life and Times of Carson Gulley" (*Wisconsin Magazine of History*, Summer 2016).

WILLIAM GOTHARD

Angela Whitmal interviewed William Gothard on January 12, 1989, for the Wisconsin Historical Society's Coming to Madison project. The following is an abridged version of the original tape.

I came to Madison in October 1928. The football season was on, and it was the year Wisconsin played Notre Dame and beat 'em. I was twenty-eight when I came here. I was working on the railroad and came through Madison going to Dakota, and when the job was finished I was going to stop off in Madison. It was such a beautiful town at that time. I stopped off here in Madison, and have been here ever since. It was during the Depression. I was lucky enough to find a job, so I just stayed here. I came to visit, then after I got a job I decided to stay. I was working at Oscar Mayer and thought it was a good place to stick with. The boys I was with, we all walked around the Square, and we all remarked about what a beautiful place this was. It was like a park. It has changed all over from when it was in 1928 and 1929. It's a mall up there now, but then, it was like a park around the Square up there. I thought it was pretty. That time of year the students were here. It was an interesting town. I got off the train. I got a free ride back to town. I went to the barbershop and started talkin' with the folks in the barbershop and through them found a place to stay. Different fellas told me, "Oh, you'll find a job someplace, if you stay here." That's the way it was.

There were only about two hundred or three hundred Black people in Madison at that time. Now, I guess there's over six thousand. So, it wasn't long before I got acquainted with some of the young fellas. One of the first fellas that worked at Oscar's, he introduced me to the foreman out there, and I got a job through one of the fellas I got acquainted with. It was easy to get acquainted around here because there weren't many Blacks here at that time. There was a funny thing. When I went to Sam Dixon's pool hall, one of the first fellas I met was a fella from my hometown, Hutchinson, Kansas. He was working in Madison. We used to play ball together. I think he helped organize our baseball team. He was a little older than I was. He didn't stay long.

My sister and brother have visited here. I had three brothers and two sisters. My dad was a carpenter. My mother did housework. I dropped out of school in my sophomore year in high school. I started roaming around. I went from Hutchinson, Kansas, to New York. My oldest brother was in New York and he had a concession there. I worked with him awhile, and I worked in a button factory for two years around there. He had a hat-checking concession in two or three nightclubs in New York. I worked with him in the nighttime, and in the daytime, I worked in this button factory for fifteen dollars a week. That was in 1926. I was a pretty good shipping clerk there. The funny thing about it was that when I came to Madison, I put my application in at Oscar's as a shipping clerk. When the plant shut down, and a lot of different departments shut down, and after I had worked there for about thirty-something years, then they put me in the shipping department. I worked as a butcher before that, but after they changed a department, that's when I got the shipping clerk job. I worked as a shipping clerk for three or four years before I retired. I had to retire out of that department. I worked at Oscar's for thirty-seven years. I left there one time and went into business for myself, but that was a lot of night work, so I gave it up and went back to Oscar's. I wasn't gone very long so I didn't lose my seniority. That's why I had the whole thirty-seven years' seniority. I was gone only about two and a half years. But they didn't consider that enough to lose my seniority. I had a cleaning and pressing business one time and then we had a restaurant. We had a barbeque place, my wife and her mother had a barbeque restaurant called the Chicken Shack. We had barbeque ribs and chicken. Those were the days when you had to have stamps for food. We were busy. We had so much business sometimes. People would line up there at night. The guy next door had a shoeshine place. He closed the shoe repair shop and made a restaurant out of it. We didn't sell liquor. People would bring their own. We worked until two or three o'clock in the morning. We turned that over to [Curt] Lucas. He had to give it up, too. Then the city talked about buying all that property out down there, so we sold out.

I lived on Dayton Street. We moved there in 1940. The church was on Dayton Street. Anytime there was something that needed to be done at the church. "Oh, Mr. Gothard will do it." So it was with the lodge. The lodge was on Blair Street. Just so happened, I was in the right place to do

things, put the trash out once a week and clean up the hall. I was raised in
the Methodist church. That's where you go to get acquainted. I was young
and liked to run around then. We'd get a group together and go to Beloit,
go to dances in Beloit. With our basketball team, we'd go to Beloit and go
to a dance afterward. The same with Rockford, we'd go to play basketball
with the colored teams down there. Most of our games were with White
teams in the vicinity, called *home talent teams*, from the high school and
kids who were out of school. Of course, that was in the wintertime. In the
summertime, we had baseball and softball teams. Sometimes we played
sixty-forty, sometimes fifty-fifty. Sometimes, it would be winner take all.
They'd pass the hat around for admission and divide up the money. We
had the Capital City Athletic Club. Some were going to school and some
were working. Most didn't make the high school team. I don't think their
grades were good enough. They wouldn't play. We had the pickup team,
we called it. There were two basketball teams, the Capital City Athletic
Club and the Lincoln Athletic Club. The Capital City Athletic Club was
the older fellas and they were the best players. If they had different games,
some would play with one team and some would play with another. We
went to different merchants. Each one would buy a suit and had his name
printed on the back.

I was with the All Stars. Most of them came out of Milwaukee. We
had a pretty good team. Those were really good players. They beat all the
White teams. The infield was the boys out of Milwaukee. The outfield was
played by about four of us Madison boys. Trotter sponsored the All Stars.
He bought the baseball suits. Then he called them the Trotter's All Stars.
He was quite a fan of us. There was no real trouble. At that time, they had
never seen Black people before. We drew quite a crowd. Madison had a
semipro team called the Madison Blues. They would get the Kansas City
Monarchs and these colored teams to play at Breese Stevens Field. Sometimes there would be five hundred to a thousand people who'd come to see
these teams play. They liked to see these Black ballplayers. We played the
home talent teams mostly. We played an Indian team called the Decorah
Indians in Columbus, Wisconsin. They were hitting the ball, not very hard,
just over the infield. The catcher finally picked up one of the bats and saw
where it was flat on one side. They were beating us before, but we caught
up with them after that. We got a big laugh out of that. All the Blacks would

come watch us play. When we went out of town, we'd have whole carloads of people go out of town to watch us.

I met my wife [Lorraine] at [Gert] Harris's Hall. Harris had a dance hall downstairs and apartments upstairs. She used to rent out the hall for parties. You didn't have to have a license back then. It was a two-story house. Had a lot of parties over there on Lake Street and Mound Streets. Right across from the railroad tracks. It was in the Triangle. Blacks owned a barbershop. Sam Dixon had a pool hall. Sam Dixon's sister owned a restaurant. Mr. Weaver had a grocery store. Mr. Hill had a grocery store. One fella had a cleaning and pressing place. Hoover's had a restaurant. Art Jones had a café, but it didn't last long. Oliver Davis had a restaurant, had mostly White customers. The social life was house rent parties.

Many Blacks lived in the Bush and south Madison. They started developing that area after the Depression. Baird Street was named after a Black man. The only place you could rent was in south Madison. I didn't want to live in south Madison when I first came here. I wanted to live close to where I worked. That's why I bought a house on Blair and Dayton Streets. John Parks, his mother died. He was going to move to Rockford and go into business. He was a dentist. We made a deal and bought the place from him.

After they got the Equal Opportunities Commission going, they made a lot of changes because they had teeth in the law. People began to move to houses all around the city. I was honored to be picked to be on the first Equal Opportunities Commission. Reverend Wright and I were the only two Blacks who were on the Equal Opportunities Commission. I was on there for three years. My time expired; I didn't want to be reappointed. I nominated Reverend Wright to be a paid manager because there was so much to do. My motion went through. He's been there ever since. Reverend Wright was an ordained minister. He was a substitute preacher. He would come to the Methodist church sometimes and preach and go to the Baptist church and do funerals. I don't know where he is from originally. He turned out to be a good worker around here. I guess he won a lot of awards for his work at the Equal Opportunities Commission. They started the Equal Opportunities Commission in 1964, but my term was from 1964 to 1966.

I was treasurer of the NAACP for twelve years, and secretary of the Capital City Masonic Lodge #2 for thirteen years. There are eleven lodges in the state and we're one of the oldest lodges in there. I joined this lodge in 1950. We had a lot of projects. I was Worshipful Master for two years, had almost every office in the lodge. We did charitable work. We tried to get good men, make them better, give them a chance to speak in public, get up and do things they ordinarily wouldn't do otherwise. It's nearly the same as a religion, but it's not a religion. The Eastern Star and the Masons are all over the United States. The Prince Hall Masonic Lodge, I guess there are nearly half a million. The Eastern Star is quite a group, too. There are about nine of those in Wisconsin. We own our building here. Beloit owns a building. Racine owns their building and there are two in Milwaukee. We're an active group, been organized since 1906 when they organized here, before I came here, and they have been going ever since. They did shut down at one time, but they reorganized.

I played golf and won a lot of trophies. I won first place pretty near in all the teams in the leagues we bowled in at one time or another. The golf trophy, I remember I played the supervisor of the whole Oscar Mayer plant. I was so glad to beat him, for the handicap championship. He wasn't too happy about that. He was a big fella. He was a good golfer. It just so happened that I won out. I liked to bowl. It was really good, a lotta fun. I had a 299 game one time. Pretty near had a perfect game. The seventh pin just up there and wiggled away. I was sick. One fella got three hundred dollars for a perfect game, but so many perfect games came in after that, they quit giving the three hundred dollars. We had an all-colored league here, the All City Merchants. They were a league I helped organize, 1965 to 1966, All City Merchants, league champs. We were called Mr. P's. He sponsored us. Trotter's sponsored us, too, and the bowling league, come to think about it. Mr. P's sponsored us after he bought Trotter's place. Oscar Mayer's, we had bowled with the Oscar Mayer teams. The Burr Oaks Bowling Alley sponsored our team for Oscar Mayer. We had a lodge bowling trophy. If there were any sports going on, it seemed like I took part in it. I never did play tennis, though. Golf, bowling, softball. Even tried to play football one time. We had a group of Blacks who got a football team together. I liked to die playing football. One of the fellas got his leg broke. Some tried to make money out of it, playing these little towns around, playing football. Some big ole boys in there, boy. Too much for me.

When I came here I went into Mosley's barbershop. He had a hot tamale place. He made good hot tamales. He had a regular business at that time.

We only had one barbershop. During the wartime, when a lot of fellas were in the army, and Mosley was sick or something and wasn't able to barber, another fella came in and did the barbering. We didn't have a barber at one time, so I said I'll help him barber sometimes. He tried to teach me how to barber. I used to cut a lot of kids' hair. I didn't have a license or nothin'. I didn't have no business doin' it. I practiced on my boys. I have two boys. I got good enough so I could cut a pretty decent haircut. But that wasn't for me. There weren't beauty parlors for the ladies to go to that I knew of. A lot of them went to Beloit. A lot of 'em could straighten hair. I remember when my sister came here, she was takin' hairdressing, beauty parlor stuff, and she had quite a thriving business going for a while in her home. She didn't have a license, though. Quite a few of those girls took that beauty parlor stuff up for a while, but they didn't stay with it. Mrs. Harris, and I forget the other girl now. There are about three different places here in town. You can go about anyplace now. Lorraine goes to a White place. There's Bennie's place. Some girls do it in their home.

Things are really different now than what they were when I came here. Blacks are scattered all over Madison now. Anyplace it seems like you go in Madison. Even in some of the restaurants around here you'll find some Blacks working or visiting. Even out to Fridays, customers come in there and that's an expensive place, I thought anyway. A fella was working out there, too. When we were running the Chicken Shack, we had more White patrons than colored. There weren't enough Blacks to take care of anything. White people liked the food, good food, though. They'll come and eat it. Ernie Mitchell, he was another. He learned from Carson Gulley. He taught Ernie how to cook. Ernie got to be quite a cook. Carson Gulley was a buddy, too. Carson and I used to play golf together and go hunting together. I happened to be with him when he died at the hospital. He belonged to the Masonic Lodge. We all took turns going up to stay with him. It just so happened that when I was up there the night that he passed. He was well known around Madison. He had a television show, show people how to cook, he and his wife. She's still living. Lucile Miller liked to play. I think I played with her once. She wanted to play, but she didn't stick to it. She was just a beginner. I liked to play when I was a caddy when I was twelve years old. I used to caddy for these guys. I think I caddied for Chick Evans when he was the world's champion. He was on tour and came to my hometown of Hutchinson. I professionally caddied for him. Oh boy, I thought that was somethin'. We got paid for caddying. We made two to three dollars a day on caddying. Oh boy, that was big money in those days. In the first caddying tournament we had, I won second place in the caddy tournament. I tried to stick with it ever since then. I tried to play left-handed, but I couldn't hit the ball very straight. So I turned and played right-handed. Those were the good old days. I bought all my school clothes when I was caddying then.

Hill's and Weaver's were the only two Black grocery stores in town. Weaver's place was up on Mifflin Street while Hill's was on Dayton and Blount Streets. Weaver's was before my time. The lodge hall was next door to where he had his store. The Hill's store didn't keep much in stock or anything, a few staples that people in the neighborhood wanted. He would never enlarge his place or try to. He said he didn't want a big place. He wanted to do something little. His wife ran the store, too.

I never had trouble living in this town with so few Blacks. A lot of others said they had trouble with 'em. I was the only Black on the bowling team at Oscar's. The only Black on the ball team. They treated me swell. Some people would ask me what nationality I was. I'd say, "I'm smoked Irish."

WALTER HARGROVE

Angela Whitmal interviewed Walter Hargrove on January 12, 1989, for the Wisconsin Historical Society's Coming to Madison project. The following is an abridged version of the original tape.

I came to Madison in 1936 from Georgia. I was about twenty-five. I came to work for the bank, and I've been here ever since. I retired from the bank. I retired from Oscar Mayer's. I left here and went to Wilmington, Delaware, the shipyards, during the war. I never liked Madison 'cause there was no work here. My wife got sick and I came back and I've been here ever since. Had a pretty good job out there. Shipyard and railroad, too. Pennsylvania Railroad.

We lived on a farm with my dad. He passed away. I lost a kid there, too. I had to get away from 'round there. I was married in the south. I had some kin, relations, lived up here. They told me about this job, so that's why I came to Madison. I wanted to get away, but I couldn't, no money. So I stuck it out until the war, and then I left here, and went to the shipyard. I should not ever have left that job. I was doing pretty good. My family was still here. They were living in the house next door. We just built this house in 1962. I had a house in the back of this one. That's what I bought first and we lived in that, oh, for a long time, and then I built this one. And I rented the little one out, the one in the back. When I went east, this was a vacant lot, so I called up my wife to see if we could buy it while I was out east. We bought it. After we bought it, we put a house on that empty lot. The pastor of Mt. Zion and me built it. He was the contractor. It took us about two years. I was helping him. But I practically built this one over here. I raised eight kids here. I had no assistance from the government, the city, never on relief. I should have been on relief. I was making ten bucks a week and the house rent was twenty-five dollars a month. I had fifteen dollars to live on a month. It was rough.

I worked at the bank on the Capital Square. I had to walk from here [home] to the bank. It doesn't snow now, but back then, we had some snow!

Walter and Annie Sue Hargrove. COURTESY OF MILDRED HARGROVE SMITH

I fell in the snow, went down in the snow. I couldn't pull up. I just had to fall over to get out of the drift. It was miserable. I didn't have five cents to ride the bus and that's all the bus fare was. I didn't have it. I had to walk there and walk back. I had to go to work at about four in the morning and get the furnaces going in the bank. They had two furnaces. Then I go do my work. During the day, I washed windows in the bank. I worked until twelve at night. When I got through cleaning, I was security for the bank until twelve at night. And then I walked home. It was so cold. I didn't have clothes like I got now because I couldn't buy them. I almost froze. Thanks to the good Lord I made it. I would not want to see anybody go through what I went through, not even my enemies. You see a person in life, you don't know what he'd been through, you don't know, especially Blacks. Some Whites couldn't get nowhere, either. The president had two colored janitors there. Kept them. Mr. Levitan, he's Jewish. He's the one that got colored in there.

There used to be a Kroger store here. You could buy bread for five cents a loaf. My wife went down to the store and asked for a loaf of bread and said, "My husband will get paid this evening. I'll bring the nickel later." He let her have it for the kids. I'll never forget that. When I got to where I was doing pretty fair, they were giving bread away. You could have all the bread you want.

I worked at Oscar Mayer in 1938 or 1939. I left Oscar's and went out east to the shipyard. I was working at Oscar's and the bank, two jobs. I thought I could better myself if I go out there, ya know, and I did. I did better myself. It was rough everywhere you went for the Negro. But there was more money out east than around here. This is a rich town, but they won't spend any money. Madison's a rich town, rich people, and million-aires here. Colored people have a hard time here in Madison. They get jobs, but some of the jobs don't mean anything. That minimum wage, but people can't make it on that today as high as stuff is. They got a lot of jobs, but what are they? People won't take those jobs. They rather go on relief. They get more. When I was coming along, I would grab anything, one dollar an hour, fifty cents an hour, anything. I always liked to have my own money. I never begged from nobody. I always made it. I tried to borrow it. I remember one day it was real cold. I was going to work and that's when I started workin' days. I know the boy had the money. I asked him for a nickel to ride the bus. He wouldn't let me have it. I had to walk. I wouldn't done nobody that way. My worst enemy, I would a given him a nickel. My face like to froze. When I got into the heat, my face ached from thawing out.

If you got an education, you could get jobs. Oscar Mayer is paying pretty good now. When I retired, I was only getting five bucks an hour and I thought that was good money. Now, they start you off at ten bucks an hour. Lot of people wouldn't believe I was makin' five bucks an hour. But that's all I was makin'. I would get two dollars bonus a night, making seven bucks, but my salary was five bucks an hour. I was glad to get it. I retired in 1975. I worked there twenty years. If they had given me my other years, I would a worked there thirty-two years, but they wouldn't give it to me. They only give me twenty-eight. You were supposed to get your years for leaving and coming back, but they wouldn't give me those years. Give me twenty-eight years, that's all. I don't know why they did that. Some people said it was because I was Black, but I don't know if that was true. They treat me all right while I was there. I never had problems. I never was late.

When I was working at the shipyard, they didn't like it you goin' in fifteen minutes before starting time. I always was at my job fifteen minutes early. This one day, I came early and was sitting beside the gate and these two guards said, "Don't you know you aren't supposed to be here at this time of day? What time do you start?" I said, "Two." So they had me get up and go with them. They acted like I was a prisoner, two big guys, with forty-fives on each side. So I went into the guardhouse with 'em and they said, "You know, we have a lot of sabotage 'round here. We don't want guys comin' in here early." I said, "Well, I'm sittin' out here where you can see me." They said, "We're tryin' to win a war." I said, "Don't you think I'm trying to help? I'm from Madison, Wisconsin. I left my family back there." They talked and talked. The guard at the gate let me in. So when I went out that night I told him, "Man, you got me in trouble." He said, "What?" He was from Georgia and I didn't know it. We got to talkin'. He said, "How ya like it here?" I said, "I don't like it." He said, "I don't either." He said, "Anytime I'm at this gate, you can come in." And I did from then on. I never had no trouble. I went when I got ready. I got along all right. That's where I should have stayed, in Wilmington. You talk about Black people; they were there. Lots of them. Isn't like it is here. When I worked in the bank when I first came here, I was glad to see a Black person come along the street. You see nothing but White, White, White. A colored person would come along, "Oh, boy. Glad to see ya." But some of 'em, the colored, wouldn't even speak to ya. I'd speak, but they act like they didn't hear me.

I was telling the guys that I was leavin' for Madison, oh man, "You're going to like that." Shoot, when I got up here, you talk about a disgusted guy. I was up here for about six or seven months before my family came. I didn't have the money to send for them. Ten bucks a week. Tryin' to live and send them a little piece of money. It was rough. They wouldn't rent to a Negro at that time. I went around. People took me around. It's rented, ya know. Found out I was a Negro. It's rented. Even if I had the money to get them up here, I couldn't get them a place to stay. That's why I bought this little place in the back. They didn't want to sell me that lot in the back of my house. The man wouldn't sell it to me. He owned a lumber company. So, I got a Jewish lawyer at the bank. I went down to the bank and the bank let me have the money. When the guy came by and saw I built this house, he was surprised. Then he tried to cover up. He said, "I got a Chinese livin' right next door to me. We're good friends. You really brought this place up. How did you manage to build?" I said, "Money. I got money to build. I got the money from Anchor Loan." A guy went up there for a loan and they told him, "If you get Hargrove to sign for ya, I'll let you have it." No, I don't sign for nobody. Nobody signed for me. I'll sign for a guy, if I know he'll pay, but some of these guys, they'll get you in trouble. But I have signed for people. I've signed to get houses. I came out all right. They paid. One guy I signed for I had trouble with, oh boy. But the rest paid, I got people out of jail, and they paid it back.

My wife never liked this place. Still doesn't like this place. I like Madison. I've been to a lot of places. But I wish I had lived in [a] town with more jobs. I would have been further ahead. Milwaukee is a much better town than this one. A lot of jobs there, ya see. But so many Black people there. They're fightin'. But to make a living, it's a much better town. One thing about Blacks, they don't pull together. They're apart. If Blacks would pull together, we could turn everything around, but they don't. They don't trust each other. It was always that way, pretty much. But a lot of them you can't trust. They get your money and you won't see nothing.

It was rough raising a family here. You had to keep on tryin'. You couldn't stop, ya know. We had three sons that played football: Charles, Dennis, and W. J. They said W. J. was good playing football. But I was working two jobs. I didn't have time to follow him. I went to a game Charles played. He was lousy to me, playing football, but they said W. J. was good. I never did see him play. I was working all the time, day and night. My wife knows more about the kids than me. It was tough. Charles went to the university. Charles got a good education. He's supposed to be home this May. But he's been saying that for a long time. He's in Los Angeles. There weren't too many Black students going to the university. There are more now than there was back then.

We always went to Mt. Zion. That's the first church I belonged to, Mt. Zion. We were up on Johnson Street, but then we built this one down here. The church had a rough time, too. Not enough money. Most people were on a lease, no money. Not too many members, maybe fifty. It was a small church, but it would be full. Now we have a pretty good church.

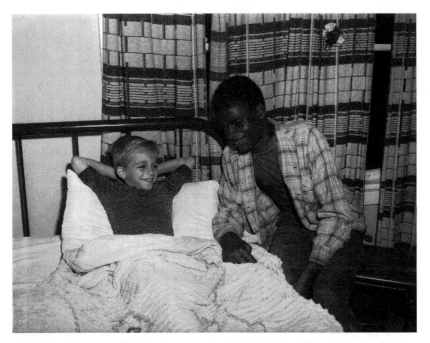

Charles Hargrove, son of Walter Hargrove, sits at the bedside of Robert Byrnes, after Charles pulled Robert from Murphy Creek on Madison's south side. The boys had gone fishing and Robert fell into the deep water. WHI IMAGE ID 65594

It's one of the biggest for the Blacks in town. When I joined, the preacher by the name of Reverend Joe Washington was there. He got on me about being a deacon. I said, "No, man, I don't want no part of that." But he kept at me. He said, "When the minister asks you to do something, the good Lord had revealed to him to ask you. If you turn it down, it won't be good luck for ya." I said, "Now, Reverend, you know you ought not to put it that way. You know, I'm not cut out to be a deacon. There are things I haven't stop doing." He said, "You pray over it and the good Lord will help you get rid of things you're doing." He kept worrin' me, kept worrin' me, and so I give in. He ordained me. And the first Sunday I was at church, not a deacon up there, but me. They had no deacons there. I was the only one there. Finally, it didn't bother me. I got used to it. Then they made me chairman of the board. The old guys were rough deacons. So I had to go up against them. And boy, I had a time. Man, I'm tellin' ya.

At a board meeting, Reverend Washington talked about one deacon and his gambling. Man, he got mad. So I told the guy what Reverend Washington said. He said, "I'll meet the board and I'll bring my gang with me." He said that, too. He never did show up. Man, they were talkin' about me. I stayed chairman of the board for twenty-five years. Every time it come up to vote, they'd vote me back in. I told them, that was it. Let somebody else have it. I've been there long enough. Let some young guys have it. I'd go to the board meetings, but later on, I cut that out. Let some young guys do it. That's what the Baptists run on, the bylaws, how the church should run, but nowadays, they skip the bylaws and go their own way. Church ain't like it used to be when I was coming up as a kid. The old preachers were just like a dad to ya. They talked to ya. Some of them were wrong.

I didn't belong to a church, but my dad did. A preacher was sitting on the school step drunk. Didn't know nothing. Now, he was one of those old preachers that kept me out of church for a long time. I see preachers doing things, and I didn't think preachers should be doing that. Drinking. I had my own soul to save. A guy looks at the leader. They're wrong, then he thinks everything's wrong. Church is a good thing, if it's run right. But today, it's money, money, money. That's not church. I know it takes money to operate, but these preachers want Cadillacs, and all fine clothes. That's not church. A lot of churches do that. These big churches can afford it. They buy Cadillacs, nice clothes, a nice home to live in. Well, the churches are takin' in thousands of dollars.

I helped to build this church we're in now. I had taken off. I was working at Oscar's. I had taken my vacation to help build the parsonage. I was doing trucking at the time. I was haulin' material for the church. Never charged the church a nickel for all the work I did. We sodded the whole place. I had a flat tire. The church couldn't help me get the tire fixed. We were that poor. I never charged the church a dime. In later years, we got it paid off. See, I was the treasurer, and we paid the church off. The Baptist convention loaned us the money to build the church. We paid them off. We bought the lots for parking. Church owned all of that for parking. We paid that off. Then we bought the house next door. The woman wanted to sell it. We bought that. We paid that off.

I turned the books over to the church. We had about forty thousand dollars. The big guys came in and wanted to remodel the church and got us way back in debt. The pastor asked me about it. I said, "Reverend, we just paid this church off. Don't let the church get back in debt." He said, "I'm going to tell them that." Next Sunday, he's preaching. Cofield, he's a coach for the university. He come in here, big head. A bank wouldn't let him have any money. Finally, Park Bank down here let him have the money. We would have got the money at a cheaper interest, three or four percent interest, but now we pay fifteen percent interest. Those big guys look at a poor guy like me, and think he can't do nothin'.

We had nice church picnics. We went to Green Lake for the Baptist convention. We got a big hotel on the lake. We had a picnic up there. We had a good time. They had picnic grounds. You can't go in there. They got a guard. When you come off the highway, you have to stop and talk to him before he will let you in. We had dinners at the church for the people. The preacher up there now is having dinners every Sunday, after the service. But that run out 'cause he couldn't pay the bills. He should not have ever started it, unless he was gonna charge each individual for eating to pay for the food he got. When we have funerals, they always have somethin' to eat after the funeral.

We did not have Black barbers and beauty shops. People would do their hair in their home. People go around and cut your hair. You weren't allowed in a White barbershop. Reverend Wright was the first one to open a barbershop here, and his wife ran the beauty shop. They built a building. They both were in the same building. Then Ben [Parks] bought it. They call it Ben's Barbershop now. When I come here, there was nowhere to get your hair cut. I don't think White folks could cut Blacks' hair. They didn't know how. Like Blacks don't know how to cut Whites' hair, but I think Ben could cut anybody's hair. He knew how. I see Whites there at his barbershop.

What I remember about Madison that's different today than way back was renting a house or an apartment. When I first came here, Blacks couldn't rent, but now, you can rent if you got the money. Today, I don't think the Whites want you in their taverns. But we got three colored taverns here now. That's a business I wanted to go in. I'm glad I didn't go into it. Yeah, I had a chance to buy one in Milwaukee. But I didn't do it. Glad I didn't fool with it. That business is something. Drunks in there, raise all kind of sand. I couldn't a stood it.

SUPPLEMENTAL ORAL HISTORIES

ON EQUAL HOUSING AND THE ETHNIC COMMUNITIES OF THE GREENBUSH

"We are each other's harvest; we are each other's business; we are each other's magnitude and bond."

—GWENDOLYN BROOKS

FRAN REMEIKA

On Equal Housing

Fran Remeika grew up in Sawyer County and moved during Prohibition to Madison, where she graduated from East High School. In 1945, she became a realtor and joined the Madison Board of Realtors. She was the first Madison realtor to sell a home in a White neighborhood to an African American family. Her interview provides insight into the obstacles endured by African Americans trying to buy a home.

Fran Remeika. COURTESY OF DIANE REMEIKA

I belonged to the National Association of Real Estate Brokers. In the 1940s, the association had a green-colored manual that contained a code of ethics listing the rules that realtors had to follow. For the most part, the manual contained codes about cheating in the realtor business and information about the relationship that brokers should have with one another. By signing this manual, a realtor made a commitment to work by it. However, I noticed a phrase in this manual that said, "You will not sell to a race or character of occupancy which will materially depreciate the neighborhood." I looked at that phrase, and I thought, "That's just because it's national, and the south is probably insisting. That's not really applicable in Madison anyway, so I don't care." I shrugged it off and signed the necessary documents saying I was going to support and abide by the code of ethics.

None of the hotels that I know of took Black people. They wiggled around it. So Agnes [Cole] and I became aware of this. We decided that we were going to find places where Black people could stay if they came to town. We started a little registry and went around and talked to the hotel managers and asked them about that. "Well, we don't have much experience with that, and it depends on the circumstances." The new registry [listed] places that would take Black people as transients, and those were not the hotels, those were the rooming houses. Thrond ["Boz"] Bozman was a friend of our company, and he did a lot buying and selling of real estate partly for fun, partly because he made money on it. He was the one that owned the property that I sold to the Doxies.

When the Doxies walked in and wanted to buy a house, I said, "Well, of course." He was just out of the war and had been a graduate of Nebraska College. He graduated [in] statistics, he came to Madison and married Mrs. Allison's daughter. He tried to find a job. The only job he could find at the time was a redcap [railway porter]. At any rate, they walked into our office and said they were looking for a rooming house. They had decided they wanted to help Blacks in the south, and one way to help them was to get them educated, and the way to get them educated was to get them some decent teachers to start with. They wanted to help the girls who were up here go to university so that they could become teachers and go back to the south and help the southern schools.

It was a girl's rooming house at the time. And I thought there was one down there on North Street because I thought it was just what they wanted

The Allison House, a well-known rooming house where Black families stayed while they searched for other housing. COURTESY OF RALPH LEE III

and in their price range and everything's fine. I said, "I'll take you to see it, and they said, "No, we don't want to see it. We want Mrs. Allison to see it." Why is that? "Well, because Mrs. Allison's going to help finance it, and if she says it's okay, we say it's okay." I said, "Don't you want to see it, too?" "No, we don't want to upset the neighbors."

Okay, I did that, I took Mrs. Allison through it, and Mrs. Allison thought it was fine, just what they needed. I guess it was about a day or two later, I was getting phone calls from the neighborhood . . . sometimes lawyers. Well, the neighbors . . . asked the city to have a building inspector come down and inspect it to see what had to be done to it to make it more livable. They [the neighbors] were hoping there'd be something that was so costly and prohibitive that the Doxies wouldn't buy it. Well, he [the inspector] came down, and he told them [the Doxies] to fireproof the boiler room, and there were a couple of little things that had to be done. [The Doxies] gave us an offer, and it was a full-price offer.

The Doxies bought the house. I called Boz and told him all about it, and I told him they were Black. He said, "I [don't] care." A few days later, I remember getting a call from the real estate [agent] saying, "We got to back off on this. Back off on this, or you're going to be in trouble. You're violating the code of ethics." Boz said, "Well, I tell you we met these people. They're very nice, they're highly educated, they're good people. You've seen the house where they are now. They are good housekeepers. They're not trash. So visit them." "Okay," says this lawyer. "We'll see about it," and he called back about ten minutes later and said, "No, we don't care. It doesn't matter. The color of their skin is what matters."

The mortgage was going to be taken out at the Home Savings and Loans that was on State Street at that time. We wouldn't tell them who the mortgager was going to be. We closed the deal as fast as we could. Then a short time after, we were notified that we had to appear before the committee—the real estate board had a committee, that's what they called it—for violating the code of ethics. So we went to that, and it was the biggest meeting I've ever seen. It was huge.

They called us up in front. It was just like a court. They asked us some questions and wanted to know what we had to say for ourselves and so forth. And I said, "Well, I just didn't consider. . . . I had discounted that part because it hadn't been considered ethical." And so they said, "Well, you can go home now, and we'll decide what to do about you. Later that day, they called us and said, "Well, okay, come back up on such and such a date and hear the sentence." So, we did a couple days later, and we had to go back and appear again. And that time they said, "Okay, you're suspended for three months, and you're fined four hundred fifty dollars for violation of the code of ethics." They patted me on the shoulder and said, "There, little girl, we know you just didn't know any better. We know you wouldn't do it again."

I got a little sassy about it, and I told them that I had just lost a husband in the Battle of the Bulge and that he was Jewish and that he had gone over there to fight discrimination, and I wasn't going to let him down on the home front. We resigned, and we told them to go to hell as far as the fine was concerned. Being suspended was not fun. Nobody wanted that. But it was interesting, there was nothing that came out in the papers about this, ever. It was kept very, very quiet.

JOE CERNIGLIA

On the Ethnic Communities of the Greenbush

Joe Cerniglia was born in 1935 to Italian American parents Charles and Georgia (Schiro) Cerniglia in the Greenbush neighborhood. Joe graduated from Central High in 1953 and served in the US Marines during the Korean War. In the 1960s, he co-founded the Madison Mustangs football team and served as their general manager for many years. His interview documents

Joe Cerniglia. COURTESY OF THE ITALIAN WORKMEN'S CLUB

the supportive relationship between the varied ethnic groups of the Greenbush neighborhood and the destructive effects of the city of Madison's urban renewal efforts on those communities.

I was fighting urban renewal and was attending all these public hearings, and this guy could not hide his bitterness toward the neighborhood. I'm thinking, why is he so bitter? The urban renewal referendum was passed in the mid-1950s. There were two separate urban renewal projects. There was the Brittingham project, which was on the south side of West Washington Avenue, and then there was the Triangle project, which was the area bordered by Park Street, West Washington, and Regent Streets. They included another four square blocks that was not in the original referendum. Then they also included Regent Street from Park to Mills Street and Milton Street. That was not in the original referendum, but they included that. They didn't have any plan. I remember when the first article came out about the referendum, and they had this beautiful drawing, picture of

205

the bushes in the right place, and then when they would go to these public hearings, they had these models, but they didn't have any plan.

I asked them one time, "Would the people who had their property taken away, would they be able to buy it back and renew it individually?" [They said,] "Well, you would think so." They just didn't know. Philip Falk was chairman of the Redevelopment Authority. Roger Rupnow was the guy in charge of urban renewal, and it was his job to acquire the property. They were proposing urban renewal all the way up [to] the university and all the way to Randall Avenue. There was a group called the Homeowners' Association that was opposing it. These were a group of people who lived in the Dayton Street and University Avenue area. They were vocal, organized, and educated. I was working with them to oppose it. We would have these meetings. They had a public meeting at the Italian Workman's Club. These were people who had a mistrust of government. They [the city] made them sign their names if they wanted to speak into the microphone and taping what they had to say in order to intimidate everyone who attended the meeting. I remember Nick Quartuccio getting up and saying, "Down with urban renewal, Down with urban renewal." We had a meeting one time at St. James Church in the basement. There was a minister there who led a group against the University of Chicago taking over a neighborhood. He suggested that we break up into smaller groups and develop questions that would be asked of the general assembly. Dr. Harry Hamilton was the moderator in our group.

So we sat down, there were about a dozen of us at a table. Dr. Hamilton said, "Does anybody have any questions they would like to ask of the general assembly?" I said, "Yes, I do. I'd like to know who is supposed to benefit by an urban renewal project, the people directly involved or the city at large or what?" Falk was circling the table, and so Dr. Hamilton said, "Here is Mr. Falk. He's the chairman of the Redevelopment Authority. Let's ask him." The first words out of this guy's mouth were that the neighborhood has been a disgrace to the city of Madison for years. I started to get out of my chair. Dr. Kenneth Luedtke reached across the table and put his hand on my shoulder and said, "No, you can destroy this guy with words." Falk said that the city fathers were at a loss when President Truman came to Madison in 1948 to dedicate the Filene House, the headquarters at that time of the CUNA movement, because the city could not get to CUNA without going through the Bush, or "that neighborhood," because it was such a disgrace. I sat there and listened. I couldn't figure out why there was such bitterness in his voice. I didn't understand why at the time, until later on, when I found out that he belonged to the Klan.

[The] Shapiros and Jimmy Puccio didn't deal with the city over selling their homes. They went to Chicago, the regional [Redevelopment Authority] people, and dealt with them to avoid the RDA here in Madison. They went to Chicago because the people in Madison who were dealing with the city were getting screwed. The Chicago regional office had more power than the city. The city had to report to the regional offices. The city got two appraisals on each property, and they were supposed to show them [the sellers] both appraisals. If the two were so far apart, either side could ask for a third appraisal. They [the city] just showed them [the sellers] one appraisal, the lowest one. And then if you didn't agree, they would take you to the condemnation commission. They would decide what your house was worth.

Now, here is another dirty trick they pulled. Once the condemnation commission put a price on the house, it became the property of the city of Madison. The money would go into an escrow account. If you were the property owner, you couldn't use the money to buy another house and on top of that, either side had six months in which to appeal the price to circuit court. Then you put the other party on notice. . . . And in all these cases, the condemnation commission gave the property owner a little more money than the city first offered them. It wasn't much money, a couple thousand dollars more—and then the city put you on notice that [they're] going to appeal and have six months in which to appeal. Well, as soon as the condemnation committee made a decision on your property, it became the property of the city. Then you would have to pay rent on your own property to the city, and the city wouldn't negotiate the rent. They would tell you what the rent was. My uncle had a house, which was one of the newer houses in the neighborhood. It was a two-story house, corner lot, brick facing on it, and kitty corner from him was the Sansone family, whose house was a corner lot, but it was a one-story bungalow. The city gave them more money than it offered my uncle. My uncle refused the city's offer and took his complaint to the condemnation committee, and the condemnation committee gave him more money. The city put my uncle on notice that it was going to appeal. Mind you, this was in the 1960s, and they said you owe us four hundred dollars rent. At that time, it was pretty substantial. I wrote a letter for him to the people in Chicago and got the rent cut in half. The city wouldn't appeal then, but for six months, my uncle paid twenty-four hundred dollars, which he should not have had to pay. This twenty-four hundred dollars was a bad deal. The city got what it wanted in the first place.

Back then, people were afraid to say or fight city hall. I was different. I was younger. I didn't own any property. The Gennas owned a nice brick building. He went to court three times to buy it back because he wanted to move it. He was denied all three times. Then the city sold it to somebody else and moved it. My uncle Vito had a nice little house. It was one of the newer houses in the neighborhood. It was in the part of the project that wasn't included in the referendum. He wanted to move it. The city said no, and then the city turned around and sold it to somebody else, who moved it a half a block away on Mills Street. I wrote about that in the paper about how [the house] was [considered by the RDA as] substandard in the Bush, but [then] a half a block away, it's not!

During the whole urban renewal thing, I wrote a real long letter to the editor. Miles McMillan was the [editor] of the *Cap Times* at the time. His secretary called me. She said, "He would like permission to print your article in two parts." I said, "No, I realize it's a long letter, but so much print has been devoted to the city side of the issue." I wrote the article, but what appeared in the newspaper was not what I said. The opening paragraph of the article in the *Cap Times* was something like, "When the city fathers were taking a walk on their lunch hour, they counted all the outhouses in the Bush. That's when the idea of urban renewal was born." So I called McMillan up, and I told him about that opening paragraph. I said, "Come on now. I assume you spent some time down there. Tell me one location where there was an outhouse. There were sheds for tools and for gardens, but I never saw one outhouse the whole time I lived in the Bush." So he reprinted the article.

One time I was in Josie's restaurant. There was one couple in there I knew with another couple. I walked by their booth. They asked me a question about the neighborhood. This guy I knew came by. He grew up in the

Fourth Ward, which was West Main Street around St. Raphael's Cathedral. The guy said that he grew up in the bloody fourth, blah, blah—braggin' about it. He said, "But I'll tell ya, the safest place for a woman was the Bush. Everybody had their eyes out, and everybody knew who didn't belong there, and they were watched."

There was a nice article about Roy Shelton in the *Cap Times*, telling about how he hung out with the Jewish and Italian kids. They all were going to a dance on the west side at a church. He couldn't go right then but was going to meet up with them later. His friends saw a little commotion at the front door. They saw Roy so they went over said, "What's goin' on?" He said, "They won't let me in." Back then, people were very frank. They thought, "You're beneath me. I can talk to you any way I want." The Italian and Jewish guys told them what they could do with their dance and left with Roy.

One of my favorite Black friends was Albert Smith. Mrs. [Marian] Smith was really nice to us. We'd sit on her front porch. Albert was a little younger than us, but although he was small, he was a good athlete. He hung around with us. Years later, all the guys went to Richard Harris's retirement party. There were a lot of Italian kids there. I went to Billy's table and said, "I heard that Albert's here at the dinner." Billy said, "He's sitting at the next table from you guys." Here comes Albert. He looked at me and then at my nametag, and gave me a big hug.

I got arrested because of Albert. The only time I've been arrested in my life, kind of because of Albert. We had a park director who was an ex-football player. They used to call him Smiley. He was always trying to impress the girls. He was showing them some trick. Just a few feet away, my brother and I were playing loop tennis, so Albert came over and said, "Hey, Smiley, we've got our football team picked." We always had a good touch football team. We always won the city championship. He said to Albert, "Okay, you're off the playground for a week." Albert said, "What did I do?" Smiley said, "You're off for two weeks." I think he was mad because Albert interrupted this trick. So I said, "Hey, Smiley, what did he do? He didn't do anything but tell you we had our football team picked." Smiley said, "And you guys are through playing." Being teenagers, well, I hit him, and my brother hits him again. In a rage, Smiley jumped off the table. My brother was real skinny then. He grabbed my brother and said, "When I tell you to drop that paddle, I mean it." Smiley started twisting his arm around my brother's back. I was boxing then, working out with the boxing team at the university. I went over to Smiley and told him, "Get your hands off of him." He said, "This is none of your business." I said, "This is my business. That's my brother. You're going to break his arm. Now, let him go." I called him a name. "What did you call me?" "You heard me." He took a swing at me. I grabbed him, flipped him over my hip, and threw him down. He got up, charged at me and yelling. I caught him with a left jab and hit him with a right, and knocked him down. Then he was really mad. All these kids are yelling, "Kill him, kill him." Nobody liked him. I knocked him down twice, and the third time I knocked a couple of his teeth out. This cop came by and arrested me and my brother.

We got off, though. Luckily, there was a policewoman there. We were supposed to see this lieutenant and detective in the Crime Prevention Bureau. We went into his office and this same policewoman was sitting there that we knew because she had been a volunteer at the Neighborhood House. So my brother and I pretended we didn't know her. The lieutenant had a phone call and had to leave, so he said to the policewoman, "You handle this." In a whispering voice, we said, "Hey, how are ya?" She said, "What happened?" I told her. She said, "I'm going to let you guys go, but I want you to go back to the park." I said, "I'll just get into another fight." She said, "No, I don't want you to stay away, because then you look like you're wrong." We went to the park, and all discipline broke down. Smiley would tell someone to do something, and the kids would say, "Oh, get off my neck, Smiley, or I'll get Joe to kick your ass again."

During the 1946–47 basketball season, Central was ranked number one in the state. The starting five was called the United Nations Five. We kidded about that. We had two Black players, one Italian player, one Jewish player, and one Irish player, and they all grew up within two blocks of each other in the Bush. Al Dockery was the best player on the team. They beat Beloit during the regular season by thirty-nine points. They played Beloit in the sectional tournament, and for some reason, the coach substituted another guy for the Jewish kid to start. They claimed that screwed up the chemistry of the team, and they lost to Beloit by one point. Beloit won the state championship that year.

This happened even when I was in school, early '50s. Central's fight song was, "Here's a toast to Central High School, Central good and true." We'd play at other schools, and when they'd start playing our song, the other kids would start singing, *Here's a toast to Central High School, n——s, wops, and Jews*. And never once did any faculty member from the other schools put a stop to it or say anything about that. We used to laugh about it. We used to say we might have lost a game or two, but we never lost a fight after the game.

In the '60s, I was starting a local football team here. Three days before our first game, we didn't have our equipment yet. The company rule was that, if you get a letter of credit from a reputable businessman for five thousand dollars, the company would release the equipment. Bill Gothard had played city leagues sports sponsored by the Board of Education. They played for the American Exchange Bank. He told me the bank was always a good sponsor. I introduced myself to the guy at the bank and told him that Bill Gothard was a friend of mine. I told him what I was trying to do. He said, "I'll call you by two o'clock and let you know." He calls me at two p.m. He said, "I talked to Bill Gothard, and he vouched for you, and said that I could trust you. Come up and pick up the letter." We got the equipment, and we had the team for eleven years.

I ran into a guy about three years ago at the Vets' hospital. He was walking down the hall. I said, "That guy looks familiar," an elderly guy, and he sat down with his wife, and they were waiting for medication; there is a screen up there saying when the medication is ready. I walked over to him, and I said, "Excuse me, are you from Madison?" He said, "Yes." "Would your name happen to be Bill Rhodes? You worked for the Board of Education, didn't you?" During the summers, he would come around to the playgrounds and bring equipment. He said, "I taught at Longfellow School, and then I taught at Van Hise on the west side." I introduced myself, and I said, "I went to Longfellow before you taught there." He said, "I think about the people in your neighborhood every single day. What a wonderful attitude they had toward education. I never had to do it because the kids were so well-behaved, but I knew that if I gave a kid a kick in the ass, the last thing he would do is run home and tell his father, because his father would drag him up here and make him apologize, not knowing why I [kicked] him. They were so supportive of us teachers, and education was so important to them. I had so much respect for them. What a change from when I went to the west side at Van Hise, where Johnny could do no wrong. It was hell out there compared to teaching in the Bush."

My brother was a Madison cop for twenty-nine years. My brother was a real handsome kid. His wife's girlfriends always said, "Oh, you're so lucky. Pete looks just like Paul Newman." We would look at pictures of all of us kids when we were little, five and six years old, and he was pretty. Well, there were three Black girls that had a crush on him. It was Clovis Johnson, Nedra [Arms], and Willa Mae [Taylor]. They would always chase him home from school. Later, when my brother was a police officer, Clovis had a job that took her to the City County Building. She would walk by the coffee shop where all the cops were drinking coffee. If my brother was there, he would see Clovis, run over to her, and give her a big hug and kiss. She said, "Peter, you're embarrassing me." He said, "I'm just getting even with you for all the times you and Willa Mae Taylor and Nedra chased me." I saw her one day, and she said to me, "Your brother is always embarrassing me." I said, "He was just getting even with you." She said, "God, he was good lookin'." Clovis was always a big girl, but she was also pretty.

Mike Shivers is always braggin' about his meatballs. I said to him, "You crook. You stole Mrs. Pullara's recipe for meatballs." Mrs. Pullara and Mike's grandmother lived next door to each other. Mrs. Pullara couldn't speak [much] English, and Mike's grandmother couldn't speak [much] Italian. They would talk over the fence and tell each other jokes and laugh. My aunt and uncle lived across the street from Mrs. Shivers. My aunt spoke English, but not very much. Her neighbor was Mrs. Pelliteri; she spoke Italian. My aunt spoke Italian. Mrs. Pullara and Mrs. Gervasi, across the street, and Mrs. Shivers all good friends of theirs. When my aunt and uncle had to move, they bought a house on the west side. My mother used to say to me, "Your aunt Theresa, she's got a nice house now; she's still down in the dumps." I said, "Ma, what does she have in common with these people on the west side? They are all college graduates." They were nice to her, but she didn't have what she had in the old neighborhood, her group of friends. She was comfortable there [in her old neighborhood]. That's what they [city officials] don't realize—urban renewal affected a lot of people.

URBAN RENEWAL AND THE FATE
OF THE GREENBUSH

The Greenbush, often fondly referred to as the Bush, was an area surrounded by West Washington Avenue, Park, and Regent Streets and pop-
ulated by working-class families of different ethnic groups in the 1930s
and 1940s. Most were of Italian, African American, and Jewish heritage.
While they did not share the same cultures, they shared a sense of community and hard work, as evidenced in the memories of those who lived
there. To the Black families of this time period, living in multicultural
neighborhoods did not mean "a Black-White amalgamation in which
all ethnic and economic distinctions would be extinguished," nor did
it mean an "absorption into some misconceived melting pot," as Tom
Wicker wrote in *Tragic Failure: Racial Integration in America*.[1] Instead,
it meant "living together in amity, respecting each other's rights and
culture."[2] It meant taking care of their families within their cultural
contexts. This latter kind of atmosphere is what several descendants
of Black families remembered about living in Madison, and especially
about living in the Greenbush neighborhood. But much of that was lost
when downtown Madison took on an urban renewal project from the
1950s to the 1960s.

The term *urban renewal* generally refers to finding ways to improve or
make progress in the center of cities, but such progress has often come at
a price for preexisting multicultural neighborhoods such as the Bush. The
phrase also refers to a federal government program that began under the
Housing Act of 1949, modified to become the Housing Act of 1954, which
turned the concept of urban renewal into law. Those acts provide the
money for this so-called progress, which to city officials and developers
meant designating new uses for land in ways that encouraged investment
by large corporations, merchants, banks, realtors, and other businesses
with property interests in downtown areas.[3] Residents who wanted to
maintain their neighborhoods stood in the way of this investment in
development. Cities take a series of steps to claim land for such purposes.
After identifying an area as blighted, a city seeks approval of a plan for

renewal from the federal government that allows them to seize the land with minimal compensation to landowning residents, allowing them to resell the land to developers at a discounted price. Meanwhile, land-owning residents have to leave their homes to find other places to live.[4]

When city officials in Madison displaced the ethnic, working-class residents of the Greenbush, they argued they were ridding blight and infusing the city with new life. Many middle- to upper-class Madison res-idents bought into this view of urban renewal as progress. They wanted to see their city clean, tidy, and cozy, and they welcomed the influx of money from the federal government and private investors. A more hidden reason was racism. Some officials in cities with urban renewal programs viewed ethnically diverse neighborhoods as a blight on the city or as hotbeds for crime and poverty, regardless of the reality. [5] The idea that families of different cultures could live together in a neighborhood was unthinkable and undesirable.

---

[1] Tom Wicker, *Tragic Failure: Racial Integration in America* (New York: William Morrow, 1996), 34.
[2] Ibid., 34.
[3] Mindy Thompson Fullilove, *Root Shock: How Tearing Up City Neighborhoods Hurts Americans and What We Can Do about It* (New York: Ballantine Books, 2004), 59.
[4] Ibid., 58.
[5] Jane Jacobs, *The Death and Life of Great American Cities* (New York: Vantage Books, 1989), 292–293.

Appendix A

Book Lovers Club Minutes

The Book Lovers Club met at the homes of Anna Mae Miller and other members to discuss articles by prominent African Americans, share poetry or music, and discuss the issues of the day. The meeting minutes, kept by club president Anna Mae Miller, provide insight into the sense of community in such groups, as well as the interests and priorities of its members. These minutes have been transcribed by Betty Mitchell Banks, granddaughter of the Millers, and used with permission.

Roll of Members

Miss Pearl Samuels, Mrs. Chestena Josey, Mrs. Estella Washington, Mrs. Essie Dortch Mack, Mrs. Mabel Jones, Mrs. Florence Wynne, Mrs. Julia Shepherd, Mrs. Anna Mae Miller, Mr. A Josey, Mr. Johnson, Mr. M A Richardson, Mr. William Miller, Mr. Oliver P Mack, Mr. Asa Washington, Mr. Harry Wynne, Mr. Irwinn, Mr. Wm Carr, Mr. Clay Turner, Mr. L B Shepherd

Nov. 2, 1909

A few friends assembled at the residence of Mrs. Anna Mae Miller, 643 East Dayton St. on the above date to organize a club or circle, the object of which was that of intellectual improvement. In order to effect an organization, it was necessary to have temporary officers where upon Mr. Oliver P Mack was elected temporary Chairman and Miss Pearl Samuels, Temporary Secretary. The members decided upon the name Book Lovers Club as suitable for the organization. The election of permanent officers resulted in the following being chosen, President Mrs. Wm Miller, Vice Pres. Mrs. Asa Washington, Secretary Mrs. OP Mack, Asst. Secretary Mr. WN Johnson, Treasurer Mr. MA Richardson. Mr. Richardson and Mr. Johnson were appointed to escort the newly-elected officers to their stations and

Mr. A Josey with much eloquence, delivered the installation address. The President in beautiful words poured forth a speech of acceptance for all the officers, where upon they assumed their respective charges. The President appointed: Programme Committee—Mrs. Josey, Miss Samuels, Mr. Mack. Committee on By-laws Mr. Miller, Mr. Josey, Mr. Johnson. Mr. Wm Miller was appointed "Reporter" of current news of the day at each meeting. Mr. Johnson was appointed "Critic" for the month of December. The Programme Committee retired in order to make up a programme for the next meeting. The following is the programme: 1. Quotations from Author by members. 2. Paper—"Life of Fred Douglass"—Mr. Wm Miller. 3. Solo—Mrs. Asa Washington. 5. Instrumental Solo—Mrs. OP Mack. Expressions of good wishes for the future welfare of the Book Lovers Club were made by the different members. Club decided upon 8:30 as the hour for meeting. After being delightfully served to a menu which consisted of hot coffee, wafers, chocolate, the Club adjourned to meet with Mr. Miller.

Friday, Dec. 3, 1909

Mrs. Wm Miller, Pres., Essie Dortch Mack, Secretary. Meeting opened with music. Next, was the reading of minutes which were received and adopted. Roll-call of members with annotations from each showed the following members present: Mr. and Mrs. Josey, Mr. Johnson, Mr. and Mrs. Miller, Mr. and Mrs. Mack. The Programme was next in order: 1. Paper on Fred Douglass by Mr. Wm Miller—showed excellent research and gave us very fine account of this excellent character. Very excellent paper. 2. Next number was a solo by Mr. Washington, but she, being absent, Mr. Johnson substituted with the solo, "Good-bye Sweetheart, Good-bye" which was very well rendered. 3. Mrs. Josey gave us a very excellent reading on "Douglass" which was quite a credit to the writer. 4. This programme closed with an instrumental solo by Mrs. Mack. A discussion of the author was indulged in by members. He was discussed in regards to his bravery, true patriotism, marked literary ability and in general, an all-around man. Mr. Josey said he may be termed the Acme of success, an ideal man, yet a man who lived ahead of his time. President urged the Committee on By-laws be ready to report by the next meeting. Current news by the Reporter was very interesting. It was news which was very complimentary to the Negro, showing that he had some friends who were willing to give him all the credit due him. Gleanings from the Report of Critic—As a whole, the programme was very complimentary, there being no real adverse criticisms. As to any grammatical corrections and errors, they would be given more attention. Critic urged that the quotations be real memory-gems, also the musical numbers have due recognition. Programme Committee handed in following for Friday, Dec. 10, 1909: 1. Poet Dunbar—Paper by President. 2. Solo—Mrs. Washington. 3. Paper—The Power of Education—Mr. JA Josey. 4. Solo—Mr. Richardson. 5. Select Reading—Miss Samuels. 6. News—Mr. Miller. 7. Critic.

December 10, 1909

President called meeting to order. Reading of the minutes was next order of business. Upon motion, the same were received and adopted. The roll was called and most of the members answered with a quotation from Paul Lawrence Dunbar, the poet under notice for this meeting. The programme was the next in order. Opening number, music—Miss Samuels, well rendered. The President, Mrs. Wm Miller followed with a very, very excellent paper on our own Paul Lawrence Dunbar. It was [a] thorough history of the young man. She also favored us with one of his "Tributes to Douglass"—an extract. A solo, "Dream On" by Mrs. Washington was well rendered. A paper from Mr. Josey on the "Power of Education" showed the true value of education. Solo by Mr. Richardson was called for, but he being absent, Mr. Mack substituted with An Ode to Mr. Josey— "go on." Select reading by Miss Samuels. She seemed especially delighted gifted with the power to deliver Dunbar. Her selection was one quite appropriate and we all feel sorry for [illegible]. The newspaper man furnished us with news—thus. A new play "The Niggar" has been written by Shaw Sheldon. Distribution of Xmas gifts in the rural districts by BT Washington. Big prize fight, Jack Johnson and Jim Jefferies, July 4, will create more sensation than anything else in this country. Jack Johnson will play 15 weeks on stage receiving $30,000.00. President sent his message to Congress. An effort on foot to have a celebration—50 years from slavery, to show progress of the Negroes. Dispute as to who proposed, Wright or BT Washington, are rivals in regard to the matter. President recommended that the Freeman's Bank be reimbursed. General discussion on Dunbar was both interesting as well as instructive. Report of Critic—All quotations very good. Paper by the President very creditable. Solos—both vocal & instrumental, good. Paper—Mr. Josey, very, very excellent. Much thought as well as careful research. Committee on By-laws made a partial report. With their consent, they were not approved until the following meeting. Programme committee reported the following programme: 1. Instrumental solo. 2. Paper—Phyllis Wheatly—Mrs. Mack. 3. Solo—Mrs. Washington. 4. Discussion. 5. Solo—Mr. Mack. 6. Current news. Adjourned to meet with Mrs. Washington, Dec. 17, 1909.

December 17, 1909

Book Lovers Club met with Mrs. Washington. President and officers presiding. Opening song—"Merry Party" song by the Club. Minutes of the previous meeting were read and approved with some corrections. Next order of business was the roll call of members with quotations from the writer. Motion & seconded to memorize verses again from Phyllis Wheatly for next meeting. Programme was in order. Mrs. Adams, a visitor, favored us with a very excellent solo. A paper on "Phyllis Wheatly" by Mrs. Mack was the next number. A solo by Mr. Washington was called for but he offered a plausible excuse. A discussion on the poet followed. Statements from the discussion: "Phyllis Wheatly was a true poet." "Was both a poet & a writer. One writer has said she was unparalleled as a writer." "When she underestimated her writings most, then the people of France, Germany, England praised her most." She wrote a poem about Washington, also on the African Painter— quite a comparison of Phyllis of her day to the Phyllis of today. A solo, "Old Black Joe" by Mrs. Mack was well rendered. President called Current news by Mr. Miller—Statistics of dark races, B.T. Washington writes a history of the Negro, William Lloyd Garrison's last words on "The Negro Problem." Gleanings from the report of The Critic— commends the opening of the Club with a song & especially a song of our people, quotations interesting, but not well learned. Solos of Mrs. Adams very much appreciated. Paper of Mrs. Mack very excellent, very scholarly in plain & concise language. Looking upon our people as our own ideals was furnished from parts of the paper. Solo of Mr. Mack was well rendered. New Items—very fine and of great importance. President called for report of the Committee on By-Laws. With the consent of the Chair, Mr. Josey read the rules. Moved to receive By-laws with the necessary corrections was carried. Report of Programme—as follows: Toussaint L'Ouverture, opening—Jubilee song, paper—Toussaint L'Ouverture, Mr. Richardson, Duet—Madames Miller & Washington, solo—Mr. Washington, solo—Mr. Johnson, Current News—Mr. Miller, Critic. Adjourned to meet with Mr. & Mrs. Mack.

Mrs. Wm Miller, Pres
Essie Dortch Mack, Secretary

January 7, 1910

Book Lovers Club met with Mr. & Mrs. OP Mack. Opening song, "Battle Hymn of the Republic." Minutes were read and adopted. Roll call of members with quotations. Next followed the Programme—address on Toussaint L'Ouverture by Mr. Richardson was very scholarly. He said from genius to real character, he was better than Napoleon. A military ruler at one time when the island progressed most. Mrs. Washington being absent, Mrs. Miller rendered a solo very excellently. Open discussion—Mr. Miller commented noble on the author. Mr. Josey discussed L'Ouverture as a soldier. Mr. Johnson favored us with a solo which was well rendered. Current news was the next in order. A Circuit Ball Club was being organized where no color line would be drawn. Other news very interesting. Critic rendered his criticism. He advised members practice more addressing than paper reading. Some corrections in pronunciations. Mr. Pully, a visitor was present. President appointed a committee consisting of Mrs. Mack, Mr. Johnson, Mr. Miller for preparation of Programme on Douglass Celebration, Feb. 22, 1910. Programme committee submitted the following programme for next meeting—Crispus Attucks opened by Mr. Johnson, solo, Mrs. Washington, discussion, quartette selected, current news, critique. After being served, Club adjourned. To meet with Mr. & Mrs. Josey, January 14, 1910.

Mrs. Wm Miller, Pres.
Essie Dortch Mack, Secretary

January 21, 1910

Opening song of Book Lovers Club, "Come Thou King" on January 21 at residence of Miss Pearl Samuels. Roll call of members with quotations from each was the next order of business. Minutes were read & approved after which the programme was in order. Absence of the members were taken note of with excuses from each. Mr. O P Mack gave us a very interesting address on Alexander Dumas, which showed us clearly that he was of Negro descent. Dumas was quite worthy of consideration. He first [illegible] in 1819. Translated Bürger's Lenore but it soon met defeat. Only book in which he wrote of himself. Memoirs—his greatest production, wrote without using his thumb. His greatest masterpiece was made when he made known he was a Negro, was claimed by a writer of him. Mrs. Mack gave us a very credible address on Dumas. Open discussion—gleanings. Monte Cristo, one of the greatest plays on the stage today, written by him. He began the revival of the Romantic School of Literature. Had a son who was also a writer but leader of the Naturalist School. Two distinct schools by father & son. Had his name signed to 1100 pieces. Solo next in order, but Mrs. Washington failed to be ready. Reading by Miss Samuels—very excellent. Current news—Colored janitor guarding bank so as to avoid inspection of bank after 7 o'clock, another case of white man marrying colored girl. American annual meeting of Negro Academy—gathering of best brains of the race. R. R. Wright received degree. Article on colored poets in Century magazine/ pictures of life series, work of people in Africa. Critique—gleanings—address very interesting, no need for further research. Critic suggested we follow a character and take from a continued [illegible]. Critic suggested that the female members speak oftener as all are a little filled with stage fright. No further business. Club adjourned. To meet with Johnson and Richardsons on January 28. Programme Committee reported. Mary Church Terrell opened by Mrs. Washington. Solo—Mrs. Wynne, Essay—Miss Jones. Quartette—selected.

January 28, 1910

Book Lovers Club met with and were handsomely entertained by Messers Johnson and Richardsons on the above date. Roll call of members showed that some were unprepared with quotations, hence the President instructed that they be subject to fines for the next offense, according to By-laws. Minutes were read and approved. The subject for discussion, Mary Church Terrell was opened by Mrs. Estella Washington. She gave us quite a nice history of Mrs. Terrell, saying she was at one time, President of National Association of Women's Club. In her lectures she states questions of lynching and problems of the Negro servant girl of the south. Mrs. Washington urged that all of us, as Mary C T, do the best we can in our own spheres. Next number on the programme was a solo by Mrs. Wynne. She, being absent, Mrs. Mayme Anderson (a visitor) substituted with a very excellent rendition of "Good-bye, Sweetheart, Good-bye." An essay from Miss Mabel Jones gave us a history of Booklyn, a town in Illinois that was governed, ruled and run by Negroes. It was a very excellent, as well as a very instructive paper. Open discussion was next in order. All the men were enthusiastic over this noble woman. Gleanings from discussion—Mary Church Terrell was a specimen of womanly beauty. She makes it a necessity why the Negro men should respect women more than ever before. Mr. Quinn, a visitor, expressed a pleasure in having seen M C T, although it was at a time when he couldn't appreciate her as he does now. Current news—by Mr. Miller. A bit of history of a tribe in Africa where the people are in a good condition, thriving, doing well. "Ancient History of Negro Race with Government," by Aski, the Great. Critique—gleanings, papers of the evening were very complimentary, treated well by writers and quite a credit to them. Solo by the visitor was very much appreciated. Talks were all very spirited. Visitors were very welcome and their talks were very interesting. Appreciation of the work done by the journalist, very great by the members of the Club. Programme for next meeting, Topic of discussion, Benjamin Banneker, opened by Miss Samuels, solo—Mrs. Wynne, instrumental solo—Mrs. Mack, Quartette selected. In connection with the first topic, Scanco— another Negro was to be discussed. Invitation was extended to visitors and two new members were added to the list. Club adjourned. To meet with Mrs. Wynne, Feb. 4, 1910.

Mrs. Estella Washington, Vice Pres.
Essie Dortch Mack, Secretary

February 4, 1910

Book Lovers Club met with Mr. & Mrs. Harry Wynne on Feb. 4, 1910 with the President presiding. The members were very much delighted to have the President present after being absent for several meetings. The members answered with quotations at roll call in the usual way. Minutes were read and approved. Programme was the next in order. Miss Pearl Samuels opened the programme with an address on Benjamin Banneker, the topic of the night. She gave us quite a nice history of Banneker, saying he was a great mathematician, the originator of an almanac. He was the protégé of some French man. Miss Samuels gave us some very interesting history of Banneker. A reading from Mrs. Wynne was the next number on the programme. It was very beautifully rendered and much enjoyed by all. Again, the Club poured forth the strains of "Old Kentucky Home." Miss Jones gave us an excellent talk on Scanco, the other subject for discussion which was quite a credit to her showing very careful research. Open discussion was next in order and all joined in expressing words of commendation which were very fitting for the subjects, gleanings from Current News, the latest discovery—the Negro is no son of Ham, not a member of the race of Ham. Negro boy is next in order for the appointment at West Point in the Military school. In Africa, law is supreme—no secret fixing of a jury. Africans have a keen sense of justice and high esteem of law. A maiden may walk through the jungles unmolested. "Wish we were in Africa," says Miss Jones. Report of Critic—Order of the night has not been good. (very noisy). Glad to welcome President, yet we have had a very worthy sub. Papers talks very good. Use the library more—all members. New business—motion to have the Douglass Celebration on Feb. 25, 1910 at St Paul AME Church. Carried. The speaker, Mr. Green of Milwaukee, would deliver a public address. Decided to have 100 tickets printed. Admission at the door, $.15. Have refreshments to sell. Reception Committee—Mrs. Josey—Chair, Mrs. Washington, Mr. Washington, Miss Jones, Mr. Johnson. Program committee reported the following program for Feb. 11, 1910—instrumental solo, Mrs. Mack, open discussion—Abe Lincoln, solo—Mrs. Wynne. Adjourned to meet with Mr. & Mrs. Miller—Feb. 11, 1910.

Mrs. A M Miller, Pres.
E Dortch Mack, Secretary

February 11, 1910

Book Lovers Club met with Mr. & Mrs. Miller Feb. 11, 1910 with the President and officers present. At the roll-call the members answered with quotations from Abe Lincoln. Minutes were read and approved. Committee on Douglass Celebration reported the following programme:

1. Opening Song—Club

2. Invocation

3. Ode to Douglass by Dunbar—Mrs. Essie Dortch Mack

4. Quartette—Mrs. Miller & Mrs. Wynne, Mr. Josey & Mr. Mack

5. Introduction of Speaker—Mr. Johnson

6. Address—Honorable W T Green, Milw., Wis.

7. Quartette—Messers Richardson, Josey, Johnson, Mack

The President approved a committee on Refreshments as follows

Mrs. Harry Wynne, Chr.

Miss Pearl Samuels

Mr. & Mrs. O P Mack

Mr. Wm Miller

Mr. Moses Richardson

Mr. Harry Wynne

Programme of the evening was the next in order with discussion on Abraham Lincoln. Vocal solo—Mrs. Wynne which was well rendered and thoroughly enjoyed by all. Current news by Mr. Miller. Gleanings—Negress in Hoboken schools leading all classes. Jack Chinn of Kentucky talking on Negroes & white folks. Minister of Haiti and his wife in society circle in Washington. New York Society leader an advocate of social equality for the races. Progress of Race in Defender very encouraging. Report of Critic—as a whole evening well spent. While being served, The Club discussed Lincoln, after which we adjourned to meet with Miss Jones, Feb. 12, 1910.

Mrs. Wm Miller, Pres.
Essie Dortch Mack, Secr.

February 19, 1910

Book Lovers Club met with Miss Mabel Jones, Feb. 19, 1910 with the President and members present. Opening song, Swanee River was poured forth in tones soft and sweet. Roll call with quotations by members showed a grabbing and scrambling since quotations were hard to find. Minutes were read and approved. Programme was the next in order. 1. Opening number—Pushkin—a reading by Mrs. Miller which was very interesting. It told us that Poushkin is Russia, all Russia. A national poet, his career was most like Phyllis Wheatly. While he was Minister of Foreign Affairs, he mingled in gaiety so much that his friends thought he would be frivolous but it was at this time he wrote his "Ode to Liberty." He met his death in a duel with his sister-in-law's husband in 1838. Thus ended life of the greatest poet of Russia. President's reading was very credible. 2. Select reading—Lincoln's speech at Gettysburg by Miss Jones was well rendered and very appropriate. 3. Address—Mr. Miller, John Brown's life, written by DuBois was very enjoyable and very interesting. Very fine that's from the pen of DuBois were given to us. Club sang "Steal Away." Gleanings from Current News. City of Cairo—colored boy about to be lynched. Negro Deputies take charge and wound several of mob. Dr. Chas. Dublin—a depiction of an Anglo-Saxon, religious hypocrite, salvation lies in learning from those he despises. Negro represents Cornell in Oratorical Contest. Open discussion was very enjoyable and much valuable information was given concerning the subject upon discussion. Report of Critic—Charged that everyone try to give a few words at least on the speaker. Speeches from visitors present. Miss Mary Jones, Mr. & Mrs. Del Jones were very encouraging. Programme committee reported following programme. Haiti—Mrs. Harry Wynne. Violin solo—Miss Samuels. Reading—Mr. Johnson. Duette—Mrs. Wynne & Mrs. Mack. Discussion concerning the public entertainment, Friday, Feb. 25, 1910 showed everything in readiness. Club adjourned to meet March 11, 1910 with Mr. & Mrs. O P Mack.

Mrs. Wm Miller, Pres.
Essie Dortch Mack, Secr.

March 3, 1910

Club met in call meeting to report concerning the entertainment.

Money taken in	$28.25
Paid out	$18.25
Turned over to Church	$10.00

March 11, 1910

Book Lovers Club meeting at the home of Mr. & Mrs. O P Mack with President presiding. Roll Call of members with quotes from different authors showed several members absent. Programme was the next in order. 1. Opening address—Haiti —Mrs. [illegible]. She gave us some very interesting notes on the topic. 2. A violin solo by Mrs. Samuels, but she substituted with reading from Dunbar, "The Rivals," was very interesting and enjoyed by all. 3. Reading by Mrs. Johnson, [illegible] 4. Duet—but Mrs. Wynne being unable to appear, Mrs. Mack substituted with a solo, which was thoroughly enjoyed. Open discussion—Gleanings—more government in Haiti than in any state of the US. Better government there than the US, any one of its states. Literary accomplishments of the island quite credible. Negro poetess, Madame Samperes. Current news—State of Negro by editor of Bohemian. The Club proceeded to elect officers for the next three months. Upon motion by Mrs. J Anthony Josey and seconded by Mr. William Martin Miller, the present officers were continued for upcoming quarter. The office of Vice-President was left vacant until the following meeting. Mr. Bell was received into membership of the Club. Two visitors were present, Mrs. Jesse Woodford, Miss Anna Barton of Baraboo. Much to the delight of those present, Mr. Harry Wynne and Miss Samuels furnished very excellent music. It was indeed quite noticeable that for the first time in the history of the organization the Secretary and Chairman of the Programme committee were absent owing to illness. Programme committee reported the following programme for Friday, April 15, topic, Bornu opened by Mr. W Johnson, Instrumental solo—Mrs. Wynn, Reading, Mrs. Josey. Critics report—Programme of the evening very fine. Suggested that we have a kind of circulating library and wherever the books are they can be renewed by phone. President appointed Mr. Johnson Librarian.

Encouraging remarks from Mr. and Mrs. Henderson, candidates for admission. Resignation of Mr. and Mrs. Asa Washington were read, motion to erase their names carried. Programme committee reported following programme, 1. King Menelik—Mrs. JA Josey 2. Solo—Mrs. CM Josey 3. Reading—Mr. Richardson 4. Violin solo—Mrs. Samuels. Adjourned to meet with Miss Pearl Samuelson, March 18, 1910.

Mrs Wm Miller, President

Essie Dortch Mack, Secretary

March 18, 1910

Book Lovers' Club met March 18, 1910 at the home of Miss Pearl Samuels. Roll-call of members with quotations by each showed some members absent. Opening song—"Sweet & Low." Minutes were read and adopted with the necessary corrections. Programme was next in order. Opening address, King Menelik by interesting history of the old king and his ability. 2. Next number was a solo by Miss Chestena Josey which was well rendered and much enjoyed by everyone in the audience. She will appear again in the future. 3. Reading—Mr Richardson—he was absent. 4. Violin solo—Miss Samuels. We were very enthusiastic over the rapid progress she has made in her performance on the violin. She will come again. Opening discussion—Gleanings, Menelik was born where he could not exert his greatest influence. A leader, a King, a ruler of people who has never been conquered. With a standing army of over 150,000, he kicked the stuffing out of the Italians who had come to conquer his country. An automobile was sent to him, but the man had to put it together, failed to arrive at the time the automobile did and when he did come, the King was riding all over town in Auto. He put it together himself. Abyssinia, the country referred to in the Bible as Ethiopia. It is the oldest civilization. Rely upon own efforts and we shall find we are some of the exponents of civilization. Mrs. Woodford, a visitor gave us a very interesting talk about origin countries. Current news—Jack Johnson owes religious prize fighting to his mother's influence. A motion that the house be open for reception of members carried. A motion that the names of members be presented at a meeting when the members are absent so that they will be members when they

come, carried. Programme committee—report on Hausaland—Mr. Wm
Miller. Solo—Mrs. Johnson. Reading—Mrs. Richardson. Instrumental—
Mrs. Mack. Adjourned to meet with Mr. and Mrs. Josey, March 26, 1910.

Mrs Wm Miller, Pres
Essie Dortch Mack, Secretary

March 26, 1910

Book Lovers Club met with Mr. and Mrs. J. A. Josey on March 26, 1910
with President and officers present. Club sang "My Country" after which
the roll was called and members answered with quotes from Hausaland.
Minutes were read and approved. Song—"Steal Away," after which the
topic was opened by Mr. Wm Miller who gave us a very interesting account of this land of milk and honey. Gleanings from his address. Hausas
inhabit a million and [a] half miles in Sudan. British established a kind of
protectorate over the country, yet this country does not owe its civilization
to outside influences. Hausers form eleven percent of all the people of
the world. Have writers, poets, teachers. Most beautiful language. Bornu
traders, mostly slave trade, though. They build walled cities in order to
be protected from raids. Almost every tribe in Africa came to them to do
trading. Slaves, cannibals, mules, leather work, salt, needles and every
variety of European goods were traded. Cairo, the city of trade. The home
of the Moroccan, largest market in the world. A land of milk and honey
possess a literature of their own. Have some 40 to 50 schools in the city of
Cairo. Mr. Miller gave us a very interesting history, portraying the wealth,
beauty and grandiosity of this African country. All the Book Lovers want
to go to Hausaland. Song by the Club. Open discussion—we need more
Hausaland and especially in Madison. Expressions of appreciation concerning Hausaland. Address on Africa by Mr. Newton. This was truly an
enjoyable treat as he spoke from his own experiences. The Club enjoyed
hearing this talk and noted a notion of thanks to Mr. Newton. The male
members of the Club with Mr. Johnson as chief formed a colony to start to
Hausaland in 1910. No women expected. Programme committee handed in
the following programme: Congo Free States—Miss Samuels. Solo—Miss
James. Reading—Mr. Richardson. There were many visitors present and

Mr. and Mrs. JA Josey served all very sumptuously. Club adjourned to meet with Mr. Johnson and Richardson, the second Friday in April.

Mrs. Wm Miller, Pres.
Essie Dortch Mack, Secretary

April 8, 1910

The Book Lovers Club met with Mr. Moses, Richardson and W Johnson on April 8. Meeting was called together by our President, Mrs. Wm Miller. Our meeting was opened by a solo by Mrs. Samuelson after which the roll was called, the members responding with quotations. Miss Pearl Samuels opened the discussion by an instruction paper and talk on Congo Free States. Mr. W Johnson warbled a soul stirring melody entitled "Dreaming" which was applauded wildly. Mr. Moses A Richardson substituted his reading with a very learned talk on the Congo Free States. The membership engaged in open discussion which was much enjoyed. Current news was given by the reporter, which furnished much information considering our own people in different spheres. Gramophone music, open discussion, current news. Club adjourned to meet with Mr. and Mrs. Shepherd, April 15, 1910.

Mrs. Wm Miller, President
MW Johnson, Acting Secretary

April 15, 1910

Book Lovers Club met with Mr. and Mrs LB Shepherd on April 15, 1910. Owing to the late arrival of the President and the vacancy of the Vice's office, the Secretary opened the meeting. Roll-call of members with quotation from each showed some members absent. Programme was the next in order. 1. Mr. Miller opened the topic which was the country, Bornu and gave us some very interesting facts. He said in part, Bornu is a country near Hausaland and has a well worked out government being subject to no master. Romba [Rabih] who was the leader of these people and was killed in 1900 kept this country so that no outside country could get possession of any part of it. 2. Instrumental solo by Mrs Mack was the next number. It was quite enjoyable. 3. Open discussion was now on. Gleanings—All eyes

are turned with interest to Africa and tell of its great progress and thrill-
ing conditions there. Bornu affords excellent food for thought. At this
juncture, Mrs Blanche Charleston of St. Paul, Minn and Secretary of Bureau of Natives was introduced to the Book Lovers Club and made a short
address to us which was very timely & much enjoyed. Other visitors, Mr.
Bundy, Mr. & Mrs. Buckner, Mrs. Pulley left words of good cheer and
extreme enjoyment. Current news came forth—Henson at North Pole—
statement of his. H A Rucker removed by Taft as Revenue Collector in
Georgia. DuBois before white YMCA in New York. Mr. Miller suggested
that we have a question box. Motion that we have a question box. Carried.
Book Lovers club was invited to be present at the GAR Entertainment
Monday April 18 at their hall as some of the members would make up
the programme. Motion that Mrs. Woodford be invited to sing with us
at entertainment, carried. Motion that the election of the Vice-President
be deferred until next meeting. Carried. Programme committee reported
the following program: Topic, WEB DuBois—Mr. Shepherd, Violin Obli-
gota, Miss Samuels, Select Reading, Miss Jones, Solo, Mrs. Josey. After
being sumptuously served the club adjourned to meet with Mrs. Harry
Wynne, on April 22, 1910.

Mrs. Wm Miller, Pres.
Essie Dortch Mack, Sec

April 22, 1910

Book Lovers Club met with Mrs. Harry Wynne, April 22 with President and
Officers present. Opening song, Annie Laurie after which the members
answered to the roll-call with quotations. Programme was the next in
order. Topic—WEB DuBois was beautifully opened by Mr. Shepherd. He
gave us a life sketch of DuBois and told of how he had always been excellent in all literary work even when [he] was a boy in high school. He urged
that whatever we do in life, let us strive to be leaders. DuBois represents
the colored people of Georgia in Legislature and helps prevent some
discriminating laws being passed. He gave us a very interesting talk of
the great man and expressed a pleasure in having seen and heard him.
Mrs. Josey read a selection from Dunbar, entitled "When the Old Man
Smokes." It was much enjoyed by all present. Club sang a selection after

which Open Discussion was in order. Gleanings—DuBois sizes up the narrowness of the Caucasian race and shows that the other races are getting tired of the same. He is a great leader, good language, clear thoughts. His book "Souls of Black Folks" is one of the greatest works. He is a man who is able to give the white people our views of the white race. Current News—Revolution in Cuba. Inquiry box was opened—All questions were put in and answered. Quite a deal of pleasure was experienced. Election of Vice-President was in order. Mr. Johnson nominated Mrs. Harry Wynne, Vice President. Motion that the nominations close, carried and Mrs. Wynne was made Vice President. Programme Committee reported the following programme. After partaking of a delightful luncheon, the Club adjourned to meet April 29 with Mr. & Mrs. Wm Miller.

Mrs. Wm Miller, Pres.

Mrs. Essie Dortch Mack, Sec.

April 29, 1910

Book Lovers Club met with Mr. & Mrs. William Miller on April 29, 1910. After opening song, the members answered the roll call with quotations. Minutes were read and approved. Programme was next in order. This being an International Programme, all members responded as follows: Bishop Turner—Mrs. Miller, Prof. Kelly Miller—Mr. Bell, Senator B K Bruce—Mr. Shepherd, Journalist J. Max Barber—Mrs. Josey, Mr. Brown substituted for Mr. Bell and gave us a pleasing instrumental solo. Prof. F. L. Williams—Mr. Miller, Dr. C.H. Parrish—Mrs. Mack, Prof. Scarborough—Mr. Richardson but he was absent. Solo, Mr. J Anthony Josey. The Club joined in singing the chorus. Pres. C. L. [illegible], Mr. O. P. Mack, Tanner the Artist—Mrs. Wynne, B. T. Washington—Mr. Johnson. Instrumental solo—Miss Samuels, but she was absent so Mrs. Wynne substituted with a solo, R. R. Wright—J. Anthony Josey. All the members gave very interesting talks on histories of the person under discussion. Much information was given and each one gave credit to whom it was due. Current News, Programme Committee, Native life, Eastern Africa—young instructed in rules of hygiene for both sexes when they are at that age best suited for it, 4 kinds of tops used by children. Africans have a kind of telephone. Drawing of Native African Children.

African states near they are coming to light and will soon be recognized. In Africa, monuments are found which are older than the oldest monuments of Egypt. Upon motion, the Club rose and gave vote of thanks to Mrs. Wynne for her excellent service. Carried. After being delightfully served, the Club adjourned to meet with Messers. Clay Turner and Wm Carr, May 6, 1910.

Mr. Wm Miller, Pres.
Essie Dortch Mack Sec.

May 6, 1910

Book Lovers Club met with Messers Clay Turner and W Carr on May 6, 1910 with the President and officers presiding. At the roll-call the members answered with quotations. A price of $.10 was collected for fines. Minutes were read and approved. Upon motion, the Programme was carried to the next meeting and this meeting turned into a soiree in honor of the birthday of the President and the departure of Mrs. Wynne. Carried. The members spent a most delightful evening in social enjoyment and after being very sumptuously served an appetizing menu, all retired to their respective homes, with the understanding that the Club would meet with Mr. & Mrs. O. P. Mack, May 13, 1910.

Mrs. Miller, Pres.
Essie Dortch Mack, Sec.

May 13, 1910

Book Lovers Club met May 13, 1910 with Mr. & Mrs. O. P. Mack with the Secretary presiding. Opening song, then the members answered to roll-call with quotations. Since the Vice-President left the city, the Club decided to elect a new Vice. Upon motion of Mrs. Mack and seconded by Mr. Josey, Miss Pearl Samuels was elected Vice President. Carried. Next in order was the Programme. Topic—India opened by Mr. Howard Bell. He gave us a history of the country. It was very enjoyable and the information furnished was very noteworthy. The violin solo of Miss Samuels was left until some future meeting. Reading by Mrs. Shepherd was the next number but she was absent. Mrs. Mack substituted her solo by reading from Dunbar.

It was very enjoyable. Open discussion was next in order. Gleanings—why does India bow to England? It is from selfishness. It is because of the Caste System. Visitors—Mr. & Mrs. Buckner, Mrs. Allison and Miss Denning, Mrs. Woodford. Mrs. Woodford gave us her parting words because she was to depart to Ethan Allen Vermont. Current News-clippings concerning the world. S. S. Convention. Mr. Brunstead on the Brownsville shooting by the soldiers. Meeting in NY to study the rising tide of race prejudice in this country both leading negroes & whites. Mrs. Wynne sent words of best regards to the Book Lovers Club. $.10 paid by Miss Samuels for fines. Inaugural speech of Vice Pres. Very excellent. No questions for Inquiry Box. Programme Committee reported the following programme: Violin solo—Miss Samuels, Topic—which is better for the Negro, Christianity or Mohammedism, opened by Mrs. Mack, Solo—Mr. William Miller. After being served, the Club adjourned to meet with Miss Pearl Samuels, May 21, 1910.

Miss Pearl Samuels, Vice Pres.
Essie Dortch Mack, Sec.

May 21, 1910

Book Lovers Club met with Miss Pearl Samuels, May 21, 1910 with the Vice President presiding. After the opening song, the members answered to roll-call with quotations. Minutes were read and adopted. The programme was the next order. Opening number—Instrumental solo—Miss Samuels. Very beautifully rendered and it showed her ability. Opening topic—Mrs. Mack who read some facts as proofs for the value of Christianity in preference to Mohammedism. Next number on programme was open discussion. Gleanings—Christianity is losing influence as it is given today. The Christian religion will, unless taught as Jesus Christ taught it, lose its influence. Whenever you take on Mohammedism, you are a Christian. Had it not been for the Battle of Tangiers, we would have doubtless been Mohammed followers. Christianity is, and always has been the moving force of the world. It has stood the test of ages and always will be left here to prove the same. Current News—Blacks and whites wedding denied by one supposed to be in favor of it. Bad advice concerning the Negro. Inquiry box was opened and everyone quite enjoyed the questions given. Program committee reported the following programme—Langston—Mrs. J. A. Josey,

St. Augustine—Mr. O.P. Mack, Select reading—Mrs. Shepherd, Reading—
Mr. Richardson, Reading—Mr. Bell. After being served the Club adjourned
to meet with Mr. & Mrs. Josey, May 27, 1910.

Miss Pearl Samuels, Vice Pres.
Essie Dortch Mack, Sec.

May 27, 1910

Book Lovers Club met with Mr. & Mrs. J. A. Josey, May 27, 1910. Meeting was opened by singing "Bless Be the Tides." Next was the roll-call
and the members answered with quotations. Minutes with some corrections were read and adopted. Programme was next in order: Opening
number—J. A. Langston—Life and history of the same—Mrs. J. A. Josey.
She gave us a very interesting reading of the character under discussion
and it was enjoyed by all. St. Augustine was born in Africa. Not much is
known of him. Was at one time a spend thrift when he became older he
came in contact with St. Ambrose and he finally became a very brilliant
young man and became head of the Latin Church. The Catholic people are proud of this writer. He wrote over 250 volumes. Knew not of
Greek but was familiar with Latin. St. Augustine, though not a familiar
character, yet he became a noble work. Select reading—Mr. Shepherd,
"Home-making" by Ella Wheeler. It was a delightful reading and gave
very pleasing, as well as wholesome advice. The advice given was well
given and quite in place for the occasion. Mr. Bell didn't appear with
his reading, but he gave quote instead, which was very pleasing. Open
discussion—we should take courage from the life of Langston and reli-
giously appreciate St. Augustine. Discussion was much enjoyed by all.
Current news—Congress wiped out the color line in the International
SS Convention by making Booker T Washington a member. The Syrians
are being kept out on account of their being brown. The Club decided
to make the next meeting a kind of Soirée in honor of the departure of
the Secretary and Mrs. Josey. Adjourned to meet with Messers Johnson,
Richardson and Bell on June 3, 1910.

Miss Pearl Samuels, Vice Pres.
Essie Dortch Mack, Sec.

APPENDIX B

Families Documented in the 1930 Census

These African American families, some of whom arrived before 1920, appeared on the 1930 census. While many of these names come up in the oral histories in this book, it's notable that not all match up. This could be due to the various methods used to record family names or inaccuracy on the part of the census taker. Additionally, some residents considered to be here on a temporary basis and not living with immediate family members were listed as lodgers. Other Blacks living in Madison at the time may not have been listed in the official census at all. David Simms, for example, reported that he came to Madison in 1927 but is not reported in the 1930 census, probably because he was a UW–Madison student and a lodger.

William Abernathy

Harry and Myra Allison and their children (Margaret, Ella, Harry, and William, and Constance)

Guy and Mayme Anderson and their seven children (Harold, Eugene, Eleanor, George, Josephine, Dorothy and Nathaniel)

William and Ruby Arms family members, Mary (mother), Florence, Frederick (daughter and son), sister Marnie, and nephew Louis

Leroy and Ozella Banks and their four children (Leroy, Peter, Fred, and Anna)

George and Anna Buckner

Edwin and Blossom Champion and their daughters (Eddie M. and Bettie)

Collins family members (Grace, Leona, Charley)

Charles and Myrtle Daniels and their children (Charline and Bernadine)

Ben and Effie Dunn and a lodger named Ely Dunn

Edward and Alice Elvard and their children (Ella, Pearl, Edward, James, and Ralph)

William Gathard

Joseph and Daisy Gentry

George and Mildred Greene and one son (James)

Carson Gulley

William L. and Gertrude Harris

George Harris

John and Amanda Hill and their three children (Freddie M., and Christena)

William Laudermilk

John S and Low B [Luberta] Masley [Mosley] and children (Jewell, Arthur, and Geraldine)

Charles and Rose Merville and children (Kenneth, Byldena, Merle, Dorothy, and Evelyn)

Anna M. Miller and children (Lucille, William M., Anna M, Dubois, and Caroline)

James and Amma Mitchell (James, Earnest, Eddie, and Ralph)

Randolph and Georgia Moncrief and son (John)

Minnie Owens

Sam and Molly Pierce and son [nephew] (Theodore)

Roy and Ann Rogers

Charles and Margaret Russell

Richard Satterfield

Louie and Julia Shepard

Joseph and Susie Washington and daughter (Lucile)

Albert and Fannie Weaver and children (Ruth, William, Eugene)

Eddie and Willie J. Withers and daughter (Minnie)

Acknowledgments

This book is dedicated to the African American families who came to Madison in the 1800s and early 1900s looking for a better life. These families demonstrated strength, courage, and pride as they raised families, created organizations, established churches, and provided help and services to those in need. I am grateful that I had the opportunity to talk to their descendants. The stories they told about their ancestors made me proud to be a descendant myself, and gratified that my family is among these Madison pioneers.

I especially dedicate this book to my mother, Mary Esther Simms, who exemplified the supportive nature of the African American community. In 1935, she arrived in Madison with my sister, Dolores, to join my dad, David Simms. Mom and Dad were hired to work in the Delta Chi fraternity house on Langdon Street, where Mom was to cook three meals a day, six and a half times a week for twenty-five young men. The pay was good and she learned from Carson Gulley and Mrs. Oliver Davis how to prepare large quantities of food. As a young woman from a small town in Missouri, she took on this challenge. She had that quiet yet courageous spirit. Well accepted in the Black community, she served in leadership positions and volunteered freely in support roles related to the politics, civic activism, and humanitarian activities of the time. She also acted behind the scenes, helping Blacks and Whites in the community wherever she could. She gave up her time and whatever extra money she had to help clothe and feed people. My mother welcomed those who were struggling or friendless into our home. I remember Mother befriending an elderly and disfigured White woman who people in the neighborhood heckled and ignored. Mary Hanna, daughter of Madison pioneer and activist Hilton Hanna, sent me an email telling me that when her mother was sick and unable to take care of things at home, my mother helped the family. Mom accepted help graciously and gave help willingly. My mother practiced her Christianity all the time. She is and always will be near and dear to my heart.

The Simms family in 1948: Mary, Muriel, David, and Dolores. COURTESY OF THE SIMMS FAMILY

This project has been living in my heart and mind for ten years. Thus, I am so grateful to have people in my life who told me that these stories must be published. First is my sister, Dolores, who gave me her thoughtful and constructive criticism of this work. Her critique, much of which is due to her extraordinary memory, led me to rethink particular sections and the style of the text. Her approval and appreciation for this work motivated me to continue at a time when I wanted to give up. Next is Betty Mitchell Banks, who has been my good friend for seventy years. Not many can boast of a friendship that has lasted that long. As the daughters of pioneer families, we talk with pride about our ancestors, remembering their wisdom and wit, and how committed, unwavering, and politically active they were. When I feel exasperated about Madison's politics, Betty's sense of humor and honesty keep me grounded. She also was gracious enough to let me include her grandmother's Book Lovers Club minutes in this book. When Betty's mother passed in 1987, Betty gave me a wooden turtle that her mother had cherished. When my mother passed in 1999, I found a bronze-covered turtle in her jewelry box. These two turtles sit side by side on my dresser.

Thanks to Bonnie Augusta for reading this manuscript, providing helpful suggestions, and encouraging me to go forward, and to Kate Conklin Corcoran for her editing knowledge and skills, and for sticking with me. I thank Ian Walter for his computer knowledge and technological skills.

I especially thank the following people, some of whom are now deceased, for sharing aspects of their lives with me. Without these special people, the idea would be still sitting in my head: Dolores Simms Greene, James L. Greene, Billy McDonald, Michael Shivers, Lois Waldon McKnight, Paul Washington, Georgia Harris Henderson, Addrena Matthews Squires, Margaret Studesville, Ralph Lee, Odell Taliaferro, Dimetra Taliaferro Shivers, Mary Hanna, Peaches Mosley Lacey, Geraldine Hopkins Clarke, Hannah Hopkins Christian, Jean Hopkins Redwood, Marie Caire Thomas, Edith Lawrence Hilliard, Edwin Hill Jr., Sara Davis Wells, Pia Kinney James, Joe Cerniglia, and Fran Remeika.

Notes

Introduction

1. Ann Allen Shockley, "Oral history: A Research Tool for Black History," *Negro History Bulletin* 41, no. 1 (1978), 787–789.
2. Linda Shopes, "Beyond Trivia and Nostalgia: Collaborating in the Construction of a Local History," *International Journal of Oral History* 5, no. 3 (1984): 153.
3. Shopes, "Beyond Trivia and Nostalgia," 152.
4. Shockley, "Oral History," 789.
5. Eve Malo and Julie Bullard, *Storytelling and the Emergent Reader*, paper presented at the International Reading Association World Congress on Reading, Auckland, New Zealand, July 11–14, 2000, 12.
6. Valerie Grim, "Integrating Oral History into the Classroom Curriculum: A Tool for Helping Students Understand the American and African-American Experience," *Teaching History* 20, no. 1 (1995): 3–19.
7. LaVada Taylor Brandon, "W/righting History: A Pedagogical Approach with Urban African American Learners," *Urban Education* 39, no. 6 (2004): 638–657.
8. Cornell West, *Race matters*, (Boston: Beacon Press, 1993): 15.

A Brief History of African American Settlement in Madison

1. "Black History in Wisconsin," Wisconsin Historical Society, www.wisconsinhistory.org/Records/Article/CS502.
2. Zachary Cooper, *Black Settlers in Rural Wisconsin* (Madison: State Historical Society of Wisconsin, 1977).
3. "Black History in Wisconsin," Wisconsin Historical Society.
4. Brooks Edgerton, "Blacks Scarce in Madison's Early Years," *Capital Times* (Madison, WI), February 1, 1984.
5. Barbara Shade, "The First Blacks in Madison Were Only Step above Slavery," *Capital Times* (Madison, WI), May 14, 1979.
6. Black Book Committee, *Black Book* (Madison, WI: National Association for the Advancement of Colored People, 1972): 6.
7. "1850 United States Federal Census," Ancestry.com, https://search.ancestry.com/search/db.aspx?dbid=8054.
8. Shade, "The First Blacks."
9. Ibid.
10. Ibid.

11. Ibid.; and "Odd Wisconsin: Jefferson's Black Descendants in Madison," *Wisconsin State Journal*, March 18, 2015, http://host.madison.com/wsj/news/local/odd-wisconsin-thomas-jefferson-s-black-descendants-in-madison/article_6a05210b-7fc2-5f42-91c5-3ac04285d80a.html.

12. Forest Hill Cemetery Committee of Historic Madison, *The Biographical Guide to Forest Hill Cemetery, Volume II* (Madison, WI: Historic Madison, 2002): 197–198.

13. Shade, "The First Blacks," 25.

14. Ibid.

15. Forest Hill Cemetery Committee of Historic Madison, *The Biographical Guide to Forest Hill Cemetery*, 200.

16. "Leo Butts Was the First African-American Football Player in 1918," *Daily Cardinal*, February 1, 2011, www.cstv.com/printable/schools/wis/genrel/020111aaa.html?frame=bottom; and "Celebrating Black History," Board of Regents of the UW Wisconsin System, www.uwbadgers.com/sports/2015/08/21/GEN_20140101938.aspx.

17. Shade, "The First Blacks," 8.

18. K. Efird, *Black Book* (Madison, WI: National Association for the Advancement of Colored People, 1970), 8.

19. Ibid.

20. Ibid., 9.

21. Black Book Committee, *Black Book* (1972), 7.

22. Ibid., 8.

23. Ibid., 8–9.

24. Forest Hill Cemetery Committee of Historic Madison, *The Biographical Guide to Forest Hill Cemetery*, 202.

25. "Sam Pierce, 66, Genial Messenger to Five State Governors, Passes Away," *Capital Times* (Madison, WI), May 15, 1936.

26. "Mrs. Hetty Pierce Dead; Reported 115 Years Old," *Capital Times* (Madison, WI), June 13, 1944.

27. "Sam Pierce, 66."

28. Rob Zaleski, "Lonely for Willy Street: Neighbors Miss Their Ted, Too," *Capital Times* (Madison, WI), August 1, 1998.

29. Ibid.

30. Forest Hill Cemetery Committee of Historic Madison, *The Biographical Guide to Forest Hill Cemetery*, 204.

31. Black Book Committee, *Black Book* (1972), 9. The Utopia Club was organized on January 1, 1918, in the home of Mrs. Charles Russell. Other members of the club were president and founder Sadie Rich, Lula Jones, Myra Allison, V'Otey Mosley, Ora Smith, Ida Henderson, Mamie F. Davis, Stella Washington, Laura Hoover, and Amanda Hill.

32. Genevieve G. McBride and Stephen R. Byers, "The First Mayor of Black Milwaukee," *Wisconsin Magazine of History* 91, no. 2 (2007): 2–15.

33. Anthony Josey, "Our Aim," *Wisconsin Weekly Blade*, June 8, 1916.

34. Ibid.

35. Shade, "The First Blacks," 9.

36. McBride and Byers, "The First Mayor," 8.

37. Ibid., 7.

38. "1930 United States Federal Census," *Ancestry.com*, https://search.ancestry.com/search/db.aspx?dbid=6224.

39. Black Book Committee, *Black Book* (1970), 11.

40. Teryl Franklin, "Old KKK Photo from Madison Mischaracterized by Conservative Author," *Wisconsin State Journal*, September 30, 2017, http://host.madison.com/wsj/news/local/crime/old-kkk-photo-from-madison-mischaracterized-by-conservative-author/article_b1506044-6d36-53fc-93e9-767158241a86.html.

41. Jonathan Gramling, "When Cotton Was King," *Madison Times*, February 6–12, 2004.

42. Ibid.

43. Jonathan Gramling, "When Blacks in Madison Were Few," *Madison Times*, February 13–19, 2004.

44. Ibid.

45. Ibid.

46. Jonathan Gramling, "Succeeding in the Struggle," *Madison Times*, February 20–26, 2004.

INDEX

Page numbers in **bold type** refer to pages with photos or other illustrations.

About the Author

Muriel Simms is a lifelong Madison resident and longtime educator in the Madison Metropolitan School District. She received her doctorate from the University of Wisconsin–Madison in 2002 and serves as an adjunct faculty member in the Doctoral Program in Educational Leadership at Edgewood College. She has published articles in several education journals, including *Elementary School Journal*, *Urban Education*, and *Democracy & Education*, and has presented her research at two educational conferences, the American Education Research Association and the University Council for Education Administration Symposium. Simms served on boards for the Charles Hamilton Houston Institute, the Friends of Cherokee Marsh, the Community Development Block Grant Review Team, Volunteers in Probation, the Brams Addition Neighborhood Association, University of Wisconsin's College Access Program, the South Madison Planning Committee, Madison's Early Childhood Care and Education Committee, and the NAACP Madison Chapter. She has received several awards for her professional duties and community service, including the Martin L. King Jr. Appreciation Award, NAACP's Unsung Heroine Award, 2012 Whitney M. Young Jr. Award from the Urban League of Greater Madison, and a "Muriel Simms Day" proclamation from the city of Madison. She was also named Wisconsin Elementary Principal of the Year in 1992 by the Wisconsin Association of Elementary School Principals and the Wisconsin and National School Board Associations. In 2003, she became interested in writing a book on Madison's pioneer African American families by interviewing the descendants of these early settlers. She golfs, creates folksy art, and collects African American dolls and stamps.